SHOCK WAVES:

THE MARITIME URBAN SYSTEM IN THE NEW ECONOMY

Edited by

George J. De Benedetti
Rodolphe H. Lamarche

INSTITUT CANADIEN DE RECHERCHE SUR LE DÉVELOPPEMENT RÉGIONAL
THE CANADIAN INSTITUTE FOR RESEARCH ON REGIONAL DEVELOPMENT

© Institut canadien de recherche sur le développement régional/
  The Canadian Institute for Research on Regional Development

Distributed by *Acadiensis Press*

ISBN   088659-035-3

Legal Deposit, 3d quarter, 1994
National Library of Canada

Printed in Canada

TABLE OF CONTENTS

PREFACE

One of New Brunswick's leading entrepreneurs recently remarked: "It may be that the Maritime provinces will become a great place to live but where it will be extremely difficult to make money." He had the uneasy sense that something is going on in the region; he could not quite put his finger on it; but he was quite sure that whatever it is, its effects will not be positive.

This book is about the Maritime urban system. Its chapters necessarily deal with a number of topics but its focus is on the region's urban centres. Although the region has been the subject of numerous studies, the analysis of its urban networks has been largely untouched. The study of the region's cities has also been neglected. This book attempts to remedy these shortcomings.

The book's title, *Shock Waves: The Maritime Urban System in the New Economy*, is to the point. What that entrepreneur senses are several shock waves that have begun to be felt in the region - globalization, the information economy, cuts in public spending. The editors were quite prescient in drawing attention to these three shocks, because they are likely to mark the region for a long time to come.

It is not at all clear what the long term impact these shock waves will have on the Maritime economy. For my part, I remain confident. Though the region will feel the sting of cutbacks in government spending, it is also slowly but surely breaking away from past forces such as some national policies, which have inhibited its growth. In addition, some areas, and among them notably Moncton, have been able to bounce back quickly from sharp reductions in government spending and presence in the local economy.

One way to assist the region in making the transition to its new economy is to understand these new economic forces at play, and to examine how the region's key urban centres are preparing themselves for the challenges ahead. I want to congratulate George J. De Benedetti and Rodolphe H. Lamarche for undertaking this work, and through it, launching a debate on what our cities must do, over what promises to be a critical decade, for the economic future of the Maritime provinces.

DONALD J. SAVOIE

ACKNOWLEDGEMENTS

We have been extremely fortunate in receiving assistance from many quarters in the preparation of this volume. It is a pleasure to acknowledge that assistance.

First, we thank all the authors for their contributions and for their cooperation throughout the process of bringing this volume to fruition. In this regard, we especially thank Professor Benjamin Higgins for having contributed three of the chapters, and for having suggested ideas in other parts of the book. He remains an inspiration to us all.

Next, we wish to thank Donald J. Savoie, Executive Director of the Canadian Institute for Research on Regional Development, for his enthusiastic support, vision, and encouragement from the inception of the project. Without his support, this book would not be possible. We also acknowledge the support of the board of directors of the Institute for their vote of confidence and their financial support for our endeavour.

We also acknowledge the contribution of Maurice Beaudin, who worked diligently to retrieve census data, which enabled us to construct the Statistical Appendix for use by the authors, and of Ginette Benoit, for her administrative assistance and for proofreading our galley proofs.

A special debt of thanks is owed Colette Allain who took responsibility for the assembly of the volume. She not only prepared the manuscripts, tables, and figures, proofread, but she patiently endured our countless corrections through successive revisions. But it is her organizational skills, experience, and her sense of professionalism, combined with good humour, for which we are most grateful.

To Eugen Weiss, who acted as our copy editor, we owe a great deal of thanks. His many corrections to the text have improved communication between writer and reader. We are also appreciative of the many suggestions he made regarding content.

We wish to acknowledge the artistic contribution of Hawk Communications in the design of our cover, and for the financial subsidy they provided in its production.

To Professor Samuel Arsenault of the department of geography at l'Université de Moncton, who designed the map in the Introduction, we express our gratitude.

Thanks to Ruth Miller, reference librarian at Mount Allison University, who went out of her way on numerous occasions to search for data, which formed the basis of the analysis in Chapter 2.

We especially thank the entrepreneurs, who consented to be interviewed by Dorothy Downing for her chapter, "Hi-Tech in Small Towns," and for sharing their experiences with us. They have given us valuable insights on how firms can operate from small centres in this age of the electronic highway and globalization. We also thank those persons interviewed in the course of the writing of the other chapters, especially those of Saint John and Fredericton.

To Maurice Beaudin, Pierre-Marcel Desjardins, Bill Cunningham, Monica De Benedetti, and the many other persons, inside and outside the Institute, who read drafts of our work and made helpful comments.

Finally, we wish to thank our families, especially our spouses, Angelique and Doris, for their patience and encouragement throughout.

George J. De Benedetti
Rodolphe H. Lamarche

INTRODUCTION

George J. De Benedetti
Rodolphe H. Lamarche

This book is about shock waves that affect our work, lives and cities in the Maritimes. Our people and our cities have survived several economic transformations, both in the distant past and more recently. And more are on their way, both from within the region and from without. Some shock waves originate in the minds of entrepreneurs, who create and, more often, adapt ideas that shape new production and management processes, generate transformations within the labour force, and invariably create new patterns of urban interaction. Some of these changes are imported, and some are imposed by decisions and conditions beyond local control. The resulting process of transformation has happened before; it continues; and it will in all likelihood accelerate.

This series of studies on the Maritime urban system was undertaken in light of the need to understand how Maritime urban centres had survived past economic transformations, and how they are adjusting to more recent changes. How had the urban centres survived the rise of industrial activity, and then the great depression preceding World War II? Has the coming of the service economy of the 1950s and 1960s made our centres more regionally inter-dependent, or more dependent on a few major national centres?

The authors set out to assess the readiness of the larger Maritime urban centres to weather three new economic shocks that are just beginning to strike the region (see Map on page 6). These are more recent shocks, and they have by no means run their course. They are: the rise of the information economy in the late 1970s and 1980s and its recent acceleration; the new international trade agreements with the United States, Mexico and through the GATT; and, finally, reductions in public spending.

Urban centres, wherein most of the country's economic production is processed, are affected every time the manner in which we produce goods and services is changed. Both the labour force and the urban areas as a whole are traumatized if the transformations are major ones. So it comes as no surprise that the three most recent shocks, two of which are likely to be major ones, would entail some restructuring of the Maritime urban system. Some centres are likely to be winners, and some, losers. It then becomes important to favour the development of those centres that have the resources to take advantage of the new economy. It becomes equally important as well to devise strategies to minimize the adverse effects on those centres that are less capable of adjusting.

The information economy is without doubt the most powerful, the most pervasive, and the most relentless of the three shocks to hit the region. Because it is a global phenomenon, there are no policies strong enough to curtail its effects, and any attempt to do so would merely put off the reckoning of its impact on the Maritime urban centres. The rise of the information economy is the result of a number of factors, some of them economic, some of them social.

Advanced societies are in a constant search to better the welfare of their citizens. In market economies there is a constant striving to produce better goods at lower prices. In the first stage of the industrial revolution, captains of industry relied on artisans to create and operate the machinery to meet these goals. Later, as the demand for more sophisticated goods appeared, firms had to turn to engineers and to scientific laboratories to create and devise the machinery and processes they needed. This dependency on scientific and technical knowledge soared during the 1940s and 50s as a result of the great wars and the subsequent rise of the service economy. The opportunities provided by the rise of the Pacific rim nations as producers of industrial goods and as new markets and sources of labour, and the linking of the telecommunication and computer technologies into a powerful management tool, eventually launched the information economy. This particular combination of technologies, often referred to as *telematics*, made it possible for companies to manage highly-dispersed factory installations producing sophisticated goods, and to keep complete control over their inventories and markets. The capacity to create and control technical information is the foundation of an information economy. Technical information is the world's newest and most important primary resource and its fastest growing industry, creating more than 800,000 new books each year, plus innumerable journals and scientific reports.

The information economy can be defined as an economy wherein the production of goods and services are dependent on a constant stream of high-tech information. Manufacturing was the first sector to be transformed by the information economy, in the early 1970s. It was soon followed by financial and banking institutions which incorporated telematics in their planning strategies. By 1981, over 50 percent of the labour force in advanced economies were either creating, managing or distributing information, or were in the business of extending and maintaining information infrastructures. The first stage of the information economy had set in. Not only did the labour force have to adjust to these new production and management processes, but urban systems wherein these activities were carried out also had to change. Some urban centres were better equipped physically and socially to meet the new demands - the winners - other centres were too weak or too late, and they became the losers in this never-ending process of economic adjustment so characteristic of market economies. This demand for better goods can even overthrow a particular type of economy, if one judges from the demise of the communist empires. An open and constant search for improvement might be considered a basic characteristic of open social systems.

It is not surprising, then, that when one studies the evolution of urban systems in the 1990s, one would pay particular attention to the impact of the information economy on the labour force within urban centres, and on the interaction networks that bind cities together. How has the Maritime urban system reacted to the first inroads of the information economy? What centres will rise in the urban hierarchy, and what are the chances of growth for the others?

A second shock wave to strike the Maritime urban system comes as a result of the globalization of world economies. Telematics has made it possible for firms to search the world for resources, technologies, and markets. Consequently, many firms have more or less abandoned the outlying regions of Canada to their own resourcefulness. It is now often more profitable for firms to spend their resources to gain access to foreign markets than to expand their domestic markets, even with the help of government subsidies. As a result, governments have reduced subsidies to outlying regions and increased them for those firms located within the larger metropolitan centres that were running into difficulties. Governments had to react when they were faced with the de-industrialization of their heartlands through international competition. The response of governments was to ensure that the large firms in the central metropolitan urban centres of the country survived by giving them the necessary financial and regulatory support to meet the new challenges. Another strategy was also employed by governments in these difficult circumstances. This was to create and gradually implement international trade agreements. Most of these agreements call for the eventual elimination of all subsidies, with the result that firms are more or less on their own. However, the lag time before their full implementation allows government some leeway to adjust. Ultimately, urban centres in one country will have to compete with urban centres elsewhere. Such trade agreements should lead to cheaper and better products in the long run, it is claimed: but they are cause for great concern to producers in the Maritimes. For a variety of reasons - from inefficient rail transportation to regulatory impediments - Maritime producers have high transportation costs, amounting to an average of 10 percent of the value added, as compared to 8.5 percent in Ontario. If subsidies are eliminated, and the structural inefficiencies are not corrected before the full implementation of these agreements, Maritime centres will face hardships from which they might never recover. For these and other like reasons, the editors felt that this globalization shock should be one of the main topics in this study of the evolution of the Maritime urban system.

Finally, the third shock is the reduction in public spending. It is also considered important, because the Maritime provinces rely heavily on government spending and transfer payments. A large proportion of the labour force in some of the larger urban centres is dependent on government, either as civil servants, or in the education, health, and defense industries. It seemed important, then, to consider which centres would be adversely affected, and how the overall urban system would be able to cope with reductions. Because governments are sensitive to political and social pressures, it is likely however, that of the three shocks, this particular shock will be managed the most easily.

The book is divided into two parts. The first is entitled "The Maritime Urban System in Transition," and its six chapters address questions that concern the urban system as a whole. In Chapter One, L. McCann makes an historical review of the impact of previous shocks on the Maritime urban system. This chapter is interesting in several ways, first because it describes how the urban centres coped with a succession of shocks that hit the area during the 1867-1939 period, and secondly because it provides some indication as to the general capabilities of the system to adjust to new shocks. In Chapter Two, R. Lamarche studies the restructuring of the regional urban system and its integration into a national system centred on Toronto. His study of the structures of the sub-networks of the region's six largest centres illustrates the impact the information economy - the first and most powerful shock - has already had on the area. Chapter Three, by P. Villeneuve and G. Vincent, describes the growing interaction between the Maritime centres and the Northeastern cities of the U.S., a feature of some importance for the area because it might signal a gradual reduction in dependency of our centres on centres in Ontario and Quebec. This would represent a major re-orientation of our system. Chapter Four, by B. Higgins, discusses the difficulties and the challenges facing the Maritime urban centres as the globalization of markets, the second shock with which we are concerned, begins to take effect. Chapter Five, by D.J. Savoie and M. Beaudin, analyzes the extent of the dependency of some of the urban centres on federal public expenditures. The last chapter of this section is by D. Downing. It elegantly describes how a number of high-tech firms have opted to settle in small towns in the area and are building highly successful operations, some of which have world-wide reach.

The second part of the book is composed of six case studies of the most important cities in the Maritime region. It is entitled "The Maritime Urban System: A Necklace of Cities, Not All of Them Pearls." The focus here, as well as in the first part, is to gauge the chances these cities have of adjusting to the rapid transformation that is occurring as a result of the three shocks. In Chapter Seven, B. Higgins analyzes the causes that could explain why Halifax is having some difficulty in asserting itself as the region's metropolis. Chapter Eight, also by B. Higgins, discusses the plight of Sydney in its difficult transition from an industrial centre to a modern city. Chapter Nine, by G.J. De Benedetti, is also concerned with the impact of the shocks on an industrial city, but here the city is Saint John, New Brunswick, where the strengths of its economy could well be its weaknesses too. Chapter Ten, by D.J. Savoie and Y. Bourgeois, discusses the resilience of the city of Moncton in the face of recent adversity, and the likelihood that it will be able to sustain its role as the hub of the region in the future. Fredericton is the object of Chapter Eleven. G.J. De Benedetti and E. Weiss describe the deliberate efforts this centre is making to build intellectual industries and become a major engineering and software centre in the region. Finally, Chapter Twelve by F. Strain is an interesting study of Charlottetown.

One gets the feeling from this chapter that all of Prince Edward Island is being drawn into the shadow of the provincial capital, and that Charlottetown and the Island as a whole have a lot to offer as a high-tech centre in a very pleasant surrounding, if only it finds the leadership and organizational resources to find its niche in these very trying times.

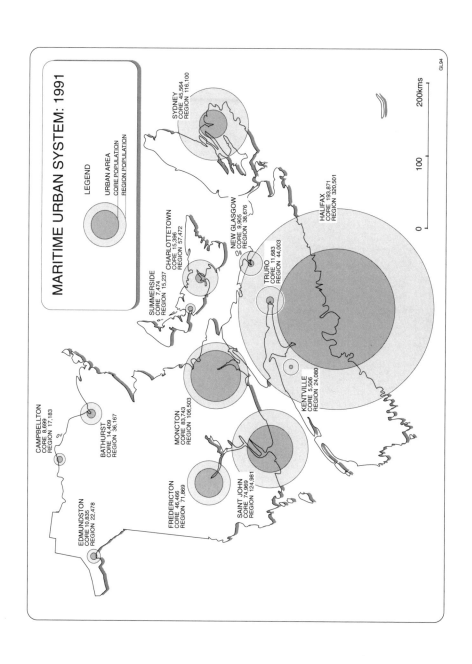

MARITIME URBAN SYSTEM: 1991

LEGEND

URBAN AREA
CORE POPULATION
REGION POPULATION

SYDNEY
CORE 45,564
REGION 116,100

SUMMERSIDE
CORE 7,474
REGION 15,237

CHARLOTTETOWN
CORE 15,396
REGION 57,472

NEW GLASGOW
CORE 9,905
REGION 38,676

TRURO
CORE 11,683
REGION 44,003

HALIFAX
CORE 193,871
REGION 320,501

KENTVILLE
CORE 5,506
REGION 24,080

CAMPBELLTON
CORE 8,699
REGION 17,183

BATHURST
CORE 14,409
REGION 36,167

MONCTON
CORE 83,743
REGION 106,503

FREDERICTON
CORE 46,466
REGION 71,869

SAINT JOHN
CORE 74,969
REGION 124,981

EDMUNDSTON
CORE 10,835
REGION 22,478

0   100   200kms

GL.94

PART I

THE MARITIME URBAN SYSTEM IN TRANSITION

1

SHOCK WAVES IN THE OLD ECONOMY: THE MARITIME URBAN SYSTEM DURING THE GREAT TRANSFORMATION c.1867-1939

L.D. McCann

As Paul Bairoch has argued, regional well-being - as well as the economic vitality of the nation and world system beyond - is tied directly to the development of cities.[1] Over time and within these spatial contexts, cities are prime shapers of economic growth and development. Through their powers of innovation and their ability to achieve economies of concentration, they offer decided advantages for the pursuit of economic activity. The various urban functions that mark a city's economic base - trade, transportation, manufacturing, producer services, and finance, for example - create employment, generate income, and therefore provide well-being for a region's population. Conversely, cities can also play a role in the underdevelopment of a region. They do so by failing to sustain the formation of basic production factors (for example, capital supplies, skilled labour, or entrepreneurial leadership) that are needed to foster ongoing economic growth and development. In short, cities sometimes fail to support the functions and structure of an integrated urban system that will facilitate and sustain the long-term opportunities and advantages needed for innovation and savings in production costs, and hence regional well-being.

The Maritimes, like all Canadian regions, is currently adjusting to the relative newness of the post-industrial economy. As the world economy restructures, redefining the division of labour between traditional core and periphery areas across the nation and throughout the developed and developing world, Maritime cities are being forced to react to a recent set of shocks that could adversely affect future urban growth and development. These shocks are the new information economy; significant reductions in public spending; and far-reaching trade agreements. However, the urban pursuit of well-being in the 1990s is taking place at a decided disadvantage because of the region's historical legacy of decline and disparity. The Maritimes lacks a dominant regional metropolitan centre that is capable of supporting strong, innovative leadership, as well as a fully-integrated urban system that provides for the advantages of concentrated economic advance.

This weakly-structured urban system, upon which so much of the region's future prosperity depends, took shape gradually during the Great Transformation that lasted from Confederation down to the close of the Great Depression. During this period, the Maritimes first shifted from a mercantile to an industrial economy, and then experienced the debilitating force of de-industrialization, particularly through the 1920s and 1930s.[2] During this *longue durée* of advance and retreat,[3] the region experienced shocks of a different but equally powerful kind: the thrust of industrialization with its attendant use of new production and transportation technologies; engagement with a highly-competitive, continental market economy; propulsive but ultimately wavering and inconsistent government policy and assistance; and the menacing outreach of metropolitan-based managerial and corporate capitalism - to cite only a few. As the Great Transformation unfolded in the Maritimes, it became increasingly clear that the region's pace of urbanization was lagging decidedly behind that of the rest of Canada. When Ontario, Quebec and British Columbia were passing the half-way point up the urbanization ladder, at the close of the First World War, the Maritimes was barely a quarter-of-the-way to establishing an urban majority. Even today, the region's level of urbanization remains well below the Canadian average.

If we accept the premise that economic vitality rests substantially, if not ultimately, on an integrated urban base that can buffer external shocks - as Bairoch suggests is essential; and if we accept the premise that a weakened Maritime urban system constitutes a serious impediment to prosperous regional development in the future, then it is important to understand the unfolding of some of the main structural weaknesses that have accompanied the process of urbanization in this region. To this end, this chapter offers an overview of the growth and development of the Maritime urban system during the Great Transformation. It examines how a number of shocks struck deeply into the so-called old industrial economy, leaving the urban system with a record of slow growth, weak integration, and marginal status that continues to plague the economic, social, and political life of this hinterland region. This is not to say that many of these inherent difficulties in the urban system cannot be overcome, but it is to say that to do so, the process by which they were created must be better understood.

Conceptualizing Urban Growth in Space and Time

Time. Place. Circumstance. What if the process of urban growth in the Maritimes took place in a different spatial and temporal context, in which the conditions surrounding the advance of towns and cities were significantly different? Would the level of regional well-being be substantially different? Such hypothetical or counter-factual questions require us to consider defining the precise conditions of space and time that have shaped urbanization in the region. The concept of space is of utmost importance. Space as a source of explanation is tied to all processes of growth and development, and urbanization is no exception. Fundamental in this regard is the conception of space as a geographic and economic continuum that extends from a centre of power to a periphery of marginal strength. Cities take the lead role, shaping the space economy and yielding contrasting patterns. Centre, core or heartland regions display a diversified profile of economic activity and a full division of labour. They are innovative, comprise an integrated urban system, and are capable of wielding, through the metropolis, considerable influence over the periphery, margin or hinterland regions. These typically are resource-oriented, display fragmented settlement patterns, and are more likely to experience dependency, underdevelopment, and disparities of all kinds.[4] Clearly, the Maritimes that comprises the provinces of Nova Scotia, New Brunswick and Prince Edward Island is a hinterland region. When first settled it was on the western periphery of the North Atlantic economy, tied principally through trade and imperial connections to decision-making in London. More recently, as the Maritimes industrialized slowly over the course of the nineteenth century and entered Confederation, it turned away from the North Atlantic towards the continental economy, linked by rail and a national market to central Canada, but still, by steamship, to the northeastern United States. Thus, in considering its urbanization record, the Maritimes has been influenced by powerful metropolitan interests in Montreal, Toronto, Boston, New York and Philadelphia. Situated more favourably in space, and with the ability to engage in a range of economic activities from a more competitive geographic position, their powerful outreach has restricted the pace of Maritime industrialization and urbanization.

Time also looms large in our consideration, if only because it is essential to apply an interpretive guide to the Great Transformation by selecting broad forces that explain the basic relationship over time between economic and urban change. Processes of change associated with the rise of capitalism - industrialization, financial restructuring, business reorganization, and government incentives, for example - meet this criterion. The years following Confederation in 1867 to the Great Depression of the 1930s were characterized by successive phases of first mercantile, then industrial, and lastly a unison of financial and managerial capitalism that modified the structures and strategies of modern industrial enterprise.[5] These shifting forms of capitalism staged a considerable act of regional transformation. From the 1850s through the 1880s, and spurred particularly by National Policy industrial incentives after 1878,[6] various merchant families in a host of staple-producing communities began diversifying local economies by either establishing or investing in various manufacturing activities.[7] The torch of industrial capitalism was then passed to the financial and managerial wizards like Max Aitken who promoted the advantages of giant corporations, trusts, banks, and chain stores in the early decades of the twentieth century.[8] Through their revolutionary business structures and aggressive marketing strategies, these largely metropolitan-based enterprises took firm control over many sectors of the regional economy by the 1920s.[9] Given this record of decline and marginalization, the infusion of federal government investment and assistance became even more critical to the regional economy.[10] It is against this shifting context both of capitalist time and of core and periphery space that we will examine the course of Maritime urban development.

Sectoral Change and Urbanization in the Old Economy

Curiously, because we generally think of Canada as being a prosperous country and the Maritimes region as less prosperous, employment data measuring the major economic sectors at the close of the nineteenth century indicate that both the Maritimes and Canada shared comparable distribution patterns across primary, secondary and tertiary activities. In 1891, about one-half of the labour force, of Canada and the Maritime provinces alike, was engaged in the staple-producing primary sector. Another one-quarter or so occupied manufacturing and construction jobs, while the remainder held a range of service-type positions (table 1). Even when logging, mining, manufacturing, and construction are grouped together in a general industrial category, as David Alexander has done for 1901, the Maritime economy still shares an overall structural similarity with Canada.[11]

But these similarities in labour force distribution conceal differences in the size of economies, and in the well-being, capital accumulation, and manufacturing types that would eventually contribute to growing disharmony in the urban and economic development between the Maritimes and Canada as a whole. Gathering strength from the substantial economic activity based in the core provinces of Ontario and Quebec, Canadian per capita production values steadily outperformed the peripheral Maritimes throughout the Great Transformation by one-third or more. For example, in 1929 the per capita production gap between Canada and the Maritime provinces was $259,000 to $156,000.[12] By this time, too, the Canadian economy's drive to industrial maturity was much more diversified and advanced than the Maritimes. Nearly two-thirds of the country's labour force now worked in the secondary and tertiary sectors, compared to about 52 percent for the east coast region (table 1). As a consequence of advances in production levels and economic diversification, regions with the greatest employment opportunities in manufacturing, trade, finance and business services attracted the majority of urban-destined immigrants and stimulated the most rural-urban migration, all leading to the strongest urbanization.[13] For Canada, the proportion of the population living in urban places with more than 1,000 people climbed steadily from just under 30 percent to some 52.5 percent between 1891 and 1931. Ontario's urbanization level rose the most, changing from 35.0 to 63.1 percent. The Maritimes, struggling to catch up, advanced significantly but went from just 16.5 to only 36.3 percent (table 1). Compared to other regions in Canada, especially the western provinces, the Maritimes gained little from the vast immigration that was building the country. Its national share of population - and hence its market potential - declined preci-

Table 1

The Industrialization and Urbanization of the Maritimes and Canada During the Great Transformation, 1890-1929[a]

	Maritimes		Canada	
	1890,1891	1929,1931	1890,1891	1929,1931
Total Population[1]	880,737	1,009,103	4,833,239	10,376,786
Percentage of Pop. Urban	16.5	36.3	29.8	52.5
Number of Urban Places (1,000+ pop)	41	53	274	503
Gross Value of Production[2]				
Primary Industries ($000s)	77,993	150,163	585,625	2,061,585
Manufacturing ($000s)	56,514	108,354	623,205	1,802,960
Changing Labour Force (%)[3]				
Primary	54.8	47.9	50.0	34.0
Secondary	21.4	17.0	25.3	45.3
Tertiary	23.8	35.1	24.7	40.7

[a] Population and labour force data are for 1891 and 1931 (Ottawa)

Sources: [1] Canada, *Census of Canada* for 1891 and 1931 (Ottawa)
[2] D. Alexander, "Economic Growth in the Atlantic Region," *Acadiensis*, 8 (1978), p. 60
[3] A.G. Green, *Regional Aspects of Canadian Economic Growth* (Toronto, 1971), Appendix C

pitously over the course of the Great Transformation. Few people from southern or eastern Europe considered the Maritimes as one of Canada's more economically-attractive destinations in which to seek employment and start a new life. Neither, in fact, did the many thousands of Maritimers who joined the exodus for "the Boston States," central Canada, or other more prosperous North American regions.[14] The urbanization level was also constrained by many occupational pluralists, people who worked in both town and country, shifting from job to job on a seasonal basis as the industrial demand for part-time labour required, yet who retained their primary residences in a rural location and not in a town or city.[15]

Structural Changes in the Urban Hierarchy

As the Great Transformation unfolded, the number of Maritime towns and cities doubled from 33 in 1881 to 67 in 1941. Most, however, remained small. At the close of the depression decade, in fact, fully 85 percent of the region's urban places still housed fewer than 10,000 people, a value little changed over sixty years (table 2). The largest urban places in 1941 were the multi-functional centres of Halifax and Saint John, with the Sydney-Glace Bay steel making and coal mining complex in industrial Cape Breton also making an important mark. But with only about 100,000 people living in Halifax and 75,000 in Saint John, the two provincial leaders in urbanization were hardly dominant places. Their rank in the Canadian urban hierarchy had diminished considerably, from fourth and fifth position just after Confederation to eleventh and twelfth status by the 1920s; and their share of regional population remained below the 20 percent level.[16] Were structural features of the urban hierarchy like these basic size characteristics a fundamental weakness in the region's quest for sustained economic development?

To answer this question, it is instructive to compare the urban hierarchy of the Maritimes to that of the much more prosperous and economically-diversified Industrial Heartland in Ontario and Quebec. Perhaps surprisingly, the hierarchical structure, that is the percentage distribution of urban places across the different population size categories, changed in remarkably the same way over time in both regions. Whether in heartland or hinterland, there was a consistently-broad base of communities in the 1,000 - 2,499 size category, upon which successively-smaller tiers of more populated centres were placed in pyramid-like fashion (table 2). The shape of this hierarchical structure suggests, as Brian Berry has argued, that in both regions there was at least a similar response of cumulative urban growth to the general process of industrialization or economic development.[17] Small settlements served an agricultural hinterland or processed staple resources; slightly larger places might take on an additional manufacturing role. This is where the similarity ends, however. A major difference between the regions, of course, was the sheer number of places, with

Table 2

The Changing Structure of the Urban Hierarchy in the Maritimes and the Industrial Heartland, 1881-1941

(by number and percentage of urban places)

Population or Size Category	Maritimes			Industrial Heartland[a]		
	1881	1911	1941	1881	1911	1941
Total Population (000s)	871	938	1,130	3,286	4,533	7,120
Percentage Urban	15.3	30.9	44.1	26.2	47.1	63.1

Urban Centres

	No.	%	No.	%	No.	%	No.	%	No.	%	No.	%
1,000 - 2,499	17	51.5	29	53.7	33	49.3	116	63.0	165	60.9	208	57.0
2,500 - 4,999	8	24.2	11	20.4	13	19.4	39	21.3	52	19.6	73	20.0
5,000 - 9,999	5	15.3	9	16.7	11	16.4	22	12.0	23	8.5	34	9.3
10,000 - 24,999	1	3.0	2	3.7	6	9.0	1	0.5	22	8.1	27	7.4
25,000 - 99,999	2	6.0	3	5.6	4	6.0	5	2.7	5	1.8	17	4.7
100,000 - 249,999							1	0.5	2	0.7	4	1.1
250,000 and over												
Total Urban Places	35	100.0	44	100.0	67	100.0	184	100.0	271	100.0	365	100.0

[a] Ontario and Quebec

Source: Compiled from Canada, *Census of Canada* for 1881, 1911 and 1941 (Ottawa).

the Industrial Heartland counting five to six times as many communities as the Maritimes. Not only did this provide a larger market that could support ongoing development, but the external (particularly localization and urbanization) economies associated with this concentration of urban places also meant decided advantages associated with production economies of scale and scope.[18] Moreover, the industrial core had more large urban centres at the pinnacle of the hierarchy whose factories and financial institutions produced more goods and services, wielding considerable sway over the hinterland regions. In particular, the rise to national metropolitan status first of Montreal in the nineteenth century and then of Toronto by the First World War - through their accumulated economic functions, concentration of capitalist power, and innovative strength - would have a profound impact on the industrial restructuring and financial decline of the Maritimes after 1900.[19]

There are other ways to examine structural change in the urban hierarchy, but one method of analysis is particularly meaningful for our purposes because it pinpoints periods of time when the internal dynamics of systemic change were responsive to external shocks. This method takes the form of creating a transition matrix to measure the growth, stability or decline of all urban places by comparing the population or size class of each urban place at any two dates, for example, between the census years 1881 and 1891 or 1931 and 1941. The summary of all comparisons yields comprehensive data on the movement of urban places within the overall urban hierarchy, as they shift either upwards or downwards from one size category to another, or else remain stable within the same grouping. This sort of analysis was done for every province and major Canadian region for each of the seven decennial periods between 1871 and 1941. Of the many possibilities developed to pinpoint shocks in time and to illustrate core and periphery influences, table 3 summarizes the decadal rates of stability and upward and downward movement for all size classes or categories of urban places in Ontario and the Maritimes from 1871 to 1941, and in so doing reveals much about hierarchical change. Ontario's urban reaction to capitalist development was quite consistent over time. Stability ranged from 73 to 88 percent across the different decades; upward movement averaged 14.6 percent; and decline 2.2 percent. Summary data for the Maritimes record similar overall results of stability and upward and downward movement.

Equally significant but more revealing, however, are regional responses to various shocks that affected urban change in particular decades. Several trends stand out. First, through the 1880s, the federal government's 1878 National Policy of industrial incentives had a more immediate impact on the rate of urban expansion in Ontario than it did in the Maritimes. The difference in percentage points was not large (15.5 compared to 12.2 percent), but the number of Ontario towns and cities experiencing growth outdistanced the Maritimes total by a ratio of five to one. Second, the closing and opening decades of the nineteenth and

Table 3

Growth Dynamics in the Urban Hierarchy of the Maritimes and Ontario, 1871-1941

(by number and percentage of urban places within size categories[a])

	Stable		Upward Movement		Downward Movement		Total Urban Places
Maritimes							
1871-81	15	65.2	8	34.8	-	-	23
1881-91	29	87.8	4	12.2	-	-	33
1891-1901	33	80.5	7	17.1	1	2.4	41
1901-11	35	79.5	7	15.9	2	4.6	44
1911-21	43	82.7	9	17.3	-	-	51
1921-31	48	90.6	3	5.7	2	3.7	53
1931-41	45	80.4	11	19.6	-	-	56
	248	82.1	49	16.2	5	1.7	302
Ontario							
1871-81	66	73.3	24	26.7	-	-	90
1881-91	106	82.2	20	15.5	3	2.3	129
1891-1901	132	86.8	16	10.5	4	2.7	152
1901-11	123	81.5	23	15.2	5	3.3	151
1911-21	138	84.1	22	13.4	4	2.5	164
1921-31	143	81.2	28	16.0	4	2.8	175
1931-41	161	88.0	19	10.4	3	1.6	183
	869	83.2	152	14.6	23	2.2	1,044

[a] See table 2

Source: Compiles from Canada, *Census of Canada* for 1871, 1881, 1891, 1901, 1911, 1921, 1931, and 1941 (Ottawa).

twentieth centuries from 1891 to 1921 gave more favourable rates of upward movement to the Maritimes, but only marginally so. In particular, expansion was a little slower in Ontario through the depression years of the 1890s, but overall these three decades generally supported sustained and transforming urban growth not only at the core and in the Maritimes but also throughout all regions of Canada.[20] Third, of much more pivotal importance over the course of the *longue durée* were the 1920s, when only 3 or 5.7 percent of Maritime towns and cities shifted ahead a size class or two, but when 28 or fully 16 percent of urban places in Ontario advanced in status (table 3).[21] This was a decade of de-industrialization and consolidation in the Maritimes; in the heartland province it was a period of renewed industrialism and rising corporate capitalism that focused on consumer durables and financial and business services.[22] Finally, the 1930s offer a curious phase of urban development. After a decade of halted growth, Maritime urban places in all size classes experienced high rates of upward mobility, whereas stability was the more prevalent pattern in Ontario's urban system. Because the United States was no longer an escape valve for out-migration - its borders generally closed to Canadian immigration since the mid-1920s - and because job prospects in Ontario and the western provinces were not very hopeful, unemployed Maritimers from the depression-torn countryside sought refuge in the region's towns and cities where relief, however rudimentary, was more than the rural municipalities could offer. Population growth of this nature, however, placed a burden on scarce financial resources, diverting investment from potential areas of sustained job creation.[23]

This review of structural changes in the urban hierarchy of the old economy identifies key phases of urban advance (e.g., the 1880s) and retreat (e.g., the 1920s) in the development of the region. Some of these changes were influenced greatly by external shocks that included the federal government's National Policy of industrial incentives as well as the later sequence of capitalist restructuring, recentering, and de-industrialization. Against this background, we can now probe the role of towns and cities in the evolving space economy of the Maritimes, and in particular examine how urban places responded to certain shocks at the intersection of time (processes of capitalist development) and space (the core-periphery process) that have shaped so strongly the region's perceived hinterland status of urban marginality.

Inheriting the Past: Staple Enclaves of Mercantile Capitalism

One of the strengths of the Maritimes, but also one of its weaknesses, is the export orientation of the regional economy. Even today, well-being is highly dependent upon external markets for traditional natural resources, upon ever-changing but of necessity specialized manufactured products, and upon newly-developing producer services.[24] Of course, all regions and their cities must export to remain economically viable, and they must also adjust to changing circumstances to sustain viability. But when necessity turns to dependency, regional well-being is placed in jeopardy. To escape this staples trap is difficult, because many of the factors that buffet an export economy - for example, government trade policy - take place externally to the region, beyond the immediate control of the exporter.

The roots of this export *mentalité* extend deep into Maritime history.[25] Features of this inherited past - particularly those consequences stemming from the type and locational constraints of staple production - continue to influence the process of regional urban development. Certain Maritime staples have always been in demand. Various fish, wood, and mineral products have met continuing success in extra-regional markets, but typically have done so in a repeated cycle of up-and-down advance and retreat, through four centuries of resource exploitation.[26] This in itself can constrain capital formation and reinvestment in linked, urban-based economic activity. It can even promote caution when caution is not called for. At the same time, there are plentiful examples in the Maritimes of resource depletion or changing demand that should have supported a more cautious approach: the false hopes surrounding the mid-nineteenth century use of Albert County oil shales for kerosene; the depletion of good quality iron ore in Pictou and Colchester counties in the 1890s; and the current, much-reduced call on coal supplies and the depletion of cod stocks - all exemplify this situation and all have influenced the performance of urban growth.[27] But within the Maritime merchant community of the mid-nineteenth century, resource depletion and substitution were not of utmost concern. Coping with changes in imperial trading policy, breaking the monopoly of the General Mining Association, accumulating capital for investment, and debating the proper role of manufacturing in the colonial economy were all considered more important issues.[28]

Dealing with the shaping power of space was also crucial. The physical geography of the Maritimes has been one of the inherent and fundamental circumstances restraining the development of the region.[29] The necessity of capturing markets in the North Atlantic economy during the mercantile era established the long-lasting legacy of a fragmented settlement system that remained as a periphery to distant core areas. The small pockets of farming, the scattered fishing outports, and the mining and lumbering enclaves that still ring the fringes of the region are inherited from this mercantile past. Conditions of soil, topography and climate not only limited the extent of agricultural settlement to less than one-tenth of the land base, but unlike the almost continuous distribution of farming across southern Ontario, these conditions held back the formation of an integrated, regional market.[30] The region's coastline - hundreds of miles in broken and twisted length - was home to thousands of fishers who lived in numerous but small fishing outports where, to ensure better-quality production and prices, family and merchant enterprises dried and salted fish locally before marketing and shipping them directly abroad. Direct community contact with ever-shifting export markets obviously bypassed a central port, constraining the metropolitan ambitions of a city like Halifax.[31] In a similar way, the assault on the forest usually favoured either isolated, export-oriented sawmills located at the junction of stream and coastal shore, or dispersed production sites found along a river's course.[32] Nor did the quest for minerals such as coal integrate the scattered distribution of rural population and the newly-emerging urban places. On Cape Breton Island, for example, mining villages on the Sydney coalfield gathered together at waterfront locations, confined by the outcropping of bituminous seams and the need for access to shipping facilities. A similar pattern of mineral exploitation also existed across the mainland coalfields of Nova Scotia in Pictou and Cumberland counties.[33]

Settlements like these in a staple economy tend to be connected mainly, as James Vance has argued, to external points lying in core areas that are situated well beyond the export enclave. They certainly do not share the internal linkages which are basic to the central-place model of settlement.[34] To illustrate how the Maritime pattern of staple enclaves was organized in response to the export economy, figure 1 recreates the economic landscape of Pictou County immediately prior to Confederation.[35] Through the eighteenth and early nineteenth centuries, Pictou County comprised a unique physiographic region. It was rather isolated and structured apart from other areas in Nova Scotia by its highland backcountry. Several rivers began in this source area, passing through a richly-soiled lowland basin to reach Pictou Harbour, around which the majority of the Scottish immigrants - the most important group of late eighteenth-century settlers - had taken up farm land. Initial resource development was rather slow, but then, stimulated greatly by the cessation of the General Mining Association's coal monopoly (1857) and the shock of reciprocity with the United States (1860-1865),[36] a number of raw materials, some lightly-processed staple products, and a few finished goods - principally coal but also timber, lumber, ships, fish, tanned hides, flour and some other agricultural products - were gathered in ever-increasing abundance from the countryside and Northumberland Strait. From the backcountry, the fluvial plains, mining villages like Albion Mines, and the sea, these staple products moved over a rudimentary network of road, rail and water - by cart, wagon, train, raft and boat - to various coastal shipping points. Pictou Town and Pictou Landing were the principal depots of staple collection. Once in hand, the staples were shipped mainly to the United States, but also to the British North America colonies, Great Britain, and the West Indies (fig. 1).

Pictou County's settlement pattern of outward orientation and external connection was repeated throughout the staple-producing regions of the Maritimes: for example, at the mouth of the Miramichi River, along the Saint John River Valley, in the Vale of Sussex, and across Lunenburg County. After two centuries of trade in response to a fragmented physical environment, mercantile capitalism had shaped a hinterland region of export enclaves. These enclaves derived well-being more from shipping goods to external markets than

Figure 1

The Economic Landscape of Staple Production and Export trade in Pre-Confederation Pictou County, c.1865

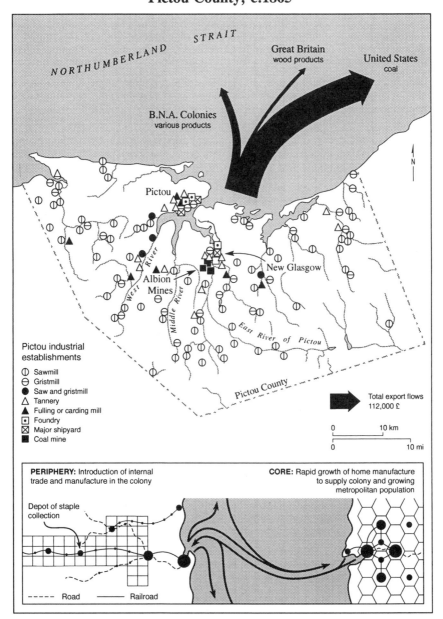

from functioning together within the Maritimes as an integrated settlement system.

The Urban System in the Era of the New Industrialism

The legacy of an inherited mercantile landscape was eventually challenged - although with only partial success - by a concerted effort of railroad building and urban-industrial growth. The inheritance is summarized succinctly by Ian McKay: "the region's links to the world capitalist economy in the period of merchant's capital. . . focused development in dependent export enclaves [and] undermined the socio-economic potential for integrated and balanced growth. . ., leaving a fragmented and dependent region vulnerable to rapidly expanding central Canadian capital."[37] To be sure, these were certainly powerful difficulties to overcome. But for several decades after Confederation, the prospects of sustained and integrated economic development - focusing on iron and steel and other secondary manufacturing - appeared quite promising. Countering the inherited difficulties and acting in support of the new industrialism were several important regional and national features that combined the shaping forces of space and time with the functioning of basic production factors. At the beginning of the Great Transformation, the Maritimes held most of Canada's important coal and iron ore reserves. Considerable mercantile capital was based in the hands of regional banks and aggressive community-minded entrepreneurs who were searching for investment opportunities in the emerging manufacturing economy. There was also a willingness to adapt new industrial technologies. The labour force was abundant, if somewhat transient in flight from the traditional staple trades and reticent about skill reclassification in the new manufacturing industries. Finally, there was the promise of federal aid to create a national industrial market through transportation and industrial development schemes and incentives.[38]

The shock waves of government-led free trade policies in the 1990s sound like echos from the past. Our review of structural changes in the urban hierarchy identified the 1880s and the subsequent decades down to the First World War as a period of sustained urban growth. Much of this advance was led by the federal government's National Policy of tariff protection, railroad building, and other attempts to build up infrastructure (e.g., harbour development) and providing various incentives (e.g., bounties on pig iron and steel). These policies were a fundamental attempt to stimulate urban-industrial growth and to integrate the Maritimes within the national economy. This was the reality of the late nineteenth century, just as today the reality is global integration and restructuring within a post-industrial economy.

Adjusting to the new nineteenth century realities meant shifting from a seaward to a landward economy. As T. W. Acheson, Eric Sager, Gerry Panting and others have shown, the process of redirecting capital from the mercantile to the industrial economy took place in many small communities and certainly in all larger urban centres throughout the Maritimes.[39] Important agents of integration and the new industrialism were the Intercolonial Railway (ICR), the Canadian Pacific Railway (CPR), and several private lines like the New Glasgow Coal, Iron, and Railway Company in Pictou County.[40] The CPR connected Saint John, New Brunswick with Montreal by cutting across northern New England. It also managed the Dominion Atlantic Railway in the Annapolis Valley. The main line of the ICR took a more circuitous route to the Industrial Heartland, running in Nova Scotia from Halifax-Dartmouth to Truro and on to Amherst, and then passing into New Brunswick at Sackville before turning towards Moncton, a major railroading hub, and then continuing northward towards Quebec through towns like Newcastle and Campbellton (fig. 2). At the close of World War I, some 4,000 miles of railroads criss-crossed the region, running from south-western Nova Scotia to Cape Breton Island, serving the length of Prince Edward Island, and embracing the perimeter of New Brunswick. Supplementing coastal shipping, the urban system of the Maritimes was now held together by a network of main trunk lines, secondary routes, and branch facilities.[41]

Clearly, railways, the new industrialism, and urbanization went hand-in-hand. Railways were used both to gather local raw materials and to ship the new producer and consumer products of the Maritimes to regional and national markets. To cite a few examples of industries protected by National Policy incentives, pig iron and steel came from Sydney, Sydney Mines and Trenton; sugar was refined in Halifax and Saint John; textiles were milled at Halifax, Yarmouth, Windsor, Moncton, Marysville, Saint John and Milltown; glassware was created at New Glasgow; nuts, bolts, and forest machinery were produced in Saint John; and boots, shoes, boilers, and rail cars were manufactured at Amherst. Location on a rail line, and preferably on a main trunk line, was therefore an essential asset for any town or city's pursuit of industrial growth and its advance through the tiers of the urban hierarchy.[42] The fastest growing industrial centres, including Dartmouth, Sydney, Trenton, New Glasgow, Amherst, and Moncton, were all well-served by the ICR (fig. 3). Besides advantages such as resource proximity, entrepreneurial initiative, and the availability of investment capital, these centres benefitted substantially from the transfer economies and other transportation savings associated with direct rail links to the major and all-important markets lying outside of the Maritimes. Communities which experienced lower rates of population growth tended to be rather removed from the more frequent services and direct access of a main line, and were less attractive to profit-seeking industrialists. Declining Digby and slow-growing Shelburne and Yarmouth in southwestern Nova Scotia exemplify this situation.

Figure 2

Railroad Construction and Urbanization in the Maritimes 1881-1921

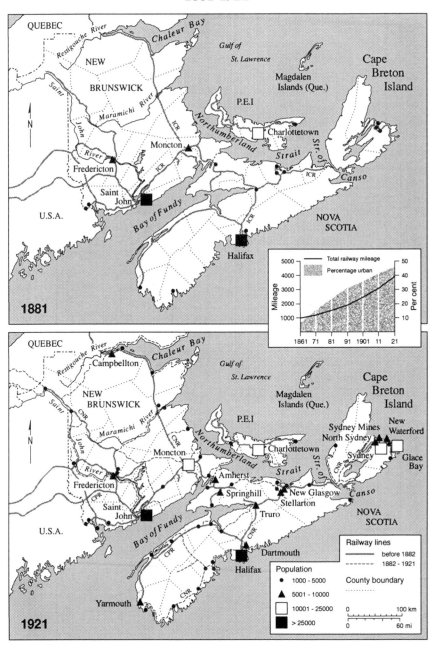

Figure 3

**Population Growth of Towns and Cities in the Maritimes
1901-1921**

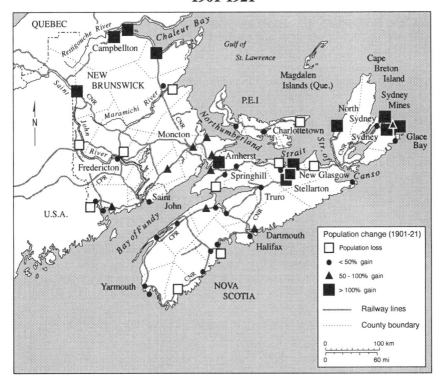

Of lasting consequence, therefore, railroad construction reinforced the pre-existing spatial pattern of staple enclaves, preserving the outward focus of the region. There was no abandonment of long-standing settlement patterns; no venture into unchartered territory; and no promotion of new town building. Instead, the railroads encouraged towns like Truro, Amherst, Sackville, Moncton, Fredericton and other older mercantile communities to break away from the sea, turning their backs, so to speak, on once-favoured waterborne connections. Even though the land-based economy had become better connected, it remained difficult to sell goods in volume in local markets. Regional consumer and producer markets of about 900,000 people and a few thousand scattered industrial firms were still very small by North American standards. In particular, the market potential of the Maritimes was limited in size and purchasing power.[43] In 1891, Ontario and Quebec had four to five times the population and industrial output of the Maritimes, and this share increased substantially over the next few decades.[44] As the New Brunswick economist B.S. Keirstead argued a few years after the close of the Great Transformation, the limited market and industrial environment found in the Maritimes could not provide the external economies necessary for sustained and integrated urban-industrial development. Therefore, for most Maritime manufacturing companies to grow in size, remain competitive, and in turn stimulate urban growth, it was essential for them to sell their products in extra-regional markets.

Industrial enterprise in Pictou County and linked communities again affords a reasonable example of the export *mentalité* of the Maritime economy, and therefore of the outward focus of the urban system. The shock of reciprocity trade closure in 1866 was followed a decade later by the shock of National Policy industrial incentives of 1878. These had an immediate effect on the industries and towns of the County. By mobilizing accumulated savings of the mercantile community and using local coal and iron ore resources, New Glasgow entrepreneurs established a succession of firms that would become, in 1901, the Nova Scotia Steel and Coal Company ("Scotia"). By 1912, it was hailed as Canada's largest vertically-integrated industrial enterprise, employing some 6,000 workers in a sphere of operations in North America that included managing the company in New Glasgow; mining iron ore at Wabana, Newfoundland; shipping iron ore to the eastern seaboard of the United States; and discharging coal at Quebec City and Montreal. Across Nova Scotia, coal mining and iron and steel production took place at Sydney Mines, Cape Breton Island, while a huge metallurgical works of mills, forges, and a railway car plant dominated the landscape of Trenton in Pictou County. The economic base of Wabana, Sydney Mines, Trenton, and New Glasgow centred on activities linked directly or indirectly to "Scotia's" multi-faceted coal, iron, and steel operations. The economies of Stellarton and Westville (coal mining), as well as North Sydney (shipping), also felt the benefits of "Scotia's" entrepreneurial hand.[45]

But despite the exchange of raw materials and producer goods that connected these places in "Scotia's" sphere of operations - all of which offers at least some evidence of forward and backward linkages within the region's urban system - the lion's share of the company's coal, iron, and steel products was shipped outside of the Maritimes. Evidence of this export orientation is provided by company data on shipments of coal, pig iron, and steel products during the decade immediately before the First World War (fig. 4).[46] The coal trade of the St. Lawrence industrial and residential market remained far more important than the sales and distribution of coal within the Maritimes. For pig iron, Ontario and Quebec together usually took over three to four times the tonnage sold to factories in the Maritimes. In fact, foundries and agricultural implement manufacturers in Montreal, Sherbrooke, Toronto, and Brantford initially favoured "Scotia's" good quality products, but competition after 1907 from Hamilton's expanding iron and steel mills soon reduced shipments from Sydney Mines to a mere trickle. "Scotia" responded by exporting various finished steel products to national markets, notably railway axles for federal government railways, but demand for such products would diminish greatly after the war. This export orientation of the coal and iron and steel industry's external linkages within the Canadian urban system - its *mentalité* - was followed repeatedly in other leading industrial sectors. For example, lumber and newly-emerging pulp and paper towns, cotton textile towns, and other communities with prominent export-oriented manufacturers (Ganong's candies in St. Stephen, Stanfield's knitwear in Truro, Robb Engineering's steam boilers in Amherst, and Enterprise and Fawcett stoves in Sackville, to cite a few) all shared this export orientation. As a result, the economic well-being of these places was most vulnerable to fluctuations in the business cycle and shifting market conditions lying beyond the Maritimes.[47]

The Double-Edged Sword of Metropolitanism

Metropolitanism is a double-edged sword: it can work to a region's advantage; or, equally so, to its disadvantage. The concept itself is an old chestnut in Canadian historiography.[48] Basically, metropolitanism heralds the rise of any city to economic, social, cultural, and political leadership by its ability to hold sway over a surrounding hinterland area. Its role as the leading transportation, trade, manufacturing, and financial centre places it at the top of the urban hierarchy. Using this prominence, the metropolis is able to compete successfully against less favoured places. The concept is thus sympathetic to our conceptualization of time and space. The metropolis is able over time to successfully mobilize the shifting forms of capitalism (for example, industrial, financial or managerial); and it acts as the spearhead of the core-periphery process that can force changes such as de-industrialization, out-migration, and declining well-being on hinterland regions.[49] For the Maritimes, the double-edged sword of metropolitanism took two basic, but interrelated forms. First, it centred on the failed attempts of both Saint John and especially Halifax to achieve metropolitan success on their own behalf; and second, it demonstrated the inability of the Maritimes to ward off competition emanating from Montreal, Toronto, and other external cities.

Halifax and Saint John experienced declining positions within the Canadian urban system during the Great Transformation. Their loss of relative national strength and their slow population growth reflect an inability to capitalize on, or to maintain, the offerings of the old economy. As trade and transportation centres in the pre-Confederation era, their shipping fleets were amongst the largest in North America; and their merchants established a substantial wholesale-trading complex (which included banking, insurance, and some commerce-serving and residentiary manufacturing) with links throughout and beyond the Maritimes. Saint John was prominent in New Brunswick and along the Fundy shore of Nova Scotia. Halifax's commercial realm extended beyond Nova Scotia

Figure 4

The Nova Scotia Steel and Coal Company: Shipments of Coal, Pig Iron, and Steel to Regional and Extra-regional Markets in the Early Twentieth Century

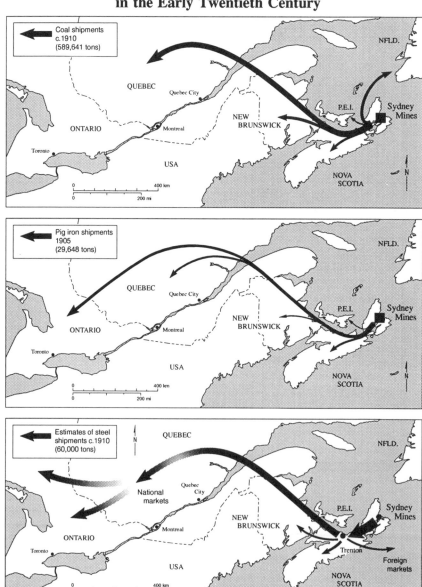

to encompass Prince Edward Island and even parts of Gaspé in Quebec. Outside the region, both cities had trading ties with other places throughout the North Atlantic economy.[50] As the world of "wooden ships and iron men" in the mercantile economy waned, however, entrepreneurs in both cities embraced the new industrialism. Gains were particularly strong in the 1880s and further advances, even if slowed by the depression of the 1890s, lasted into the early 1900s. Saint John's manufacturing sector (principally sawmilling, machinery, and hardware) was linked closely to New Brunswick's forest sector. By contrast, Halifax was generally unable to process any of the province's staple resources because it lacked immediate, cost-efficient access to their sources. Instead, a diverse, but largely unrelated line of consumer products was manufactured there - for example, cotton textiles, sugar, hardware, rope, clothing, paint, railway cars, and boots and shoes. Thus, the manufacturing structures of both cities were not strongly positioned, even though each city was a provincial leader. Saint John's make-up was too narrowly-focused on the forest industries, and Halifax's shallow diversity did not benefit from localization or urbanization economies. Moreover, although both cities managed to capture regional markets in some product lines, attempts to gain a national toehold in ubiquitous industries - like textiles, clothing, or boots and shoes - proved difficult. Despite countering with bonusing and at times quite aggressive marketing tactics, success in the age of financial capitalism was limited. It became difficult to ward off competition from the Industrial Heartland. After 1900, industries like cotton textiles were increasingly subjected to takeover attempts by Montreal corporate interests and, in some cases, even closure by their new owners. Under pressures like these, many local companies were forced to cut back production and focus instead on smaller, less rewarding regional markets.[51]

The metropolitan outreach of central Canada soon extended into traditional areas of regional dominance - trade and ocean shipping. Both Halifax and Saint John competed for winter port status. Federal government assistance was crucial to meet this goal. Fast mail contracts, steamship subsidies, grain terminals, and other harbour facilities and improvements were sought and obtained. But here, too, the double-edged sword struck against the region. These winter port gains were achieved at considerable loss of independence, for "in developing a strategy for securing facilities, the civic and business elite in their negotiations emphasized Saint John's [and Halifax's] appendage relationship...[to] Montreal's pivotal position."[52] But Montreal was not the only external influence. Both Halifax and Saint John soon lost control to shippers and agents for international steamship lines. The hinterland ports had become, in effect, largely intermediaries for handling trade in the rapidly changing international shipping scene.[53]

This intermediary role also applied to wholesale and retail trade where the incursion of wholesaler distributors and retail chains from Montreal, Toronto, and other continental cities cut a wide swath across the Maritimes after the turn of the century. In the wholesaling field, central Canadian manufacturers, some with branch plant ties to American multinational enterprise (Canadian General Electric, Canadian Westinghouse, and Singer Sewing Machines, to cite a few) set up distribution facilities in Halifax and Saint John. Moncton was also a preferred location, which further dampened the metropolitan ambitions of the coastal cities. The product lines of these distant manufacturers were not assembled in the Maritimes, only distributed and serviced. Consequently, job creation was limited, as were the salaries of these less-skilled service jobs. Similarly, national retail chains, another agent of managerial capitalism, made inroads against local businessmen. Eaton's, Woolworths, Metropolitan Stores, Agnew Surpass, Birks, and other major Canadian and American retailers became household names to Maritime consumers. Regional businesses fought back, but were sometimes at a cost disadvantage, even forced to purchase products from the very central Canadian manufacturers and distributors against whom they were competing.[54]

Beyond transportation, trade, and manufacturing, the critical mark of metropolitan status is achieved by gaining control of financial activity - establishing trusts, selling insurance, raising capital through the stock market, and most important of all, dominating banking. Halifax and Saint John developed all of these businesses when making the transition to industrial and financial capitalism. In Halifax, for example, the Bank of Nova Scotia, the Merchants Bank, Eastern Trust, the Halifax Insurance Company, and other financial institutions functioned prominently in the late nineteenth century as provincial leaders in their fields. They actively supported regional industrialization, such as the alliance between Pictou County's Nova Scotia Steel and Coal Company and the Halifax legal, banking, and industrial community. Some of these financial concerns also acted in an export capacity, using surplus savings to finance development well beyond provincial boundaries. In fact, some scholars argue that regional banks became too enthusiastic about exporting capital out of the region, to the detriment of urban-industrial development in the Maritimes.[55] A recent study contradicts this assertion, concluding that the Bank of Nova Scotia "treated its established Maritime customers with a generosity more readily characterized as shoring up the declining Maritime economy than promoting its demise."[56] By the turn of the century, however, the pattern of head office leadership was changing. Citing various reasons, including the need to be closer to a larger financial community and major customers, the Bank of Nova Scotia relocated to Toronto and the Merchants (soon to become the Royal) Bank moved to Montreal. This was also the migration path followed by some leading Maritime businessmen like Max Aitken, Nathaniel Curry, Arthur Nesbitt and Izaak Walton Killam, all of whom were dedicated to the maximization of profit, and who worked their way into the elite ranks of the central Canadian business community. As Gregory Marchildon argues, ". . . their primary loyalty was not to their region, but to their class. . . [their decision to live and invest outside of the region] was a reaction to the already declining profitability of Maritime enterprises, not the cause of that decline."[57] By going, however, Halifax and Saint John lost people of great innovative ability, and became all the more subject to the financial actions of Montreal and Toronto.

Shock Waves at the Close of the Great Transformation

The double-edged sword of metropolitanism was sheathed for the moment, but its actions had a profound and long-lasting impact on the Maritimes. While Canada suffered through the Great Depression of the 1930s, the Maritimes experienced an even longer period of economic hardship. It began early in the 1920s, when the region suffered greatly from the recession which followed shortly after the close of the First World War, and continued through the 1930s in devastating fashion. The net impact was decline or stasis, as one shock wave after another hit the Maritimes.

For some urban places, the root of the problem rested with the need to trade beyond the region - the long-standing *mentalité* of many Maritime communities. Except for the growing American demand for pulp and paper, and the positive impact this had on the growth of towns such as Liverpool in Nova Scotia and Bathurst, Dalhousie, and Saint John in New Brunswick, the traditional staple industries were buffeted by the up-and-down shocks of an unstable economy. This took many forms: technologies were changing (e.g., larger diesel trawlers in the off-shore fishery and centralized freezing depots affected fishing towns); resources were being substituted (e.g., diesel fuel for coal hit hard at inefficient coal sites); and markets for many resources were being either closed through protection or simply evaporating with reduced demand.[58] Changes like these were major factors in the long-term population losses during the 1920s and 1930s of a number of regional fishing, lumbering, and coal mining towns, including Annapolis Royal, Canso, Chatham, Joggins, Louisburg, Lunenburg, Parrsboro, North Sydney, St. Stephen, Wedgeport, and Westville. Most were export enclaves - places at the edge - more weakly positioned than the manufacturing towns located on the trunk rail lines that tried to integrate region and nation.

But as comparison of urban population growth in figures 3 and 5 clearly shows, location on a major rail line was no guarantee against the shock of industrial restructuring and other disrupting factors that fell upon the region. "Busy Amherst," which once ranked as Canada's twentieth largest manufacturing centre in terms of value of production, and which had experienced a population growth rate of just over 100 percent from 1901 to 1921, suffered a fifteen percent loss between 1921 and 1941.[59] The same pattern of decline prevailed in other once dynamic towns: New Glasgow (from +102 to +2 percent); Sydney Mines (+161 to -2 percent); Moncton (+94 to +30 percent); and Milltown (-3 to -5 percent) illustrate this situation. For all of these towns and some others, the loss of population was directly linked to the loss of jobs in various manufacturing industries.[60]

Figure 5

Population Growth of Towns and Cities in the Maritimes 1921-1941

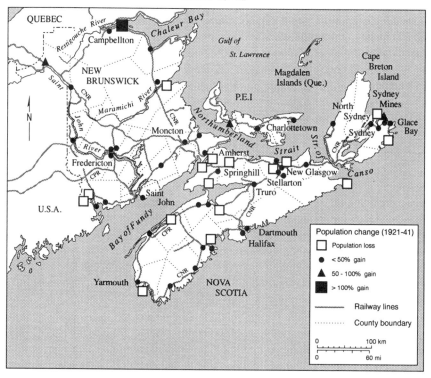

Of course, no one explanation can be offered to account for the loss of manufacturing jobs and the subsequent impact on the sluggish performance of the urban system. Certainly, the export orientation of important manufacturing industries was a factor. Increasingly, Maritime businessmen were forced to compete against central Canadian firms which were accumulating considerable benefits from more favourable external economies and internal economies of scale. With an environment of cheaper production costs, metal-making and metal-working firms in Hamilton, Toronto, and Brampton, for example, could parlay these savings into meeting or exceeding the extra cost of shipping their products to the Maritimes.[61] In related fashion, given this increasingly favourable cost position, a central Canadian corporation, which had recently bought out a Maritime competitor, now could justify to national shareholders the reasons for its action, taken to allow it to close down the Maritime branch plant. Other scholars contend that exploitive policies towards deskilling labour, while also failing to invest in new technologies, were critical reasons for making firms uncompetitive on the national scene.[62] In some cases, the quality of resource endowments affected production costs and investment strategies, hindering urban-industrial development.[63] Poor, if not incompetent, financial management is also cited as a concern.[64] Some argue that rising freight rates, especially after World War I, also played a role in hindering market accessibility; others suggest otherwise.[65] Further, with massive out-migration from town and countryside, totalling around 100,000 people in the 1920s, local market potential and capital formation were obviously held in check.[66] Clearly, many factors affecting either the region at large, or the particular nature of a local town, were at work to slow or impede the urban-industrial growth process in the 1920s. The cumulative weight of all these factors, whether general or particular, was the much publicized de-industrialization and restricted urbanization that characterized the final decades of the Great Transformation.[67]

Conclusion

Maritime towns and cities share a problem. The regional urban system comprises the traits of a hinterland area where fragmentation, weak integration, narrowly-based urban economies, and the lack of a dominant regional metropolitan centre are more characteristic than the obverse. These traits exist because the regional economy functions from a relative position of limited strength, shaped adversely by the contextual forces of capitalist time and core-periphery space. There is no one explanation that neatly summarizes how these forces have intersected to force underdevelopment on the region. It is clear, nevertheless, that over time most of the towns and cities in the Maritimes have found it extremely difficult to overcome external factors that impinge on the region. To counter this situation, various government-led strategies of revival have been attempted. For example, two important regional development strategies of the last few decades have been attempted to redress the situation first by sponsoring a growth pole solution, and second by investing in highway construction to foster integration. Success has been only partial and unevenly shared throughout the region. While Halifax is slowly emerging as the region's most prominent city, it has met with only limited success in functioning as a growth pole and integrating force. It services the Maritimes well as a regional transportation, distribution, producer-service, government and financial centre. Certainly its status is more secure than that of Saint John's.[68] But it is not an innovator. Nor has it stimulated the kinds of industrial linkages between and among cities that can overcome the regional problem of urban fragmentation. It remains a "centre at the edge," much removed from major decision-making that shapes the Canadian space economy in the post-industrial era.[69]

This chapter has suggested that the problems that Halifax and other towns and cities face took shape during the Great Transformation, when attempts at economic development and reorganization of the space economy around industrial centres were high on the agenda of regional entrepreneurs and government officials. This effort was particularly evident in the immediate post-Confederation era. Possessing coal and iron, capital and labour, entrepreneurship and access to technology, the region held many of the factors of production that were essential to accomplish the transformation. At the same time, there were internal difficulties that had to be overcome. One was the physical environment of the region, that is, the quality, extent, variety, and accessibility of natural resources. Later, in the twentieth century, their depletion, substitution, and high production costs amongst other factors would plague the sustained development of the urban-industrial economy. As the transition to the new industrialism was made, however, the legacy of mercantile capitalism was an export *mentalité*, a belief in the value of pursuing growth by satisfying external demands for staple products rather than by building-up an urban system of strongly-linked or integrated urban places. The railways did not, in essence, alter this condition; they merely provided another conduit that reinforced the perceived need to ship products out of the region. Inevitably, the region's towns and cities found that they were at a cost disadvantage when producing many lines of manufactured goods for the export market. Not only did they suffer the tyranny of a peripheral location, but they also lacked the agglomeration economies that could place them in a more competitive position. Without internal integration within the regional urban system, which creates these more favourable external economies, and which in turn lead to reduced production costs, the region's industries were susceptible to possible take-over and closure, and certainly to competition from the distributors of products made in more economically-favourable locations. This was perhaps the ultimate shock - the realization that in a core-periphery space economy there are both winners and losers, where the losers are usually the towns and cities of the distant periphery.

NOTES TO CHAPTER ONE

1. Paul Bairoch, *Cities and Economic Development: From the Dawn of History to the Present*, trans. Christopher Braider (Chicago, 1988), p. xvii.

2. For a discussion of the Great Transformation and its application to an interpretation of the changing geography of late nineteenth and early twentieth century Canada (c.1891-1929), see Donald Kerr, Deryck Holdsworth and Susan Laskin, (eds.), *Historical Atlas of Canada*, vol. III (Toronto, 1992), pp. 13-5. See also D. A. Muise, "'The Great Transformation': Changing the Urban Face of Nova Scotia, 1871-1921," *Nova Scotia Historical Review*, 11 (Autumn 1991), pp. 1-42.

3. On the nature and meaning of the *longue durée* in historical analysis, see Fernand Braudel, *On History*, trans. Sarah Matthews (Chicago, 1980), pp. 27-34.

4. The differences between core and periphery areas are considered more fully in L. D. McCann, "Heartland and Hinterland: A Framework for Regional Analysis," in *idem*, (ed.), *Heartland and Hinterland: A Geography of Canada*, 2d ed. (Scarborough, 1987), pp. 3-37.

5. Alfred Chandler, "The United States: Seedbed of Managerial Capitalism," in *idem* and Herman Daems, (eds.), *Managerial Hierarchies: Comparative Perspectives on the Rise of the Modern Industrial Enterprise* (Cambridge, Mass., 1980), pp. 9-40. See also Alfred Chandler, *The Visible Hand* (Cambridge, Mass., 1978) and *idem*, *Scale and Scope* (Cambridge, Mass., 1990).

6. T. W. Acheson, "The National Policy and the Industrialization of the Maritimes, 1880-1910," *Acadiensis*, 1 (Spring 1972), pp. 3-29.

7. L. D. McCann, "The Mercantile-Industrial Transition in the Metals Towns of Pictou County, 1857-1931," *Acadiensis*, 10 (Spring 1981), pp. 29-64.

8. Gregory P. Marchildon, "John F. Stairs, Max Aitken and the Scotia Group: Finance Capitalism and Industrial Decline in the Maritimes, 1890-1914," in Kris Inwood, (ed.), *Farm, Factory and Fortune* (Fredericton, N.B., 1993), pp. 197-218. See also Christopher Armstrong, "Making a Market: Selling Securities in Atlantic Canada before World War I," *Canadian Journal of Economics*, 13 (1980), pp. 438-54.

9. L. D. McCann, "Metropolitanism and Branch Businesses in the Maritimes, 1881-1931," *Acadiensis*, 13 (Autumn 1983), pp. 112-25.

10. Ernest R. Forbes, "Cutting the Pie into Smaller Pieces: Matching Grants and Relief in the Maritime Provinces During the 1930s," *Acadiensis*, 17 (Autumn 1987), pp. 3-24.

11. David Alexander, "Economic Growth in the Atlantic Region, 1880-1940," *Acadiensis*, 8 (Autumn 1978), pp. 47-76.

12. Ibid., pp. 51-62. On earlier regional inequality, see K. Inwood and James R. Irwin, "Canadian Regional Commodity Income Differences at Confederation," in Inwood, *Farm, Factory and Fortune*, op. cit., pp. 93-120.

13. Leroy O. Stone, *Urban Development in Canada: An Introduction to the Demographic Aspects* (Ottawa, 1967), pp. 9-42.

14. Patricia A. Thornton, "The Problem of Out-Migration from Atlantic Canada, 1871-1921," *Acadiensis*, 15 (Autumn 1985), pp. 56-77.

15. The links between occupational pluralism, industrialization, and urbanization are discussed in L. D. McCann, "'Living a Double Life': Town and Country in the Industrialization of the Maritimes," in D. Day, (ed.), *Geographical Perspectives on the Maritime Provinces* (Halifax, 1988), pp. 93-113. See also S. A. Saunders, *Economic History of the Maritime Provinces* (Fredericton, 1984 [1939]), pp. 55, 77; *idem*, "Forest Industries in the Maritime Provinces," in A. R. M. Lower, (ed.), *The North American Assault on the Canadian Forest* (Toronto, 1938), pp. 368-69; and L. Anders Sandberg, "Dependent Development, Labour, and the Trenton Steel Works, Nova Scotia, c.1900-1943," *Labour/Le Travail*, 27 (Spring 1991), pp. 127-62.

16. The changing rank of Halifax and Saint John within the Canadian urban system is analyzed in L. D. McCann, "Staples and the New Industrialism in the Growth of Post-Confederation Halifax," *Acadiensis*, 8 (Spring 1979), pp. 52-3; and The Carleton University History Collaborative, *Urban and Community Development in Atlantic Canada, 1867-1991* (Ottawa, 1994).

17. Brian J. L. Berry, "City Size Distributions and Economic Development," *Economic Development and Cultural Change*, 9 (1961), pp. 573-88. See also Wilbur Thompson, *A Preface to Urban Economics* (Baltimore, 1965), especially pp. 11-60; Eric E. Lampard, "The Evolving System of Cities in the United States: Urbanization and Economic Development," in Harvey Perloff and Lowdon Wingo, Jr., (eds.), *Issues in Urban Economics* (Baltimore, 1968), pp. 81-139; and L. S. Bourne, *Urban Systems: Strategies for Regulation* (Toronto, 1975), pp. 157-83.

18. James G. Gilmour, *Spatial Evolution of Manufacturing of Southern Ontario, 1851-1891* (Toronto, 1972). For a conceptual discussion of these issues see P. Lloyd and P. Dicken, *Location In Space* (New York, 1977), pp. 197-300; and Alfred Chandler, *Scale and Scope: The Dynamics of Industrial Capitalism* (Cambridge, Mass., 1990).

19. The metropolitan influence is well treated in J. M. S. Careless, *Frontier and Metropolis: Regions, Cities, and Identities in Canada before 1914* (Toronto 1989); and is also a theme in L.D. McCann, (ed.), *Heartland and Hinterland: A Geography of Canada*, 2d ed. (Scarborough, 1987), especially pp. 3-37 and 175-245. On the timing of metropolitan ascendancy, see L. D. McCann and Peter J. Smith, "Canada Becomes Urban: Cities and Urbanization in Historical Perspective," in Trudi Bunting and Pierre Filion, (eds.), *Canadian Cities in Transition* (Toronto, 1991), pp. 84-9.

20. This comment is based on the results of the urban growth matrix analyses for each decade from 1871 to 1941.

21. This analysis, of course, focuses on movement across rather broadly-based class sizes or categories. Another way of looking at advance and retreat is to measure simple population gain or loss. In Nova Scotia alone, some eighteen of thirty-seven urban communities actually lost population in the 1920s, their losses ranging from less than one percent to as high as forty-two percent. The urban communities of New Brunswick and Prince Edward Island suffered similar setbacks. Few Ontario towns and cities lost population in this decade.

22. For an overview of these and other decades in the regional economic growth and development of Canada, see Alan G. Green, *Regional Aspects of Canada's Economic Growth* (Toronto, 1979); Ken Norrie and Doug Owram, *A History of the Canadian Economy* (Toronto, 1991); and Kris Inwood and Thanasis Stengos, "Discontinuities in Canadian Economic Growth, 1870-1915," *Explorations in Economic History*, 28 (July 1991), pp. 274-86.

23. See, in particular, Forbes, "Cutting the Pie into Smaller Pieces," op. cit.; and *idem* "The 1930s: Depression and Retrenchment," in *idem* and D. A. Muise, (eds.), *The Atlantic Provinces in Confederation* (Toronto, 1993), pp. 272-305. The problems of unemployment and its relation to urban development are also considered in Carol Ann Ferguson, "Responses to the Unemployment Problem in Saint John, New Brunswick, 1929-1933," (MA thesis, University of New Brunswick, 1984); and Canada, Dominion Bureau of Statistics, *The Maritime Provinces in Their Relation to the National Economy of Canada* (Ottawa, 1948).

24. See, for example, Pierre-Marcel Desjardins, "Trade in Atlantic Canada: Trends and Opportunities Under Trade Liberalization," Discussion Paper No. 1, The Northumberland Group Series, The Canadian Institute for Research on Regional Development (Moncton, 1994).

25. According to James Henretta, a *mentalité* exists where there is "a direct relationship between the material environment, on the one hand, and the consciousness and activity of the population on the other." See his "Families and Farms: *Mentalité* in Pre-Industrial America," *William and Mary Quarterly*, 3d ser., 35 (1978), p. 14. The theme of *mentalité* has been taken-up more in the United States than in Canada,

but see T. W. Acheson, "New Brunswick Agriculture at the End of the Colonial Era: A Reassessment," *Acadiensis*, 22 (Spring 1993), pp. 5-26.

26. This is a theme that is discussed and mapped at length in the various volumes of the *Historical Atlas of Canada*, published recently by the University of Toronto Press.

27. These particular examples are treated in Hugh M. Grant, "Public Policy and Private Capital Formation in Petroleum Exploration," in Paul A. Bogaard, (ed.), *Profiles of Science and Society in the Maritimes Prior to 1914* (Fredericton, 1990), pp. 137-60; McCann, "The Mercantile-Industrial Transition in Pictou County," op. cit.; and Hugh Millward, "Mine Locations and the Sequence of Coal Exploitation on the Sydney Coalfield, 1720-1980," in Kenneth Donovan, (ed.), *Cape Breton at 200* (Sydney, 1985), pp. 173-88.

28. Marilyn Gerriets, "The Impact of the General Mining Association on the Nova Scotia Coal Industry, 1826-1850," *Acadiensis*, 21 (Autumn 1991), pp. 54-84; Eric Sager with Gerry Panting, *Maritime Capital: The Shipping Industry in Atlantic Canada, 1820-1914* (Montreal 1990); T. W. Acheson, "The Great Merchant and Economic Development in Saint John, 1820-1850," *Acadiensis*, 8 (Spring 1979), pp. 3-27; Graeme Wynn, *Timber Colony* (Toronto, 1980); and Ian McKay, "The Crisis of Dependent Development: Class Conflict in the Nova Scotia Coalfields, 1872-1876," *Canadian Journal of Sociology*, 13 (1988), pp. 9-48.

29. Such a claim for the physical factor is sometimes dismissed as the viewpoint of environmental, geographical, or locational determinism, but for a balanced perspective see Graeme Wynn, "The Maritimes: The Geography of Fragmentation and Underdevelopment," in L.D. McCann, (ed.), *Heartland and Hinterland: A Geography of Canada*, 2d ed. (Scarborough, 1987), pp. 175 and 180-86. John Kenneth Galbraith, for one, in his *The Nature of Mass Poverty* (Cambridge, Mass., 1979), pp. 3-5, holds that physical conditions alone cannot explain poverty. I agree. Here I am arguing that aspects of physical geography have contributed to the shaping of a fragmented settlement system that in turn limits the strength of competitive enterprise.

30. Local markets, some with ties to New England and Newfoundland, were the more common pattern. See, for example, Robert McKinnon and Graeme Wynn, "Nova Scotian Agriculture in the 'Golden Age': A New Look," in Douglas Day, (ed.), *Geographical Perspectives on the Maritime Provinces* (Halifax, 1988), pp. 47-60; A. R. MacNeil, "Cultural Stereotypes and Highland Farming in Eastern Nova Scotia, 1827-1861," *Histoire sociale/Social History*, 19 (May 1986), pp. 19-38; *idem*, "The Acadian Legacy and Agricultural Development in Nova Scotia, 1760-1861," in Inwood, *Farm, Factory and Fortune*, op. cit., pp. 1-16.

31. David Sutherland, "Halifax Merchants and the Pursuit of Development, 1783-1850," *Canadian Historical Review*, 59 (1978), pp. 1-17.

32. Graeme Wynn, "A Region of Scattered Settlements and Bounded Possibilities: Northeastern America, 1775-1800," *The Canadian Geographer*, 31 (1987), pp. 319-38.

33. McKay, "The Crisis of Dependent Development," op. cit., pp. 30-1; and Stephen Hornsby, *Nineteenth Century Cape Breton: A Historical Geography* (Montreal, 1991).

34. James Vance, Jr., *The Merchant's World: The Geography of Wholesaling* (Englewood Cliffs, N. J., 1970), especially pp. 150-67 which outline his mercantile model of settlement.

35. The location of economic activity is derived from several sources, including A. F. Church, *Topographical Township Map of Pictou County*, c.1865. The export data are from "Customs Records for the Port of Pictou, 1833-1875," RG 13, vols. HA-186, Public Archives of Nova Scotia. The inset of Vance's mercantile settlement model is from Vance, *The Merchant's World*, op. cit., p. 151.

36. Rosemary Ommer, "Anticipating the Trend: The Pictou Ship Register, 1840-1899," *Acadiensis*, 10 (Autumn 1980), pp. 67-89.

37. McKay, "The Crisis of Dependent Development," op. cit., p. 16.

38. The literature on industrialization and the mobilization of factors of production during the Great Transformation is now very substantial. The seminal paper on this theme is by T. W. Acheson, "The National Policy and the Industrialization of the Maritimes, 1880-1910," *Acadiensis*, 1 (Spring 1972), pp. 1-28. For a recent review of this literature, see Kris Inwood, "Maritime Industrialization from 1870 to 1910: A Review of the Evidence and its Interpretation," *Acadiensis*, 21 (Autumn 1991), pp. 132-55.

39. Acheson, "National Policy and Industrialization of the Maritimes," op. cit.; Eric Sager, "'Buying Cheap and Selling Dear': Merchant Shipowners and the Decline of the Shipping Industry in Atlantic Canada," in Peter Baskerville, (ed.), *Canadian Papers in Business History*, vol. I (Victoria, 1989), pp. 59-75; and *idem* and Gerry Panting, *Maritime Capital*, op. cit.; and McCann, "The Mercantile-Industrial Transition," op. cit.

40. Ken Cruikshank, "The People's Railway: The Intercolonial Railway and the Canadian Public Enterprise Experience," *Acadiensis*, 16 (Autumn 1986), pp. 78-100; *idem*, "The Intercolonial Railway, Freight Rates and the Maritime Economy," *Acadiensis*, 22 (Autumn 1992), pp. 87-110; and E. R. Forbes, "Misguided Symmetry: The Destruction of Regional Transportation Policy for the Maritimes," in D. J. Bercuson, (ed.), *Canada and the Burden of Unity* (Toronto, 1977), pp. 60-86.

41. This mileage represented about one-eighth of the Canadian total of 32,559 miles of trackage in operation in 1911. M. C. Urquahart, (ed.), *Historical Statistics of Canada* (Toronto, 1965), p. 532.

42. This issue is examined in D. A. Muise, "The Federal Election of 1867 in Nova Scotia: An Economic Interpretation," *Collections of the Nova Scotia Historical Society*, 36 (1968), pp. 227-51. For a classic interpretation of the railway and urban growth relationship, see George Rogers Taylor, "American Urban Growth Preceding the Railway Age," *Journal of Economic History*, 27 (September 1967), pp. 309-39.

43. On the importance to urban growth of market size and accessibility to markets, see Allan R. Pred, *The Spatial Dynamics of U.S. Urban-Industrial Growth, 1800-1914* (Cambridge, Mass., 1966), especially pp. 49-75.

44. Allan Green, *Regional Aspects of Canada's Economic Growth* (Toronto, 1971), Table II-9, p. 43.

45. For further discussion on the integrating role of "Scotia" in the space economy of the Maritimes, see L. D. McCann, "Fragmented Integration: The Nova Scotia Steel and Coal Company and the Anatomy of an Urban-Industrial Landscape, c.1912," forthcoming in *Urban History Review/Revue d'histoire urbaine*.

46. Data on coal, pig iron, and steel shipments were obtained from the following sources: Nova Scotia, Department of Mines, various *Annual Reports, 1901-1912* (Halifax); "Markets for Pig Iron, 1904-1908," Thomas Cantley Papers, MG 3, no. 525, Public Archives of Nova Scotia; and Nova Scotia Steel and Coal Company, *Report of the General Manager...1905-1912* (New Glasgow).

47. On these conditions and the export nature of manufacturing industries, see Canada, *The Maritime Provinces*, op. cit., pp. 59-63; Michael Hinton, "The National Policy and the Growth of the Canadian Cotton Textile Industry," paper delivered at the Conference on Quantitative Methods in Canadian Economic History, Wilfred Laurier University, 1984; and Gordon M. Winder, "Beyond Industrial Districts: Linkages among Foundries and Machine Shops," paper delivered at the Annual Meeting of the Association of American Geographers, (San Francisco, 1994).

48. J. M. S. Careless, "Frontierism, Metropolitanism, and Canadian History," *Canadian Historical Review*, 35 (1954), pp. 1-21. For a critical review of the concept, see Don Davis, "The 'Metropolitan Thesis' and the Writing of Canadian Urban History," *Urban History Review/Revue d'histoire urbaine*, 14 (1985), pp. 95-114.

49. McCann, "Heartland and Hinterland: A Framework for Regional Analysis," op. cit., pp. 22-7.

50. T. W. Acheson, *Saint John: The Making of a Colonial Urban Community* (Toronto, 1985); and Sutherland, "Halifax Merchants and the Pursuit of Development," op. cit.

51. This information on the development of manufacturing in Halifax and Saint John is summarized from Robert H. Babcock, "Economic Development in Portland (Me.) and Saint John (N.B.) during the Age of Iron and Steam, 1850-1914," *The American Review of Canadian Studies*, 9 (Spring 1979), pp. 3-37; John A. Watt, "Uneven Regional Development in Canada: A Study of Saint John, N.B., 1880-1910," unpublished Ph.D. dissertation, University of Waterloo, 1981; McCann, "Staples and the New Industrialism," op. cit.; and David A. Sutherland, "The Personnel and Policies of the Halifax Board of Trade, 1890-1914," in Lewis R. Fischer and Eric W. Sager, (eds.), *The Enterprising Canadians: Entrepreneurs and Economic Development in Eastern Canada* (St. John's, 1979), pp. 95-110.

52. Elizabeth W. McGahan, *The Port of Saint John: Volume One: From Confederation to Nationalization, 1867-1927* (Saint John, 1982), p. 249.

53. Sager, "Merchant Shipowners and the Decline of the Shipping Industry in Atlantic Canada," op. cit.

54. The material on the changing wholesale and retail trade is derived from McCann, "Metropolitanism and Branch Businesses," op. cit.

55. See, for example, R. T. Naylor, *The History of Canadian Business*, vol. I (Toronto, 1975), p. 150; Acheson, "National Policy," op. cit.; and James D. Frost, "The 'Nationalization' of the Bank of Nova Scotia, 1880-1910," *Acadiensis*, 12 (Autumn 1982), pp. 3-38.

56. Neil C. Quigley, Ian M. Drummond and Lewis T. Evans, "Regional Transfers of Funds through the Canadian Banking System and Maritime Economic Development, 1895-1935," in Inwood, *Farm, Factory and Fortune*, op. cit., pp. 219-250.

57. Gregory Marchildon, "John F. Stairs, Max Aitken and the Scotia Group: Finance Capitalism and Industrial Decline in the Maritimes, 1890-1914," in Inwood, (ed.), *Farm, Factory and Fortune*, op. cit., pp. 197-218.

58. The literature on the problems confronting the Maritimes through the 1920s and 1930s is very substantial, but see in particular: Eugene Forsey, *National Problems of Canada: Economic and Social Aspects of the Nova Scotia Coal Industry*, McGill University Economic Studies, no. 5 (Toronto, 1926); Canada, Dominion Bureau of Statistics, *The Maritime Provinces in Their Relation to the National Economy of Canada* (Ottawa, 1948); Royal Commission on Dominion-Provincial Relations, Public Accounts Inquiry, *Dominion of Canada and Provincial Governments: Comparative Statistics of Public Finance* (Ottawa, 1939); E. R. Forbes, *Maritime Rights: The Maritime Rights Movement, 1919-1927* (Montreal, 1979); *idem*, "The

1930s: Depression and Retrenchment," op. cit.; David Frank, Class and Region, Resistance and Accommodation," in E. R. Forbes and D. A. Muise, *The Atlantic Provinces in Confederation*, op. cit., pp. 233-71; and Wynn, "The Maritimes: The Geography of Fragmentation and Underdevelopment," op. cit., pp. 194-8.

59. The industrial experience of Amherst is well-told in Nolan Reilly, "The General Strike in Amherst, Nova Scotia, 1919," *Acadiensis*, 9 (Spring 1980), pp. 56-77.

60. L. D. McCann, "Industrialization and the Maritimes," Plate 24 in D. Kerr, D. Holdsworth, and S. Laskin, (eds.), *Historical Atlas of Canada: Addressing the Twentieth Century*, vol. III (Toronto, 1990). On the need to exercise caution when interpreting employment losses in the 1919-1922 period, see Phillip J. Wood, "The Dominion Bureau of Statistics and the Deindustrialization of the Maritimes, 1919-1922," *Acadiensis*, 22 (Spring 1993), pp. 139-43.

61. See the table of such cost differentials in McCann, "The Mercantile-Industrial Transition," op. cit., p. 60.

62. Sandberg, "Dependent Development," op. cit.

63. Kris Inwood, "Local Control, Resources and the Nova Scotia Steel and Coal Company," *Historical Papers* of the Canadian Historical Association (1986), pp. 254-82.

64. David Frank, "The Cape Breton Coal Industry and the Rise and Fall of the British Empire Steel Corporation," *Acadiensis*, 7 (Autumn 1977), pp. 3-34.

65. Forbes, "Misguided Symmetry," op. cit.; and Cruikshank, "The Intercolonial Railway, Freight Rates and the Maritime Economy," op. cit.

66. Thornton, "The Problem of Out-Migration," op. cit.

67. For reviews of the region's decline, see Eric Sager, "Dependency, Underdevelopment and the Economic History of the Atlantic Provinces," *Acadiensis*, 17 (Autumn 1987), pp. 117-37; and James B. Cannon, "Explaining Regional Development in Atlantic Canada," *Journal of Canadian Studies*, 19 (1984), pp. 65-86.

68. The Carleton University History Collaborative, *Urban and Community Development in Atlantic Canada*, op. cit., pp. 76-88.

69. L.D. McCann, "Halifax: Centre at the Edge," *Horizon Canada*, 3, 26 (1985), pp. 608-13.

2

A CHANGING MARITIME URBAN SYSTEM: FACING RESTRUCTURING AND INTEGRATION

Rodolphe H. Lamarche

Urban systems are intimately tied to their economic environments, and their vitality or anemia reflects the characteristics of the economic processes at work within their borders. In recent years the Canadian urban system and its Maritime component have been subjected to a series of major stresses and shocks which have permanently altered the Canadian and Maritime urban structures. The powerful restructuring impact of the service economy is clearly demonstrated in the first section of this chapter. However, other economic shocks such as recent reductions in public spending, new international trade agreements and the rise of the information economy - an offspring of the service economy - are also influencing urban system development in varying degrees. This chapter deals with the impact of these three shocks on the Maritime system. Of the three shocks - reduced public spending, new international trade agreements and the information economy - the one least likely to have a profound effect on system structure is the reduction in public spending. The recent international trade agreements, which are in many ways only the latest in political and economic adjustments brought on by the service (1950s) and information (1970s) economies, will undoubtedly have strong permanent effects. It is somewhat difficult to measure precisely how the Maritime urban system has reacted to all these stresses and to determine how individual urban centres will stand up to the more recent shocks. The difficulty lies in proving the cause-effect relationships between economic processes and their urban adjustments. The need to understand the processes of change and the development of adequate policy responses is a matter of urgency. (Savoie, 1992)

By their nature, urban systems have a much lower rate of adaptability to change than do economic systems. Economic systems are dominated by large firms which have focused objectives, which are defined mainly by a few prominent individuals, and are pursued diligently. Firms can and must adapt to change or they become unable to maintain their market share. This explains, to a large degree, the concentration of effort and persistence demonstrated by firms in adopting innovative production and management processes to this ever-changing environment. Urban systems, however, respond to a more fluid set of constraints. They are subject to a broad spectrum of cultural and political pressures and cannot pursue objectives with the same focused persistence of intent as economic organizations do. Their huge investment in infrastructure is an important factor in accounting for the slower pace of evolution of cities. However, in Canada at least, social and political factors are just as important in explaining the inertia of urban centres. It takes considerable time and effort to build common goals when the power of decision-making is diffused throughout the communities and the provinces. The resistance from institutions, groups and individuals who have a lot to lose in the process is hard to overcome. If resistance to change within the communities is widespread and succeeds in inhibiting change to a point where a number of firms within a given urban centre find that they are incapable of acting with sufficient freedom, they have to either move to more responsive locations or risk the chance of going down with their community as competitors take over their markets.

Because our purpose as regional development analysts is to understand development processes, it is important to remember that *urban problems*, like regional disparities, have as their main cause the inability of urban and regional systems to sustain a rate of evolution in step with economic transformations. So, it is important to be able to measure the capacity of an urban system or a given urban centre to adjust because it then becomes possible in many instances to create policies that enhance a city's existing capacity to evolve, its flexibility to react to change. In other instances where it is clear that social and political structures are inhibiting change to a point where an urban centre is likely to be doomed to stagnation, it might be possible to enact policies and programs to dispel such rigidity before sclerosis totally marginalizes an urban centre within the national system. More than ever, problems have to be diagnosed swiftly and steps taken early, before all growth impulses are gradually switched away from one recalcitrant urban centre to others.

Because the Maritime urban system is located on the periphery of the Canadian urban system, it has been subjected to even greater than average pressures with regards to urban restructuring. Following each major stress period, the Maritime system has been left with a smaller number of active urban centres that are closely integrated into regional and national networks. It is quite important for the provincial economies and authorities that this integrating process be monitored closely, because the increased rate at which new stresses are appearing is quite alarming and leaves little leeway for experimentation with urban system development. Only the centres that are totally dominated by primary industries seem able to resist integration to a certain degree, but they have other serious problems which are also caused by modern economic processes.

The purpose of this chapter is to illustrate the impact of economic stress on the integration of the Maritime system and to measure how individual Maritime urban centres have been able to cope with these shocks. It is in effect an attempt to measure the capacity of Maritime urban centres to adapt to change.

It is also an attempt to identify the centres that are most likely to grow within the new information economy.

The chapter is divided into four sections. The first section briefly outlines the economic transformations that have had the most impact on urban systems in recent decades. The second section describes the effect of the integration process on the Maritime urban system. The third section looks at the growth patterns of the Maritime urban labour force during the 1981-1991 period and attempts to determine how well suited it is to the demands of the new economy. The fourth section uses an advanced shift-share technique to compare urban industrial structures and urban dynamics. The fifth section applies a systems analysis technique to measure the relationship between network activity and the location of head offices within the Maritime urban system.

Economic Transformations and Major Urban Stresses

The main economic transformations that have altered the Maritime urban system in the recent decades are the rise to prominence of the service economy of the 1950s, the appearance of the Pacific rim nations and the subsequent proliferation of the multinationals in the 60s and 70s, the world-wide economic crisis of 1981-1982 and the recession of 1990. In each instance the economic system has reacted by turning to innovative technologies to meet the challenge. The major technologies that were at the origin of the information economy have been the computer and communications technologies. The union of the two has had a tremendous impact on production and management processes. The introduction of high-tech instruments in the production of goods and services and management processes has resulted in a greater concentration of research and development within the larger urban centres and the movement of head offices from regional to national centres. There was some speculation that the *information economy* would lead to a more decentralized form of urban structure. However, this has not yet occurred. Highly decentralized urban systems are possible only in *information societies*, a form of social organization that cannot be attained with the present telecommunication infrastructures. It is possible and even probable that electronic highways under construction will move us into an information society during the next few years. But here again one can expect that the urban system will be slow in evolving. Decision-making processes are now concentrated within a few major metropolitan centres in the country. Not only has the urban system been restructured but high-tech innovations have called for a new type of workforce, and few regional centres have been able to cope with either of these consequences. It is quite important for development analysts to realize that while the service economy was predominantly under the direct control of governments, the information economy is a large measure beyond it.

Thus the three economic shocks referred to in the introduction to this book - decreased public spending, new international trade agreements and the rise in information activities - have led to a concentration of economic control within a few large Canadian centres, with Toronto acting as the national node. Had it not been for the federal nature of the country, it is likely that the emigration of head offices from the periphery to the national node would have been even greater. The impact of these forces on the Maritime urban system is only beginning to show.

The Integration of the Canadian and Maritime Urban Systems

That the Canadian urban system has suffered a major restructuring since the 1950s is quite evident from a brief examination of tables 1, 2 and 3, and of figure 1. The rise of the service economy in the 1950s and 1960s was followed by a huge increase in the number of multinationals during the 1970s. By 1979 there were over 11,000 multinational firms directing more than 86,000 branch plants, of which 75 percent were located in industrialized countries. (Wadley, 1986, p. 27) Multinationals were the main agents in the transmission of technology from industrialized countries to other parts of the world. The management processes they empowered restructured the economic processes of industrial countries which led, in Canada as elsewhere, to a huge increase in inter-urban passenger traffic. Note that approximately 68 percent of domestic air passenger trips are of a business nature. Over the three decades from 1960 to 1990 the average annual increase in air traffic has been six times greater than the average increase in population. This growth has not been evenly distributed over the three decades, as one can see from figure 1. Huge annual increases are reported for the 1960s and 1970s followed by a severe drop *in growth* of traffic during the 1980s. One could interpret this either as an indication that the economic crisis of 1981-82 had stunted all new growth, or that the existing linkages were sufficient to service the new economic structures, or again, there might be a third explanation as table 2 and figure 2 suggest. One can surmise from table 2 that the surge in the 60s and 70s was needed to provide the extended interaction networks metropolitan centres required in a service economy. However, table 2 and figure 2 also suggest that a new stage of urban development - the information economy - is really under way in the 1980s and this should come as no surprise, as one would expect a crisis of the magnitude of the 1981-82 recession to induce urban system change. Table 2 and figure 2 show that *a few urban centres continued to experience growth throughout the 1980s.* But it seems that growth was restricted to the national node, Toronto, and only a few major regional nodes such as Ottawa, Halifax, Victoria and St. John's. Other centres had either very little growth or a reduction in traffic during this difficult period, centres such as Sudbury, Quebec, Calgary and Edmonton. This latest growth pattern could be an indication of another level of urban integration. (It seems that an information economy has to be structured around a few national nodes with a limited number of regional nodes.) This also implies

Table 1

Population Growth in the Canadian Metropolitan Areas 1961-1991

Rank	CMAs	1961	1971	1981	1991	Relative average annual population growth %			
						1961-71	1971-81	1981-91	1961-91
1	Toronto	1,919,409	2,628,043	2,998,947	3,893,046	3.69	1.41	2.98	3.43
2	Montreal	2,215,627	2,743,208	2,828,349	3,127,242	2.38	0.31	1.06	1.37
3	Vancouver	826,798	1,082,352	1,268,183	1,602,502	3.09	1.72	2.64	3.13
4	Winnipeg	476,543	540,262	584,842	652,354	1.34	0.83	1.15	1.23
5	Ottawa-Hull	457,038	602,510	717,978	920,857	3.18	1.92	2.83	3.38
6	Calgary	279,062	403,319	592,743	754,033	4.45	4.70	2.72	5.67
7	Edmonton	359,821	495,702	657,057	839,924	3.78	3.26	2.78	4.45
8	Halifax	193,353	222,637	277,727	320,501	1.51	2.47	1.54	2.19
9	Quebec	379,067	480,502	576075	645,550	2.68	1.99	1.21	2.34
10	Windsor	217,215	252,643	246,110	262075	1.63	-0.26	0.65	0.69
11	Regina	113,749	140,734	164,313	191,692	2.37	1.68	1.67	2.28
12	Victoria	155,763	195,800	233,481	287,897	2.57	1.92	2.33	2.83
13	Saskatoon	95,564	126,449	154210	210,023	3.23	2.20	3.62	3.99
14	Thunder Bay	105,085	112,093	121,379	124427	0.67	0.83	0.25	0.61
15	London	226,669	286,011	283668	381,522	2.62	-0.08	3.45	2.28
16	Saint John	98,083	106,744	114048	124,981	0.88	0.68	0.96	0.91
17	St. John's	106,666	131,814	154820	171,859	2.36	1.75	1.10	2.04
18	Sudbury	127,446	155,424	149,923	157,613	2.20	-0.35	0.51	0.79
	Average	464,053	594,792	673,547	814,894	2.48	1.50	1.86	2.42
	Standard deviation	614,439	799,422	867,913	1,059,440	1.01	1.27	1.06	1.41

Source: Canadian Censuses.

Figure 1

Metropolitan Population Growth and Inter-urban Passenger Flows, 1960-1991

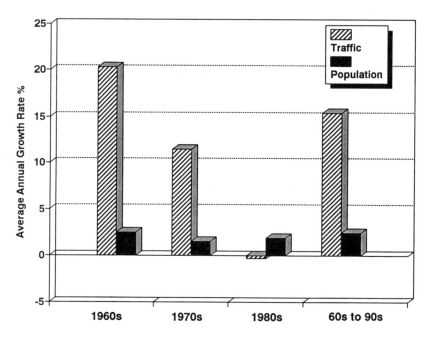

Source: Canadian Censuses - Statistics Canada, Catalogue 51-204, various years.

Table 2

Inter-Urban Domestic Passenger Traffic

Rank	CMAs	Outbound Flows				Relative annual average growth in traffic (%)			
		1963	1970	1980	1990	1963*-70	1970-80	1980-90	1963-90
1	Toronto	466,645	992,745	2,137,150	2,593,320	16.11	11.53	2.13	16.88
2	Montreal	341,485	633,105	1,033,720	1,104,970	12.20	6.33	0.69	8.28
3	Vancouver	145,170	412,890	1,085,220	1,144,370	26.35	16.28	0.55	25.49
4	Winnipeg	120,780	312,980	580,700	556,760	22.73	8.55	-0.41	13.37
5	Ottawa-Hull	119,720	305,575	607,280	783,340	22.18	9.87	2.90	20.53
6	Calgary	105,890	355,045	1,121,460	861,000	33.61	21.59	-2.32	26.41
7	Edmonton	101,885	302,515	939,440	561,860	28.13	21.05	-4.02	16.72
8	Halifax	68,065	159,665	335,780	447,530	19.23	11.03	3.33	20.65
9	Quebec	67,205	86,360	160,440	98,720	4.07	8.58	-3.85	1.74
10	Windsor	57,345	89,725	128,930	69,750	8.07	4.37	-4.59	0.80
11	Regina	44,780	102,770	222,090	212,180	18.50	11.61	-0.45	13.85
12	Victoria	37,725	86,420	196,520	242,290	18.44	12.74	2.33	20.08
13	Saskatoon	29,435	84,735	206,070	202,830	26.84	14.32	-0.16	21.82
14	Thunder Bay	29,010	74,355	177,620	151,480	22.33	13.89	-1.47	15.64
15	London	28,095	55,860	75,180	62,820	14.12	3.46	-1.64	4.58
16	Saint John	25,315	46,015	69,360	81,650	11.68	5.07	1.77	8.24
17	St. John's	25,200	56,125	143,390	187,100	17.53	15.55	3.05	23.79
18	Sudbury	10,145	40,765	85,110	61,470	43.12	10.88	-2.78	18.74
	Average	101,328	233,203	516,970	523,524	20.29	11.48	-0.27	15.42
	Standard deviation	119,038	250,721	553,311	629,433	9.32	5.15	2.56	7.86

*1963 was the first year data on air passenger was made available.
Source: Statistics Canada, Catalogue number 51-204, various years.

Figure 2

Population and Traffic Growth Rates
in Selected Canadian Centres 1961-1991

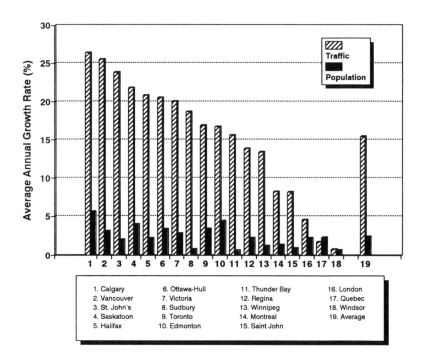

1. Calgary	6. Ottawa-Hull	11. Thunder Bay	16. London
2. Vancouver	7. Victoria	12. Regina	17. Quebec
3. St. John's	8. Sudbury	13. Winnipeg	18. Windsor
4. Saskatoon	9. Toronto	14. Montreal	19. Average
5. Halifax	10. Edmonton	15. Saint John	

Source: Canadian Censuses, Statistics Canada Catalogue 51-204, various years.

Table 3

Interaction Ratios for Selected Cities: 1966 to 1990

Year	Average for all Centres	Montreal	Vancouver	Ottawa	Halifax	St. John's	Moncton	Fredericton	Sydney	Saint John	Charlottetown
1966	0.1388	0.6995	0.3471	0.2659	0.1879	0.0981	0.0634	0.0475	0.0460	0.0519	0.0115
1968	0.1436	0.6812	0.3899	0.2854	0.1962	0.0933	0.0600	0.0449	0.0488	0.0529	0.0135
1970	0.1436	0.6530	0.4005	0.3067	0.1970	0.0830	0.0518	0.0469	0.0466	0.0464	0.0187
1972	0.1452	0.6305	0.4133	0.3221	0.2013	0.0944	0.0555	0.0465	0.0494	0.0416	0.0278
1974	0.1474	0.5961	0.4345	0.3384	0.2022	0.0930	0.0578	0.0467	0.0490	0.0459	0.0305
1976	0.1495	0.5658	0.4279	0.3252	0.2050	0.0945	0.0526	0.0457	0.0454	0.0444	0.0347
1978	0.1496	0.5246	0.4434	0.3256	0.1964	0.1042	0.0491	0.0433	0.0418	0.0395	0.0343
1980	0.1461	0.4869	0.4897	0.2857	0.1742	0.0883	0.0440	0.0335	0.0321	0.0320	0.0256
1982	0.1395	0.4509	0.4733	0.3056	0.1864	0.0849	0.0409	0.0350	0.0295	0.0297	0.0261
1984	0.1330	0.4546	0.4542	0.3196	0.1883	0.0864	0.0399	0.0347	0.0271	0.0311	0.0277
1986	0.1189	0.4182	0.4904	0.2737	0.1641	0.0711	0.0319	0.0260	0.0207	0.0265	0.0231
1988	0.1120	0.4001	0.4337	0.2765	0.1532	0.0666	0.0319	0.0209	0.0153	0.0228	0.0198
1990	0.1172	0.4278	0.4237	0.3049	0.1936	0.0875	0.0407	0.0320	0.0268	0.0309	0.0294

Source: Statistics Canada, Catalogue number 51-204, various years.

a reduction in importance for most of the nation's secondary urban centres. Because the growth patterns are not clearly defined in table 2 and figure 2 it is very likely that there are several different conflicting processes at work simultaneously within the urban system. However, it seems plausible from the rates reported in table 2 that a few of regional centres have developed into major regional nodes and others are having difficulty in maintaining their position within the Canadian hierarchy. It might appear that an average annual growth rate of 16.9 percent over the three decades for Toronto is low, as compared to rates for other centres. But then Toronto had already assumed a national role even before the 1960s and an average increase of 16.9 percent of the huge volume of traffic coming out of Toronto was undoubtedly sufficient for its operations, and, based on that, it needed only minor increases in the 1980s. There is a similarity of pattern between the growth of the Toronto and Vancouver networks, and a huge difference between the Vancouver and Montreal patterns. These particular similarities and differences do not show up clearly in table 2, but they can be better perceived using a systems analysis approach, as we shall illustrate.

A systems approach is an appropriate technique for urban analysis because urban systems are open social systems which always tend toward greater complexity of their structures and greater interdependence of their centres. Modern urban systems are forced in this direction because economies are required to produce more complex goods at better prices and in greater quantity and this can only be achieved in highly integrated urban networks. In an *information economy*, the natural outcome of growing complexity of production and management processes is a greater level of integration of the urban centres. Note that in an information society, it might be possible to achieve similar levels of production and management capabilities in an urban system that could be less physically integrated.

In a systems technique the main national urban centre, in our case, Toronto, is defined as the central node and the interaction activity of all other nodes is compared to that of the central node. The interaction ratio is the simplest of all system measurements. This ratio compares the total output from a given centre to that of the central node. If the interaction ratio is equal to a value of 1, the output of the centre equals that of the main node, an unlikely occurrence. If the ratio has a value smaller than one, then the centre has less interaction than the main node, as one would expect. What is most relevant to the understanding of the changes occurring in an urban system are the trends in the interaction ratios of individual centres over a period of time during which an urban system is being subjected to a series of stresses. If an urban centre increases its activity at a greater rate than the national centre, the interaction ratios will be on the rise, a clear indication that the system is becoming more interdependent. If the interaction ratios of most centres are dropping, then the main node is expanding at a greater rate and exerting a greater dominance. If the ratios of a single centre are dropping when most centres are experiencing higher ratios, it is likely that this one centre is being pushed out of the mainstream interaction networks, and away from the transmission links along which the growth impulses flow.

For our analysis we have used the origin-destination of domestic air-passenger traffic between the larger urban centres in Canada and the Maritimes because interpersonal contacts play the major role in decision-making processes and passenger flows depict fairly accurately the business interaction networks in the Canadian urban system. Table 3 reports the interaction ratios of a system composed of eighteen of the larger urban centres in Canada plus seven smaller centres that serve as communication nodes for the fifteen economic regions of Atlantic Canada for the period extending from 1964 to 1990.

Table 3 in effect confirms that in recent decades there has been a major restructuring of the Canadian and Maritime urban systems, and that these changes have occurred during periods of economic stress. Note the dramatic decrease in the Montreal ratio. In 1966 Montreal had a volume equal to 70 percent of Toronto's, but Montreal faded to a low of 43 percent by 1990. Vancouver experienced a much different pattern, going from 34.7 percent in 1966 to 49 percent in 1986 and 42 percent in 1990. The various phases of restructuration and integration that the Canadian and Maritime urban systems have undergone during the 1966-1991 period can be deduced from table 3. When the average interaction ratio values for all centres are on the rise, as was the case during the 1966-1978 period, the smaller metropolitan and agglomeration centres were expanding their communication links and were being integrated into larger regional systems. The restructuration of the whole system was tremendous during this period, for even as the smaller networks were expanding, Toronto was also expanding, albeit at a lesser rate. Many of the smaller systems, such as the Maritime system centred on Halifax, and another small western system centred on Winnipeg, have been integrated into larger regional networks based on Toronto in the East and Vancouver-Calgary in the West. Note that Toronto plays a dual role first as a regional node then as the national node. That public and private businesses in the smaller centres felt the need to expand their links at this rate is a clear indication that the world-wide stresses and economic transformations outlined earlier could only be met through more sophisticated transmission networks of production and management processes that could only be carried out in a more integrated urban system. The service economy that had started to develop in the 1950s had achieved maturity by the mid-1970s. All urban centres made a valiant effort at building their networks during this period but some had more success and probably more foresight than others.

From 1978 on and particularly after 1981 *the average interaction ratio values decreased.* After 1978 the Toronto network growth surpassed that of all other centres although a few regional centres did experience large growth rates, as was the case for Vancouver. We can interpret these figures in several ways. We could conclude that the smaller regional centres had built up their networks during the earlier period to a degree sufficient for their needs within a service economy. Later during the mid-1970s and after the crisis of 1981-82 further adjustments had to be made and this was achieved through an additional expansion of the national node. This is a logical explanation if we accept the notion that an urban system in a market economy tends towards greater complexity of structure and operation and the information economy was the natural outcome of this process. The interaction ratios for the years 1978 through 1990 reflect the restructuring brought by the rise of the new information economy. It first appeared in the early 1970s and grew so fast that by 1981, 51 percent of all jobs in Canada and the United States were information related. (Rubin, 1983; Serafini, 1980) Because the economic processes had evolved anew, the urban system had to adjust again through greater integration and interdependence.

Some Maritime centres were more successful than others in this latest stage of change as one can see from tables 1, 2 and 3. Halifax remains the dominant regional centre with Moncton a distant second. Both of these centres have some initial advantages that should favour their development as major nodes within the Maritime region in an information economy, in spite of the negative effects of the recent three shocks outlined earlier. It would seem the Maritimes cannot function without a minimum number of dominant regional centres, and these two centres offer some of the best prospects. All urban centres in the Maritimes are going to have to adapt to the information economy. The strengths and weaknesses of the labour force with regards to the demands of an information economy will be one of the main factors in deciding whether or not an urban centre will find a niche within the regional urban network.

Labour Force Growth Patterns in the Maritime Urban Centres

In Atlantic Canada there are sixteen urban centres classified as either metropolitan or census agglomeration areas, thirteen of which are located in the Maritime provinces. In our study of labour force growth patterns we have used this set of sixteen centres as a basis of comparison for the study of growth patterns in the Maritime urban centres. (The tables of the Statistical Appendix at the end of the book give the complete set of the labour force statistics used in this section.) The average rate of growth over the 1981-1991 period for the sixteen urban regions was 19 percent. During this same period the overall employment growth rate in Canada was 18 percent and in Atlantic Canada 16 percent. The industries that had the highest average growth rates were the hotel and restaurant (33 percent), health (32 percent) and business and personal services (27 percent) industries. The industries that sustained losses or very little growth were the manufacturing (-7 percent), primary (-1 percent) and transportation (1 percent). Public administra-tion (20 percent) and teaching (18 percent) did provide a significant number of new jobs.

Since average values are primarily determined by the larger units in a set, it comes as no surprise that the larger urban regions have labour force growth patterns similar to the regional average. However, there are important differences as well. Halifax had an overall employment growth rate of 22 percent, yet a rather high rate in construction (26 percent) and a low rate in public administration. Halifax also had an impressive increase of 5 percent in its manufacturing labour force, in sharp contrast with the general trend. In other industries the Halifax rates followed the general pattern. Saint John, N.B., has a growth rate of 15 percent, which is 4 percent below the general average. Moncton, Fredericton and Charlottetown had employment growth rates above average. The highest rates of growth were in the health, hotel and restaurant and business and personal services. There were losses in the manufacturing and primary industries.

The variance in growth rates for smaller centres is always much greater than that of the larger centres, because the smaller centres are often single-industry towns. Of the smaller centres, Bathurst was the centre to experience the greatest growth (67 percent) over the 1981-1991 period. The main sectors responsible for the high rate were construction, health and business and personal services. The construction of a huge electrical facility in the region is responsible for Bathurst's high rates. Most of the smaller centres had lower than average growth rates, New Glasgow (-3 percent), Summerside (12 percent), Campbellton (10 percent), Edmundston (12 percent) and Truro (16 percent). Kentville, although it is a small urban centre with a labour force of only 10,600 (1981), had a large overall growth of 24 percent due mainly to its manufacturing sector.

In short, only a few of the smaller urban centres experienced growth over the period whereas the larger, with the exception of Saint John, and medium-sized centres, with the exception of Sydney, had above average growth rates. Centres whose growth resulted from increases in the teaching, health, hotels and restaurant, and public administration sectors are likely to have difficulty in creating new jobs over the 1991-1996 period as a result of projected reductions in public spending in these sectors. Note that it is quite common for an urban centre that is faced with the closure of a major industry to temporarily dampen the trauma by expanding its service sector. This was the case for Summerside on Prince Edward Island after the closure of its military base, and Moncton after the closure of its CN shops. However, this is only a temporary measure. Unless a city has other capabilities, its rank within the urban system will drop in the long run. This could also be the case for St. John's and Saint John. Such temporary expansions of service sectors are possible only if public spending is on the increase, which of course is not likely in the immediate future.

In centres where growth has been more evenly spread across several industrial sectors, one can foresee better prospects for the future. This seems to be the case for Halifax, Moncton, Fredericton and Charlottetown. Both Halifax and Moncton are in a position to increase their participation in the information economy as regional nodes. Moncton and Saint John benefit from the presence of the highly dynamic NBTel Corporation and its specialized information technologies, and Halifax, as the Maritime region's largest centre, can draw on a variety of urban factors to promote its growth. The increase in the number of software companies that have chosen Fredericton as a centre of operation, coupled with the declared intentions of the New Brunswick government to promote information activities within the province, should see this city develop its business and consumer information service industries to a considerable degree. It seems that all three centres have had increases in the two industries that are most relevant to an information economy: infrastructure, the business information services and the administrative sector. These cities have a truly dynamic entrepreneurial labour force, a feature which will be the *most important ingredient* in the growth of information services on the electronic highway if this infrastructure is fully implemented in the Maritimes over the next decade. Everything hinges on how quickly governments see information services to business and *consumers* as a major new source of jobs and income, and accordingly provide the necessary incentive, leadership and organization. An early start in this line of development will be of major significance for these three Maritime centres. The initial advantage will determine whether their only function within the Canadian urban system will be to serve as distribution nodes for information products developed elsewhere or whether they will also participate as innovators in the growing demand for information services.

Urban Industrial Structure and Regional Dynamics: A Shift-Share Analysis

The capacity of Maritime urban centres to absorb stresses and shocks and to rise within the Maritime urban hierarchy depends to a large degree on each city's dynamism and the strength of its industrial structure. To measure regional dynamics and industrial structures in order to compare urban centres with regard to these two factors, we have adopted a shift-share technique, developed by Ray and Srinath in 1990. One of the main difficulties in measuring regional dynamics of a set of cities stems from the interaction effects that city size has on growth. It is a common perception that size is everything when assessing growth opportunities. The original shift-share technique, developed by Jones in 1940 and widely used thereafter, failed to address the issue of the impact that size could have on growth. Because the Jones technique did not isolate the interaction effects between the factors of city-size and industrial structure, one was never certain about the true measurement of the impact of a city's regional dynamics or its industrial structure on its growth patterns, simply because city size tended to dominate all factors. When size is taken into account, it then becomes possible to have a much better notion of the dynamism of a city, or its *region effect,* as Ray and Srinath prefer to call it. Measuring the regional dynamics of a region or its *region effect* can be viewed as follows: All labour force growth not attributable either to city size or to peculiarities of the industrial structure is the product of other factors, which are summed up in the term *region effect*. The *region effect* measures the impact of all factors that are not explicitly included in the analysis. Even though we cannot specifically identify them, we can still measure how many jobs are related to these other unspecified factors, much as someone can measure the growth in a tree without specifying all the factors involved.

In our application of the Ray-Srinath technique we standardized the data with respect to city size, industrial structure and the male/female distribution in eleven major industry categories. The technique is particularly useful when comparing just two entities at a time, either two regions, or, as in this case, two urban centres because a direct comparison of two units reveals which of the two had the better dynamics, the better industrial structure and the better interaction effects.

We have compared all the urban centres with each other and have found some indications that might explain why some of the Maritime urban centres show more resilience than others in times of stress. In the discussions that follow, it is important to remember that the impact of the various effects is measured in growth rates. A difference of 3 percent would mean an increase of 4,689 jobs for Halifax, which had a labour force of 156,295 in 1981, and only 311 jobs for Edmundston, with its labour force of 10,360 in the same year.

The male/female distribution factor was included into our analysis because 66 percent of all jobs created during the 1981-91 period were in the female labour force. We assumed that this factor would not be decisive here, because the study deals only with urban centres which have similar labour force distributions, but then the industries that grew the most in 1981-91 were the service-related industries, industries that are female-dominated. Had the analysis included the surrounding rural regions, we would have been inclined to assume that this factor would have played a more significant role. As we had surmised, the differences in the male/female distribution pattern had very little impact generally on growth patterns. In only one instance did this factor prove quite significant in terms of job numbers, and this was in the comparison between Halifax and Sydney. The difference in rates was only 1.4 percent, but it translates into 1,083 jobs in favour of Halifax. Elsewhere the differences in growth rates attributable to male/female distribution were slight. Table 4 demonstrates how helpful a comparative analysis of this type can be. The *category effect* in this case is the *male/female distribution effect*.

The difference in raw rates between Halifax and Moncton is nil in table 4. Moncton has an advantage of 6.19 percent in region effect, but a comparatively weaker industrial structure. Had Halifax had a region effect equal to Moncton's, 9,670 additional jobs would have resulted. Because Halifax had an industry effect rate of 1.9 percent higher than Moncton's, its industrial struc-

Table 4

Differential Analysis in the Growth Rates: Halifax-Moncton, 1981-91

	Labour Force rate/jobs	Std. L.F. rate/jobs	Region Effect rate/jobs	Industry Effect rate/jobs	Category Effect rate/jobs	Interaction Effect rate/jobs
Halifax, N.S.	18.01%	19.61%	1.03%	0.92%	0.23%	-2.74%
	28,155	30,652	1,614	1,430	356	-4,283
Moncton, N.B.	18.00%	25.80%	7.22%	-1.00%	0.02%	-6.82%
	8,790	12,601	3,526	-491	9	-3,330

Differential Analysis in the Growth Rates: Halifax - Moncton

Raw Rates	=	Region Effect	+	Industry Effect	+	Category Effect	+	Interaction Effect
0.02%	=	-6.19%	+	1.92%	+	0.21%	+	4.08%
29	=	-9,670	+	3,000	+	327	+	6,372

Source: Calculations based on Canadian Censuses.

ture accounted for 3,000 additional jobs. Of the two centres, Halifax had a much better interaction effect (4.1 percent), which is interpreted as meaning that industries locating in Halifax had a better chance of developing the same industry in Moncton. Comparisons of this type are useful in that they focus the attention onto the two main attributes of an urban centre, its regional dynamism and its industrial structure.

Differences in industrial structures were more significant than male/female distribution but less so than region effects. Some urban centres had better-than-average industrial structures while others did not. A better-than-average industrial structure in this modified shift-share analysis means that a given region had a large segment of its labour force working in industries that had on average the largest increases. A region - as was the case for Bathurst - might have experienced considerable growth in the construction and primary sectors, but because these two industries were not generally on the rise during the decade such a centre would not have its industrial structure classified as particularly good. The Bathurst industrial structure did not behave at all as did the industrial structures of other regions, and should be looked at more carefully because of the special conditions prevailing at the time in Bathurst.

The greatest differences in industrial structures were reported for the pairs Halifax and Saint John, and Halifax and Moncton. In the first instance, Halifax had an industry effect of 2.4 percent higher than Saint John's and in the second comparison Halifax's rate was 1.9 percent higher than Moncton's. The 1.9 percent advantage Halifax had over Moncton in table 4 means than the industry pattern in Halifax was better than Moncton's and translates into a 3,000 job increase for Halifax. Halifax also had a better industrial structure than Sydney, as one would expect because jobs in the manufacturing sector during the decade were on the decline. Of all the comparisons made between the medium and smaller centres, the most significant was the comparison between Fredericton and Edmundston. Fredericton had a 2.9 percent rate advantage over Edmundston, even though Edmundston also has a university campus and has an important regional hospital complex.

That the Maritime urban system was under tremendous stress during the 1980s can be seen from figure 3. The region effect rates reported in figure 3 are not comparative figures but separate measurements of the region effect for each centre. They provide a measurement of the effect on growth of all the factors that are not explicitly stated and are justifiably labelled the *effect of regional dynamics* on labour force growth. Of all the larger centres in the Maritimes, the only ones to show positive values apart from Moncton, are the provincial capitals. That Moncton has been able to maintain a positive value despite the loss of the CN shops is quite remarkable. Moncton's location as well as its large pool of entrepreneurs is the most likely explanation. Halifax, because of its size, and Moncton, because of its dynamics, are therefore the two most likely urban centres to emerge as the dominant regional urban nodes in the new Maritime

Figure 3

Regional Urban Dynamics 1981-1991
Region Effect Rates

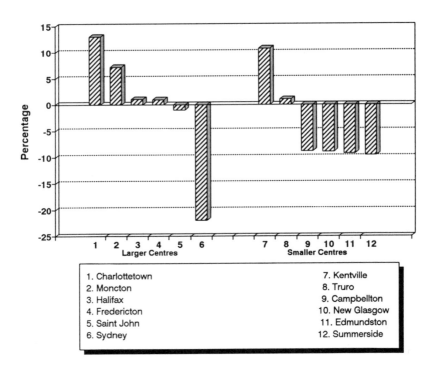

Source: Calculations based on Canadian Censuses.

urban system. The smaller urban centres apart from the provincial capitals are not likely to fare well in the future if one judges from these region effect values. Kentville is an interesting exception. The case of Saint John is particularly puzzling; in some respects, such as sub-network structures, it resembles Moncton but in other respects, it has several drawbacks.

Finally, one should compare the differences in interaction effects. When the difference in rates of the interaction effects between two cities is high, one concludes that any given industry will fare better in the city with the higher interaction effect. Of all the larger cities in Atlantic Canada, Halifax reports the highest interaction effects. Its interaction rate exceeds that of Saint John by 3 percent and Moncton's by 4 percent (table 4), differences which translate in the latter case into some 6,372 jobs for Halifax. Because the data is standardized for city size, the larger interaction effects reported for Halifax *cannot be attributed directly* to the fact that it is the largest city in the Maritimes. However, it seems reasonable to attribute such high interaction effects to other conditions that are related to size, such as that once a city reaches a certain threshold-size, everything about it is changed, and it can easily have more than twice the appeal of cities with half the population. The interaction effect might be the *urban effect* that Ray and others sought to measure when they first applied the Jones technique. Interaction effects are important and caution us to point out that regional dynamic values such as those reported in figure 3 are not the only factors that are important to growth. Cities that do have a large entrepreneurial pool of business people should make determined efforts to project an image of the city that has a large number of appealing characteristics: a metropolitan flavour, environmental consciousness and security.

Network Activity and Head Office Location

In 1968 when Tornqvist first outlined his urban model to account for changes in urban systems, he divided interactions between urban centres into two categories: interactions that maintained and serviced existing networks, and interactions that induced changes in the urban system structures. The first category included telephone calls, news networks, banking and other financial flows. The second category included a single type of interaction: interpersonal contacts. In his view, real change to urban systems occurred only when high-level decision makers gathered and determined the locations of future developments. However, that was in 1968. Much has changed since the oil crisis of 1973 and the great economic recession of 1981-82. The impact of the oil crisis of 1973 and the recession brought Aydalot (1984) and Stöhr (1984) to state that those crises had been so severe as to alter permanently the spatial patterns of industrialized countries. Probably the most significant change has been the rise of the information economy, in conjunction with the huge growth in the number of multinationals that now dominate the production and management processes. It therefore seemed that the location of head offices within the Canadian urban system would now be a major factor in explaining the restructuring of the Canadian and Maritime urban systems. Determining the impact of the loss of one or more head offices, on any given sub-network of an urban centre in the Maritime system, seemed of great interest, mainly because we have seen a migration of head offices from the Maritimes to central Canada over the years. (McCann, 1983) A model that could define the role head offices have in urban growth would be more closely attuned to present-day realities, and would also confirm Pred's concept of growth. Pred (1977) demonstrated that growth in urban systems occurred along transmission networks first set out by large multi-locational firms. The only technique that can actually measure sub-network changes of this nature is a systems analysis technique, as we have indicated earlier.

The systems analysis model we use to generate the results we report in the following paragraphs is based on topology, a branch of mathematics which deals with geometric forms. The interaction ratios in table 3 are an integral component of this approach. But the most interesting aspect of the model is that it can measure precisely the proportions of the total interaction flowing into a given urban centre through each of its sub-networks, and this in effect means that we can account for all the flows in the sub-networks, both direct and indirect. Also the model allows us to distinguish between the *capacity* of each sub-network and the *actual usage* that is made of this capacity. Finally, the model, when it is used in conjunction with regression analysis, allows us to establish the relationships between the number of head offices to which each sub-network is attached, as well as the sub-network's capacity and its usage.

Because the Maritime system is closely integrated into the national urban system and has numerous linkages with Newfoundland, a set of twenty-five urban centres was included in the analysis of sub-network structures of the Maritime centres. In table 5 there is a list of centres and the number of head offices in each centre, as reported by Dun and Bradstreet for the fourth quarter of 1993. Figure 4 is a stylized diagram of a city's sub-network structure, in this case Halifax's, and it is provided to help visualize the complexity of direct and indirect flows in urban interaction.

The flows between Toronto and Halifax generate secondary flows with other centres that also affect the total flows in and out of Halifax, because head offices interact with all their branches and with other firms as well. One can see this in table 6. The number of direct trips from Halifax to Toronto in 1991 amounted to 147,600 trips, but on this one Halifax sub-network, the trips totalled 168,829. At least 21,229 secondary trips were generated as a result of the highly integrated nature of modern urban-economic systems. The row *Total* in table 6 gives the total number of direct trips out of each of the six selected centres to all other twenty-four centres included in the system. The other rows indicate the number of trips moving through each of the sub-networks of each of the six centres. Because of the short distances separating a number of the Maritime cities

Figure 4

Halifax Sub-networks - 1991

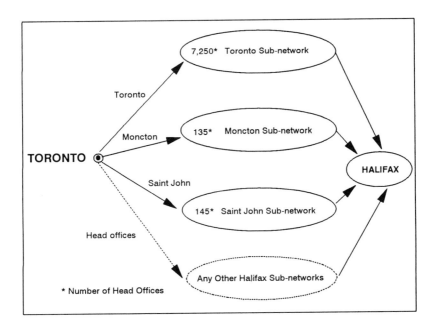

Source: Dun and Bradsteet, 1993, File 520: D & B - Canadian Dun's Mkt. Ident. (R) 1993/Q4.

Table 5

Total Number of Head Offices in Selected Urban Centres*

Toronto	7,520	Windsor	274
Montreal	4,656	St. John's, Nfld.	257
Vancouver	3,136	Saint John, NB	145
Calgary	1,878	Sudbury	139
Edmonton	1,608	Moncton	135
Ottawa	1,039	Fredericton	122
Winnipeg	980	Thunder Bay	119
Quebec	939	Sydney	80
Halifax	462	Charlottetown	68
London	446	Gander	16
Saskatoon	333	Stephenville	11
Victoria	320	Deer Lake	7
Regina	281		

*Source: Dun & Bradstreet, File 520: D & B - Canadian Dun's Mkt. Ident. (R) 1993/Q4.

one can assume that some of the interaction patterns reported in table 6 are underestimated. The dominance of Toronto, which acts as both the national node and the regional node of Eastern Canada, is quite evident; over *one third* of all trips out of the six centres flows through their Toronto sub-network, 15 percent and 11 percent through their Montreal and Ottawa sub-networks respectively. The links between Halifax and the other five centres is ten times greater than the Maritime sub-networks of the other five centres. By 1991, the Maritime urban system has been completely and directly integrated into the Canadian national urban system. The strength of Halifax's position within the Maritime system is also clearly visible, first by its ties to Toronto and secondly by the strength of its sub-networks.

Consider figure 4 again, and note that there are two components to any given sub-network of any given city. Each sub-network is anchored at one end in Halifax and the other end is anchored in one of the remaining twenty-four centres included in the system. Thus, each sub-network consists of two parts. In the sub-network that links Halifax to Moncton there is first a *set of links* that binds Halifax and Moncton together, and to all the other centres with which they interact, and second, there is *the direct link* between Moncton and the national node, Toronto. The total number of trips that arrive in Halifax through its Moncton sub-network depends, in a strict mathematical sense, on a combination of these two elements. The multitude of linkages that bind Halifax and Moncton to all the other centres is in a true sense a measure of the *capacity* of this sub-network, and the system model provides an accurate measure of this capacity in the form of a *multiplier coefficient*. However, the actual number of trips generated on this sub-network also depends on the level of interaction that the opposite node, in this case, Moncton, has with the national node. The *product* of the two values provides the exact number of trips that flow into Halifax through this sub-network. The point about all this is that *the usage* of a given capacity is highly dependent on the opposite node, and as figure 5 clearly demonstrates, the *usage* is very highly correlated with the number of head offices in the system.

In figure 5, we can see the relationship between activity on the sub-networks and the number of head offices. The drop in interaction increases considerably as the number of head offices at the opposite node decreases. Had we included only the head offices with more than 50 employees, the curve would have been more pronounced and the drop in interaction would have been much steeper. In short, figure 5 demonstrates that for the six urban centres listed in this figure, the drop in activity on their sub-networks is non-linear, which indicates that the smaller centres are much more sensitive in this regard. For example, referring back to figure 4, the drop in activity on the Halifax's sub-network to Moncton would be greater, if Moncton were to lose a head office, than the drop would be on Halifax's network with Saint John, should that centre lose a head office. This explains to a large degree the tremendous negative impact Sackville

Figure 5

Sub-network Traffic and Number of Head Offices 1991

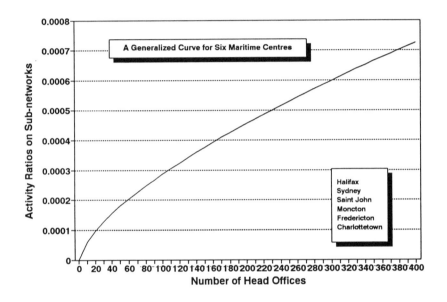

Source: For head office count, Dun and Bradstreet, File 520: D & B - Canadian Dun's
Mkt. Ident. (R) 1993/Q4. Activity ratios based on Statistics Canada, Catalogue
51-204, 1991.

Table 6

Sum of Direct and Indirect Flows Into an Urban Centre From Its Maritime Sub-networks

Sub-networks	Destination Centres					
	Halifax	Sydney	Saint John	Moncton	Fredericton	Charlottetown
From:						
Toronto	168,829*	19,316	23,616	31,434	23,199	23,932
Montreal	68,450	8,379	11,646	16,764	10,959	9,601
Ottawa	50,992	5,913	6,714	8,192	9,058	8,368
Halifax	-	8,079	6,312	4,969	5,848	6,300
Sydney	8,176	-	626	720	604	545
Saint John	6,525	671	-	-	423	552
Moncton	5,529	849	483	453	507	461
Fredericton	5,690	576	396	446	-	549
Charlottetown	6,768	574	547	423	621	-
Other sub-networks	-	-	-	-	-	-
Total**	460,630	58,840	69,570	88,090	73,700	68,480

Source: Computations based on Statistics Canada, Catalogue 51-204, 1991.

* The values in table 6 report the total number of outbound direct and indirect trips from a centre through its sub-networks. There were 147,600 direct trips from Halifax to Toronto. An additional 121,229 indirect trips were generated by the network.

** Total outbound direct trips to the other 24 centres.

N.B. sustained recently when the head office of a major wholesaler moved to Halifax. This also points out the great loss Moncton would sustain if the ACOA head offices were to be relocated.

Another indication that the head office location is a major factor in network activity can be seen from figure 6. The curve was derived from average values for the six centres listed in the figure, and reports the percent increase in activity on a sub-network for each additional head office. Here again one can see that the smaller centres in the Maritime urban system are very sensitive to either a gain or loss of a single head office. Regional business leaders and provincial decision makers should make every effort to promote *a climate* and *an infrastructure* that would induce head offices, or regional head offices, to move to those Maritime centres that are most likely to grow within the new economy, in spite of the stresses that have affected the region in the last few years.

Finally, we sought to establish the relationship between the capacity and the usage of any given sub-network of the Halifax system. The two curves of figure 7 are somewhat strange but interesting in this regard. One curve, the traffic curve, graphs the percentage of Halifax's traffic that is carried by each of its sub-networks against the number of head offices in these sub-networks. This is a curve of the actual usage, in relative terms, of these sub-networks. The second curve, the multiplier curve, links the capacity, not the actual usage, of the sub-networks to the number of head offices in the sub-networks. This capacity or multiplier effect is also measured in percentage terms. Note that if the number of urban centres in the Halifax system were increased, the overall capacity of the system would also increase. However, this would not necessarily mean a real increase in sub-network usage but only an increase in capacity. Usage only increases if real flows are carried by the sub-networks. Figure 7 indicates that only when the sub-networks have a large number of head offices does the traffic curve actually surpass the multiplier-capacity curve. Note that the usage of the sub-networks rises tremendously once the number of head offices reaches a threshold point. Figure 7 is in effect stating that even if an urban system has considerable interraction capabilities the potential of any of its sub-networks is reached and surpassed only when the sub-network itself is tied directly to other centres with large number of head offices. Similar curves were obtained for the other centres of the Maritime urban system. This is a clear indication that an urban system in an advanced economy is dominated by the organizational structures of the large firms located within the system.

Conclusion

The Canadian and Maritime urban systems have been profoundly affected by the succession of economic transformations and shocks to hit the industrialized world since the 1950s. The Maritime urban system now is nothing like the description put forth by Boisvert in 1978. The loosely-integrated and fairly independent sub-provincial systems are no more. The biggest change has been the total dominance of Toronto over the Maritime system. Two great surges of system restructuring

Figure 6

Percent Increase in Sub-network Activity
With Each Additional Head Office

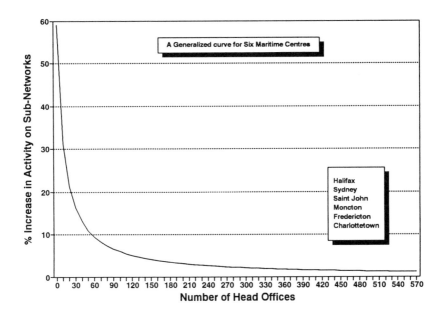

Source: For head office count, Dun and Bradstreet, File 520: D & B - Canadian Dun's Mkt. Ident. (R) 1993/Q4. Activity ratios based on Statistics Canada, Catalogue 51-204, 1991.

Figure 7

Sub-network Capacity and Usage
on the Halifax Sub-networks

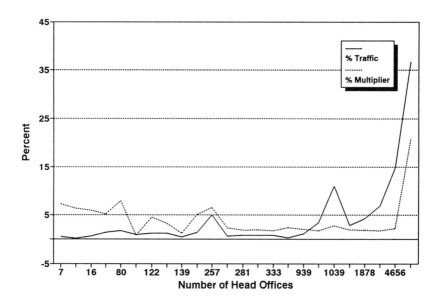

Source: Dun & Bradstreet, Calculations based on Statistics Canada, Catalogue 51-204, 1991.

have occurred. The first and most important, so far, occurred in the 1950s and 1960s with the service economy, and the second, in the 1970s and 1980s, came with the rise of the information economy.

Giarini (1983) and Gershuny (1983) have provided ample proof of the powerful impact the call for services has had on the economic processes. However, they gave little indication how urban systems would be affected, either because the reaction of the urban centres to economic change was too slow to catch their interest, or because they had no way of measuring urban system change, or, again, because they might have been too caught up in the economic processes themselves to notice the spatial impacts of these transformations. However, there is no doubt that the *service economy* has been the economic transformation that has had the most dramatic impact on the Maritime urban system. The effect of that transformation has been the greater integration of a number of the larger urban centres into a national urban system centred primarily on Toronto. There is very little doubt that Halifax emerged during this period as the Maritime's prime regional node.

The second most important economic transformation to alter the Maritime urban system has been the rise of the information economy, and with it, the rise in the multinationals. We note its beginnings in the mid-1970s. A tremendous increase in the production of new technological information, as well as the convergence of the telecommunication and computer technologies, have been its trademark so far. However, the implementation of a *fully-developed information society* could not be achieved in the 1980s, not even because of the 1981-82 crisis which served to heighten its momentum, because of two limitations: first, a lack of sufficient computing power and adequate user-interface technology; and secondly the delay in building the electronic highway, which hinges on digital transmissions through fiber-optic networks. All through the 1980s, railway and telephone companies combined their resources to build fiber-optic networks right across the United States and Canada, at a total estimated cost of $100 billion. It also seems the Americans and Japanese took a different approach in the search for an information society and the wealth it would generate. The Japanese spent tremendous amounts of money on a strategy, developed in 1977, to cover the islands with a network of 25 technopolises. Each technopolis, (the first appeared in 1984), was to be based on three ingredients; a set of high-tech industries, a number of scientific institutions and a highly developed urban core in which the transportation infrastructure was to be of paramount importance, as subsequent studies were to show. (Stöhr, 1992) It is interesting to note that the Americans first set out to deregulate their telecommunications. This deregulation was to provide the impetus for development. Most of their early efforts in computer technology seem to have been to develop the highly specialized chips the electronic highway would require, and the fifth generation computers, leaving to the Japanese the task of developing the high density memory chips, a major success story in its own right. Until all the technological problems could be solved, it was impossible to create the information society, and create the jobs the new services and infrastructures would demand. The scene is now set, with one exception. How do you go about administering such an electronic highway? The establishment and trials of the internet infrastructure now in operation are, it seems, a testing ground for these management aspects; management of consumer information networks is a new technology in its own right as the French have discovered; had they not been able to overcome these management problems, their whole Minitel network would have floundered. (Marchand, 1987)

The information economy began to have some impact on the Maritime urban system when the fiber-optic networks began to stretch across the nation and through the provinces. The Maritime telecommunication companies have done extensive work and developed the necessary expertise in these matters. Within the next five years the fate of the Maritimes will be determined in this regard. Will we have a number of urban centres capable of producing and delivering goods and services and jobs for an information society? Or will all our urban centres be nothing more than distribution centres? Will we have lost all manufacturing capabilities, except in the primary and transformation sectors? Or will we be able to create from an educated labour force a new economy capable of creating goods and services for an information society? An information society will also have a *manufacturing component*, of a different type, but a major source of jobs for those who are going to service and feed the electronic highways. The new information society, and its new economic activities, have a potential worth estimated at a *trillion dollars U.S.!*

The reductions in public spending will not be an overpowering shock for the urban centres in most instances, except probably in Halifax and Newfoundland. All of the larger urban centres in the Maritimes have a fairly good pattern of industrial activities and should be able to sustain these reductions, especially if new regional development efforts are geared at creating an information economy and society. Federal and provincial governments will have to approach this carefully because funds are so limited and the new international agreements, when they come into full effect will prevent government subsidies for such endeavours.

Finally, the NAFTA and other international trade agreements will have some impact on the urban centres in the region, and only the most robust will be able to compete. In the long run, the agreements will prohibit government subsidies, and this will force the urban centres to rely solely on their own resources. Only a few of the centres, other than the primary producers, will have the capacity to meet the challenge. When the agreements come to full implementation, and if the information activities are not well established in the most important centres of Maritime Canada, the Maritime urban centres will face another round of restructuring and difficulty. The prospects are good if strategies are devised and launched within the next five years. If not, the Maritime urban system will be in great difficulty.

REFERENCES

Aydalot, P., "À la recherche de nouveaux dynamismes spatiaux", in Aydalot (ed.) *Crise & Espace* (Paris: Economica, 1984).

Boisvert, M., *La correspondance entre le système urbain et la base économique des régions canadiennes* (Ottawa: Conseil Économique du Canada, 1978).

Gershuny, Jonathan, "The Future of Service Employment", in O. Giarini (ed.), *The Emerging Service Economy* (Toronto: Pergamon Press, 1987), pp. 105-126.

Giarini, Orio, "The Service Economy: New Strategies for Creating the Wealth of Nations" in O. Giarini (ed.), *The Emerging Service Economy* (Toronto: Pergamon Press, 1987), pp. v-viii.

Jones, J.H., "A memorandum on the location of industry," Appendix ii to the *Royal Commission on the Distribution of the Industrial Population* (the Barlow Report), HMSO Cmnd 6153, pp. 149-280, 1940.

Lamarche, R.H., "The Maritime Provinces in an Information Economy," in Donald J. Savoie and Ralph Winter (eds.), *Les Provinces Maritimes: Un regard vers l'avenir/The Maritime Provinces: Looking To The Future* (Moncton: Canadian Institute for Research on Regional Development, 1993).

Lamarche, R.H., *Capitalizing on the Information Economy: A New Approach in Regional Development* (Moncton: Canadian Institute for Research on Regional Development, 1990).

Marchand, Marie, *La grande aventure du Minitel* (Paris: Larousse, 1987).

McCann, L.D., "Metropolitanism and Branch Businesses in the Maritimes, 1881-1931," *Acadiensis*, 13 (Autumn, 1983), pp. 112-25.

Pred, Allan, *City-Systems in Advanced Economy: Past Growth, Present Processes and Future Development Options* (London: Hutchinson and Company Ltd., 1977).

Ray, Michael, *Standardising Employment Growth Rates of Foreign Multinationals and Domestic Firms in Canada: From Shift-share to Multifactor Partitioning* (Geneva: International Labour Office, 1990).

Rubin, Michael Rogers, *Information Economics And Policy in the United States* (Littleton Colorado: Libraries Unlimited, 1983).

Savoie, D.J., *Regional Economic Development: Canada's Search for Solution* (Toronto: University of Toronto Press, Second Edition, 1992).

Serafini S., Andrieu M., Estabrooks M., "Post Industrial Canada and the New Information Technology," *Canadian Futures*, 1.2 1980, pp. 81-91.

Srinath, K.P. and Ray D.M., "Use of Standardization in the Analysis of Rates" (Los Angeles: Proceedings of the American Statistical Association Conference, CA., 1990).

Stöhr, W., "La crise économique demande-t-elle de nouvelles stratégies de développement régional?" in Aydalot (ed.), *Crise & Espace* (Paris: Economica, 1984).

Tornqvist, G., "Flows of Information and Location of Economic Activities," *Geografiska Annaler*, 50B, pp. 99-107, 1968.

3

MARITIME CITIES AS A PART OF THE NORTH AMERICAN URBAN SYSTEM

Guy Vincent
Paul Villeneuve

The growing interaction between the Maritime urban centres and the United States Northeast centres - an adjustment to the three shocks?

> *L'immense étendue de terres qui occupe toute la partie septentrionale du continent américain, et que l'on a délimitée politiquement sous le nom de 'Puissance du Canada', ne constitue point un ensemble géographique . . . Si la population du Canada se groupait en une masse compacte, elle pourrait se développer librement en une individualité politique distincte, sans avoir à souffrir de la bizarre frontière politique tracée au sud de son territoire; mais l'immense contrée, d'une superficie plus vaste que les États-Unis, n'est encore que faiblement peuplée, et les habitants se sont répartis suivant une ligne sur la frontière. (Élisée Reclus, 1890, p. 257)*

What can be said about Reclus' verdict a century later? How does it apply to the Maritimes? How can we account for the position held by the Maritimes within Canadian interaction patterns? More precisely, how can we describe the relationship between the East-West and North-South interaction fields, and what are the roles of Maritime cities in the interplay between these two fields? These are the crucial questions this chapter tries to answer.

The Canadian space-economy can be seen as resulting from an intermittent tugging between North-South and East-West fields of interaction. From time to time, and for varying reasons, one field tends to predominate over the other. Currently, tendencies furthering continental integration are relatively strong in North America. Two sets of reasons, reinforcing each other, may have favoured North-South interaction over East-West interaction in recent years. First, agreements such as the North American Free Trade Agreement (NAFTA) tend to facilitate North-South trade. Second, the centrifugal forces operating within the Canadian political space, particularly in Quebec and the West, might negatively affect East-West interaction.

To what extent, then, are strong continental integration trends a danger for Canadian unity and integrity? The answer to this question may depend largely on the specific forms taken by the spatial interaction patterns through which integration occurs. Increasing North-South interactions which are restricted to adjacent Canadian and American regions may pose a greater threat to Canadian integrity than interactions that are diffused throughout the continent. If interactions between the Maritimes and New England increase more rapidly than interactions of the Maritimes with the other regions of North America, including the rest of Canada, the resulting geoeconomic zone may, in time, appear more viable than the present situation. If, on the other hand, Maritime interactions become more diffused throughout the continent, then the strength of their linkages with the rest of Canada may diminish, but they may do so in a manner which is less threatening to the integrity of the country. In fact, diffused and diversified patterns of exchange may be a way to maintain autonomy.

This chapter deals first with the historical circumstances setting the North American fields of interaction into motion. Secondly, the hypothesis of restricted versus diffused interaction is further developed, making use of available theories about the role of cities in the formation of interaction fields. Then, preliminary empirical tests are conducted which utilize air passenger flows between Maritime cities and a selection of North American metropolitan areas. Finally, case studies of two transportation firms are presented as complementary information in order to further substantiate our hypothesis.

Evolution of East-West and North-South Relations

Within the span of a century, Canada moved from the orbit of Europe to that of the United States. The first significant field of interaction in Canadian history was centred in Europe, and particularly in London. Following the collapse of the British Empire, the economic shadow enveloping Canada now came from the South, rather than from the East. Throughout Canadian history, the overriding objective has been to counteract this strong North-South attraction between the different regions and their American counterpart by creating an East-West interaction field. Tariffs were instituted, railways were built. Yet, the physical geography of the continent resisted stubbornly. For example, the more expensive and poorer quality, coal from distant Nova Scotia was still less attractive to Southern Ontario steel producers than that of Pennsylvania. (Wolfe, 1968, p. 201) Other contemporary examples of irresistible North-South interactions include power lines, pipelines, tourism and professional sport.

Because of the limited size of its economy and its regional fragmentation, Canada's internal market rapidly appeared a difficult one to unify. The presence of a huge American market lying a few hundred kilometres South also reinforced tendencies towards fragmentation: "Les complémentarités nord-sud [y] sont plus évidentes que les complémentarités est-ouest." (Claval, 1989, p. 205) As early as 1937, André Siegfried tried to evaluate the North-South and East-West relations in Canada. He noticed that North-South relations tended to get stronger in periods of peace and prosperity. One of the reasons for this intensification, he argued, was the growing demand for Canadian natural resources during these periods. East-West relations tended to strengthen in harsh periods, through political centralization exercised by the federal state, which would act as an alternate regulator and replacement of a slowed private sector.

However, prosperity, fuelled by natural resource exports, can have unexpected consequences. Since natural resources belong to the provinces, these jurisdictions have tended to develop their own continental and international ties with their clients, once again opening up the question of the balance between East-West and North-South economic relations. Furthermore, the revenues generated by these exports can be invested, as they were in the 1950s and 1960s, in social programs such as in education, health care, and urban planning and development. Because these are administered by the provinces, an imbalance of revenue tends to produce interprovincial differentials.

The unification of Canada was implemented, largely, by the construction of an East-West transportation network in which the Canadian Pacific Railway Company was heavily involved. The development of the CP Ltd. perfectly illustrates the evolution of continental economic trends. Where once it was a symbol, and one of the principal instruments of national unity, it has since been busy extending its control outside Canada, with business preoccupations overshadowing national goals. (Goldenberg, 1984, p. 157) Recently, seeking to present a new image, CP unveiled a new logo in which the U.S. Stars and Stripes are blended with the Canadian Maple Leaf, which made very clear the firm's intention to tap a larger share of the American market (fig. 1). This national unity symbol "going South" is a striking example of the re-direction of continental relations.

Metropolitan Fields of Interaction

Figure 1

Large corporations, such as CP Ltd, operate out of metropolitan areas and contribute much to the structuring of fields of interaction focused on metropolises. Usually, these fields cut across provincial and state boundaries. In reality, provinces and metropolises constitute two organizational levels which mold Canadian spatial dynamics. Metropolitan regions play a key role in Canada's territorial integration while provinces are, above all, an element of spatial differentiation. (Villeneuve, 1990)

Cole Harris (1987) has shown how provincial boundaries correspond poorly to the hinterlands of the larger Canadian cities. Settlement, nevertheless, took place within these boundaries, contributing to forge distinct provincial identities throughout Canada. Metropolises, on the other hand, are part and parcel of the relation between technology and empire (Innis, 1972): Transcontinental railways throughout Canada; manufactures at the centre; markets from one ocean to the other, and beyond; and later, Air Canada, CBC, and the Trans-Canada highway. A country as wide as Canada would have been inconceivable without this technological arsenal, which served to establish the complementary relations between metropolises and their hinterlands that eventually led to national integration.

National integration was initiated out of Montreal and was then pursued from Toronto and Ottawa. But, in the period of prosperity following World War II, regional metropolises have risen and challenged central Canada's metropolitan triangle. This change has also been helped along by the fact that Montreal itself has become a regional metropolis. (McCann, 1987; Coffey and Polèse, 1993) Conversely to Montreal, whose hinterland has shrunk, Halifax, during this period, has become the undisputed regional metropolis of Atlantic Canada. What do these changes in metropolitan interaction fields mean for the Maritime urban system?

Before turning to tentative empirical answers to this question, let us consider briefly the historical basis for possible North-South metropolitan interaction fields. Some years ago, Vance (1970) identified several North-South supranational urban alignments going back to the mercantile period when North America was still in the European orbit. According to Marshall (1989), seven fields of interactions cross the continent from North to South (fig. 2). Most find their origin in the East-West fields, established through relations between North America and Europe. The cities forming each alignment were, historically, more similar than complementary, but the advent of automobiles and airplanes, as well as the growing autonomy of the continent, favoured North-South exchanges, contributing in this way to the formation of complementarities within each alignment. The East Coast alignment is of interest here. It extends from New Orleans to Montreal and Quebec City, including Maritime cities. The cities in this alignment were trans-shipment points during the colonial era, but the long term diversification of their economic base accompanied the development of complementary ties among them, especially among those on the Atlantic Coast.

Considering that Canada sends 75 percent of its exports southwards and imports around 25 percent of United States exports, one may want to know whether these flows, as well as other flows of, say, people and information, are constrained by such North-South alignments as the one on the Atlantic Coast, or

Figure 2

Metropolitan Alignments in North America

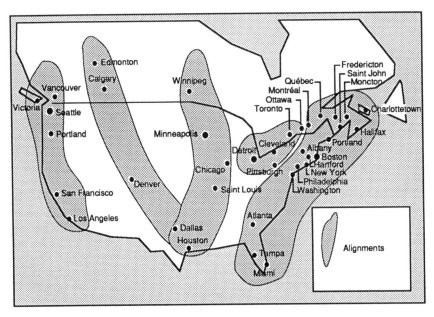

whether they are diffused over the continent. What are the chances that these alignments become the principal interaction fields and the main framework of the continent? In a world where information has become the primary resource for economic growth and identity formation, new solidarities and new cross-border regional identities may develop and challenge East-West identities. A number of redrawings of the North-American regional map have been attempted, based on emerging new regionalism. Joel Garreau's (1981) is probably the best known to date. The front cover of his book reads: "Forget the traditional map - new realities of power and people are making this continent into The Nine Nations of America." On the other hand, things could evolve quite differently if each province or region diversifies its interactions on a continental scale, and not along any North-South channel. Such multidirectional and diffuse interactions between the parts of North America could result in multiple level action spaces, a reality that most of us already experience in our everyday lives. The new action space, not necessarily operational for most of us, would be continental space, including Mexico. It will more likely be, for a number of years to come, an action space shaped mainly by telecommunications, but it may be worthwhile to ask if we can see it emerge in the travel patterns of, say, air passengers.

Air Passenger Flows as Integration Indicators

Some of the questions raised so far can be addressed empirically by examining changes in air passenger flows between the Maritimes and the rest of North America. For the time being, we are more interested in the form taken by these flows than in their consequences for the formation of new regional patterns. The following analysis attempts to verify a simple hypothesis derived from the above discussion. The first part of the hypothesis relates to the growing importance of North-South interaction compared to East-West interaction in Canada. If this growth holds, it should be noticeable in the flow data. The second part of the hypothesis relates to the form taken by North-South interaction, with special emphasis on its direction; does it follow the above mentioned alignments, or does it show a diffuse or fuzzy pattern in all directions?

Air passenger data are particularly suited - and just about the only data readily available - to test our hypotheses. Since air transportation is widely used for business and tourist purposes, these data can portray key movements of people between cities and help trace action spaces of individuals. These action spaces reflect both the existing interaction fields, and contribute to ward the moulding of the fields of tomorrow. Air passenger data between Canadian cities and between Canadian and American cities are published yearly (Statistics Canada, annual catalogues 51-204 and 51-205).

The logic behind the use of these data is quite simple. Approximately 70 percent of air passengers are business travellers. These establish and maintain relations between or within enterprises from one region to another. It is fair to assume that a number of these contacts are made across the Canada-United States border. By means of increasingly frequent and close relationships, business strategies from both sides of the border could converge and favour North-South patterns. If a group of firms chose similar development strategies, this could lead the North American cities where these firms operate to adopt similar planning and development strategies. One end result would be the creation of urban patterns where affinities between cities grow more strongly along North-South lines than East-West. The result over time could be the enhancement of North-South cultural patterns.

In order to submit this thinking to a preliminary empirical test, the authors selected fourteen Canadian cities. The choices were such as to represent each Canadian region. The Maritimes were, however, intentionally over-represented, in order to more closely assess their position in potential and eventual reordering of continental interactions. The Maritime cities considered were Sydney, Halifax, Charlottetown, Moncton, Fredericton and Saint John, while Quebec City, Montreal, Ottawa, Toronto, Winnipeg, Regina, Calgary and Vancouver completed the national picture. The data set contained the number of air passengers among these fourteen cities, and between each of them, and an array of twenty-three American cities for 1970 and 1990. Again, the American cities were carefully selected in order to represent each region, with a slight over-representation of the North-East (fig. 3). Also, metropolitan populations and airline distances were included in the data.

Figure 3

Cities Considered in the Study

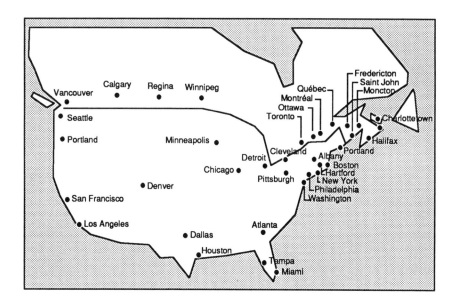

This data set has been submitted to an analysis based on the gravity model. Where the first objective is to extract the most evident variations in the flow pattern, before specifically comparing the variations between East-West and North-South relations. The most evident variation depends on the size of the urban areas and the distance between them. Flows are directly proportional to size and inversely proportional to distance, although because of the transportation mode considered here, flow intensity will be minimal on distances below 200-300 km, then will rise abruptly with distances up to 600-700 km, finally tending to diminish with even-longer distances.

The simplest way to measure size and distance effects (G for gravity) between cities i and j is:

$$\log G_{ij} = \log(P_i P_j / D_{ij}),$$

which supposes that the gravitational effect is directly proportional to the product of the population of both urban areas and inversely proportional to flight distance between the two cities. $\log G_{ij}$ values are then used as the independent variable in a regression model to account for the most obvious part of the variance in the air passenger interaction volumes (I for interaction), for each Canadian agglomeration, at both points in time. These interactions are also expressed in logarithms in order to linearise the relation:

$$\log I_{ij} = a + b(\log G_{ij}) + \log(e_{ij}) \qquad (1)$$

The term e_{ij} is of interest here. It designates the residuals, that is, the part of the interaction variance not explained by the gravitational effect. A strongly integrated East-West gravitational field would be evident if the residuals for Canadian cities were highly positive, meaning that East-West interaction would be more intense than anticipated solely with respect to the size of the cities and the distance between them. On the other hand, if the North-South gravitational field were well integrated, this would be indicated by positive residuals for American cities. Finally, no pattern in the residuals would indicate a diffuse interaction. The comparison between 1970 and 1990 allows the possibility to evaluate the evolution of both gravitational fields. A shift in the interaction patterns in conformity with the theoretical discussion above would correspond to diminishing residuals in the East-West field and increasing ones in the North-South field. Moreover, the interaction field of a given city is becoming more diffuse, and reaching further away, if its interaction gradient (the b parameter in the gravitational equation) diminishes between 1970 and 1990.

Twenty-eight gravitational equations, such as equation (1), have been evaluated using least squares (six Maritime cities and eight other Canadian cities for two-time periods). Generally, the equations were not significant: they accounted for a small proportion of the variance, with the coefficients of determination ranging from 0.00 to 0.24. Obviously these coefficients of determination are very low and could be cause for concern. However, they do reveal an interesting fact about interaction patterns of Canadian cities. Canadian cities interact differently with American cities than they do with other Canadian centres. The regression line of our model serves more as a boundary between the two sets of interacting patterns than as a representation of the total interaction activities of Canadian cities. However, we can get a better understanding of these interaction patterns by examining the scatter graphs as we do in figures 4-a and 4-b, or by modifying our initial equation to account for the nationality of the cities involved, as we do later on in the study.

Cartographic representation of the residuals, expressed as percentages of the corresponding observed values, that is $[\log(e_{ij}) / \log I_{ij}]*100$, appears to be the most effective method to test the above hypotheses. Results for Maritime cities will now be described and compared to those for other Canadian cities.

Maritime Cities in a Continental Context: Marginalization and Polarization

Sydney demonstrated for 1970 what would seem to be a normal interaction pattern with Canadian cities. Roughly, interaction decreased as distance increased, Quebec City was the exception with a negative residual. The pattern appeared rather similar with American cities, with higher negative values tending to increase with distance. Indeed, interaction with some of the most distant cities showed negative residual values close to zero. Changes between 1970 and 1990 appeared rather dramatic (fig. 5). There was a clear specialization of destinations throughout North America, since a number of cities did no longer interacted with Sydney. Consequently, American cities which were still interacting with Sydney now showed high positive residuals, although they remained below those of Canadian cities. Generally, the cities with the lowest residual values in 1970 cut their interaction with Sydney in 1990. A further comparison of the two points in time, showed a strong East-West interaction, maintaining itself simultaneously with the emergence of selective North-South interaction. One interesting fact was the "closing-in" of Sydney and Pittsburgh, two cities which have a common economic base, possibly generating complementary relations. Clearly, an important reorganization of air transportation between Sydney and North American destinations seemed to have taken place. In fact, these data suggested that either there were no passengers from Sydney heading to a number of American cities, or that Statistics Canada rounds off insignificant numbers.

For 1970, Halifax showed high positive residuals for its interaction with other Canadian cities. These values ranged from 16 to 30 percent except for Quebec City (5.6 percent) and Regina (7.7 percent). Two trends were noticeable between 1970 and 1990: the residuals tended to diminish in the interaction with Maritime cities, whereas they tended to increase, although slightly, with other Canadian cities. Among American cities, only New York and Boston showed positive values for 1970. To these latter two cities, Tampa and Miami were added in 1990. The trend, on the other hand, seemed rather diffuse. The difference between 1970 and 1990 values indicated an increase in interaction with most American cities, except the easternmost ones, save Portland, and a decrease with Maritime cities along with Montreal, Toronto and Regina. This trend was

Figure 4-a

Air Passenger Flow and Interaction - Halifax

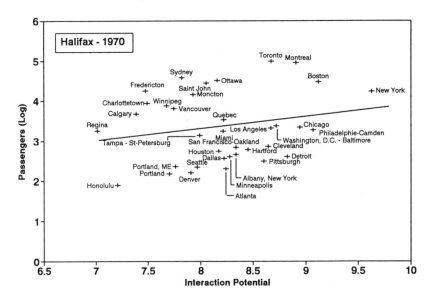

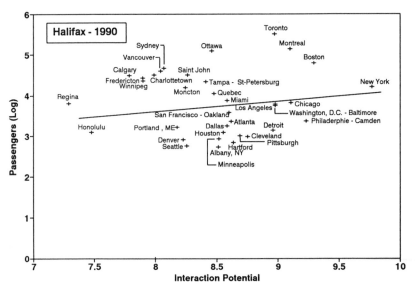

Figure 4-b

Air Passenger Flow and Interaction - Sydney

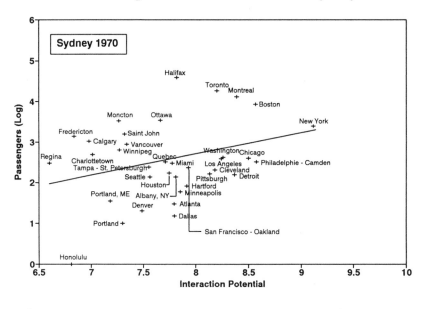

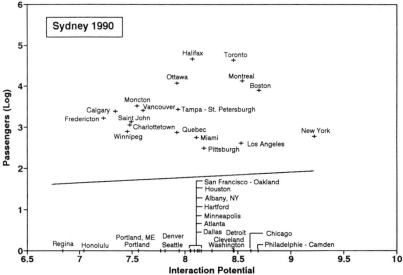

Figure 5

Sydney: Rationalization and Polarization

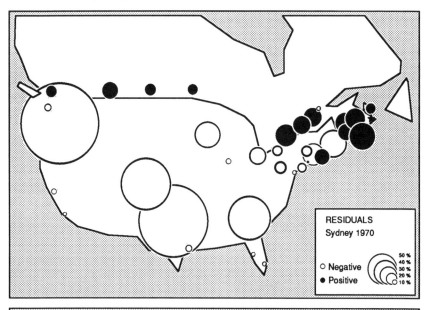

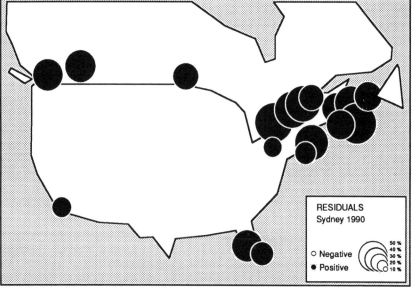

no surprise considering the already high values of Canadian cities among themselves, compared to that of American cities, but the results seemed to indicate an increased North-South interaction, while East-West links were still highly superior, and the increasingly important role of Halifax as the regional pole in a continental context (fig. 6).

Charlottetown showed an even more radical pattern of interaction, similar to that of Sydney. For 1990, the positive residual values were limited to Canadian cities, Boston, and New York, which resulted in the loss of contact with most American cities, and high negative values for the remainder. In fact, only interactions with Halifax, Ottawa, and Toronto showed positive residuals. Two important decreases are worth noting: Boston from 31.3 to -38.2, and New York from 18.9 to -47.3 percent. The losses of contact and important decreases between 1970 and 1990 tended to marginalize Charlottetown and limit its role as the regional pole of Prince Edward Island, which role could be eroded eventually when the province will be permanently linked to New Brunswick (fig. 7).

The Moncton, Saint John, and Fredericton patterns were very similar. In 1970, their values showed a strong East-West field of interaction, with an emergent, but polarized, North-South pattern quite similar to that of Sydney, but not as dramatic. Indeed, Boston, New York, Miami, and Tampa showed positive residual values with these three New Brunswick cities, while most of the other North-East cities reported high negative values. As was the case for Sydney and Charlottetown, these high negative residuals translated into losses of contact by 1990. However, the emerging North-South interaction out of Moncton gave it a more widespread pattern by 1990 with the addition of high positive residuals for Los Angeles and Chicago. It should be noted that the interaction between Moncton, Charlottetown, Fredericton, and Saint John (though not between Saint John and Charlottetown) was considerably reduced. Although Moncton, Saint John and Fredericton have sustained losses and might appear, at first glance, to have been marginalized, they have retained their most important continental contacts, and are now "connected" to important American clusters that can redirect passengers continentally and internationally. The term polarization, rather than marginalization, would better describe the process that they have undergone. Moncton and Saint John have an advantage over Fredericton by having a "stronger" connection with continentally-central Chicago.

Marginalization of Maritime Cities in Canadian Urban Interaction?

When looking at other Canadian cities' patterns of interaction, Maritime cities seemed to suffer from marginalization. The exception was Halifax, which appeared to have become the regional pole. Every city seemed to extend its relation southwards in a rather diffuse manner. Often, this extension was detri-

Figure 6

Halifax: Maritime Pole

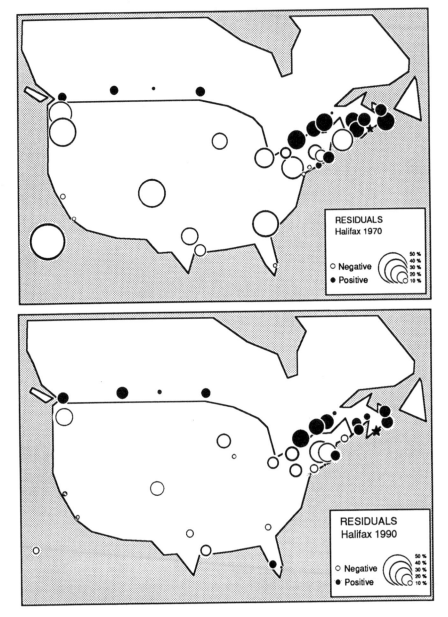

Figure 7

Charlottetown: Marginalized Maritime City

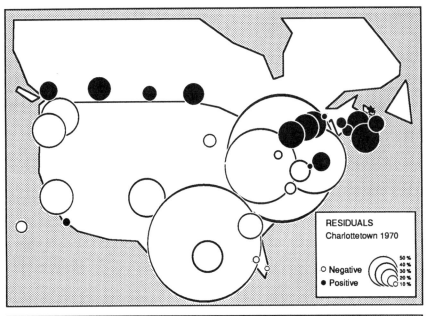

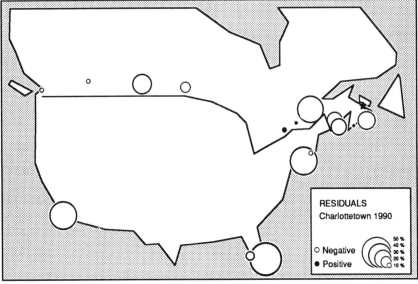

mental to Maritime cities. This pattern was noticeable even for Ottawa, which would have been expected to act as a "guardian" of East-West relations.

This increase in southward interaction, at the expense of Maritime cities, did not seem to be the case with Quebec City. In fact, it maintained high residual values with Maritime cities, and the gains were comparable to those of most North American cities, except for several losses of contact and, interestingly, a decrease in interaction with Ottawa. Montreal and Ottawa maintained moderate interaction with Maritime cities, particularly with Halifax. Montreal showed a high increase of contact with Moncton, whereas Ottawa showed a small increase with Sydney, Halifax and Charlottetown, and a decrease with all three New Brunswick cities.

Not surprisingly, Ottawa displayed a re-orientation of its interaction continentally with important economic and political poles, such as Toronto, New York, and Washington, as well as nationally with the regional poles of Halifax, Winnipeg, Calgary, and Vancouver. The trend shown by the difference of residual values for both periods, however, indicated an eventual "americanization" (as opposed to continentalization) of its interaction, in that most of Ottawa's gains were mainly obtained south of the border. Nonetheless, the Maritime cities were not marginalized in Ottawa's traffic pattern.

Toronto's East-West interaction appeared stronger than North-South for both 1970 and 1990. Yet, although some showed positive residual values, Maritime cities, with the exception of Halifax, seemed marginalized by their comparatively weak magnitude (fig. 8). The trend portrayed by the difference between 1970 and 1990 is a perfect example of American continentalization and Maritime marginalization. Losses were observed from East to West, in the Great Lakes region, and Hartford, Albany, and, surprisingly, New York. The gains were diffused all over the United States. Why Charlottetown was the only eastern Canadian city displaying gain remains to be explained.

Winnipeg and Regina showed somewhat similar patterns. They seemed to maintain predominantly East-West patterns of interaction, and to increase their interaction with neighbouring cities across the border. Unexpectedly, though, their residuals with respect to Maritime cities and their gains were relatively high, especially for Regina. Part of the explanation lies in the fact that residual values were so low in 1970.

Calgary and Vancouver showed a stronger East-West integration than North-South. However, the interaction with their distant counterparts on the Eastern seaboard was weak compared to other Canadian cities, since the magnitude of their residual values - with southern "oil cities" for Calgary, and Pacific cities for Vancouver - is somewhat equivalent or, in a few instances, inferior. Halifax was still exceptional in showing higher values, thus re-affirming its position as the regional pole. The tendencies, however, are different for both cities. Vancouver's interaction increased predominantly with central and eastern

Figure 8

Toronto: Marginalizing Maritime Cities

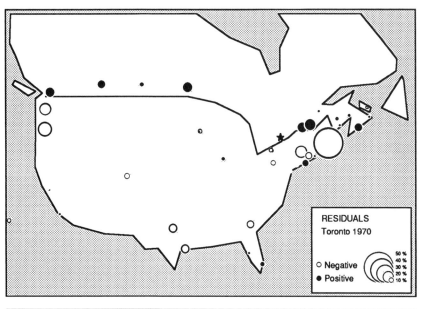

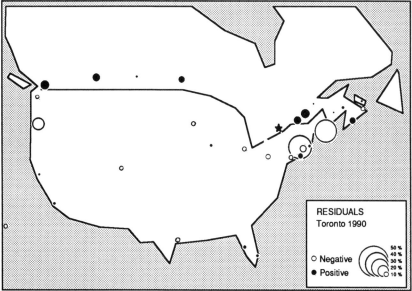

American cities and decreased with most Canadian cities, while Calgary displayed increased relations with Pacific and Atlantic cities, including Maritime cities.

By examining the fields of interaction of selected Canadian cities, it appeared that the Canadian gravitational field was still stronger than that of the United States, although the differentiation tended to diminish. This decrease operated in a rather diffuse manner, and no clear North-South alignments were specifically identified, with the exception of Calgary and Vancouver.

The Maritime cities showed similar behaviour. While 1970 data seemed to indicate an eventual segmented interaction with American Northeastern cities, 1990 data displayed a "fuzzier" interaction. However, Halifax showed positive residual values with cities located on the East Coast, but residuals with several others in Eastern United States were negative. On the other hand, the Maritime cities appeared to be gradually marginalized by Canadian cities. Meanwhile, Maritime cities seemed to be increasingly well connected to the air transportation network in the United States. In fact, the Maritime connections with some American cities tended to be better than among themselves. Would this fact alone be the reason for their marginalization by other Canadian cities? Or, on the contrary, could their marginalization by other Canadian cities explain an air network restructuring?

One last analysis can add substance and nuance to these preliminary conclusions. In order to better evaluate the effect of the Canadian-American boundary on interaction patterns, we introduced a dummy variable in the gravitation equation. Canadian cities were given a value of 1 and American cities were given a value of 0 on this variable, noted F_{ij}. Its coefficient, c, measured the vertical distance between the two regression lines that would have been obtained if analyses were performed separately on Canadian and American cities. This new equation reads as follows:

$$\log_{ij} = a + b(\log G_{ij}) + c(F_{ij}) + \log(e_{ij}) \qquad (2)$$

The addition of F_{ij} considerably improved the gravitational model's performance. Table 1 displays the results.

The general decrease in r^2 between the two dates indicated more randomness in interaction patterns. In other words, interaction levels were not as easily predicted in 1990 as they were in 1970, which is in line with the hypothesis of greater "fuzziness."

The increases in the b's, although small, tend to suggest that, with the exceptions of Ottawa, Toronto, and Vancouver, a unit change in G produced a larger change in I in 1990 than it did in 1970. Since G combines both the sizes of the cities and the distance between them, it is difficult to infer whether the change in the b's is attributable to variations in population or travel costs, or both.

Table 1

Regression Results

	1970			1990			Differences		
	b	c	r^2	b	c	r^2	b	c	r^2
Sydney	1.16	1.79	0.76	1.43	3.19	0.62	0.27	1.40	-0.14
Halifax	0.89	1.74	0.83	0.92	1.73	0.61	0.03	-0.01	-0.22
Charlottetown	0.90	1.87	0.69	1.07	3.04	0.57	0.17	1.17	-0.12
Moncton	1.00	1.95	0.71	1.31	2.60	0.41	0.31	0.65	-0.30
Fredericton	0.74	1.86	0.66	0.87	2.75	0.46	0.13	0.89	-0.20
Saint John	0.85	1.46	0.68	1.18	2.68	0.44	0.33	1.22	-0.24
Quebec	0.94	1.36	0.77	1.36	2.70	0.52	0.42	1.34	-0.25
Montreal	0.68	1.11	0.64	0.98	1.25	0.52	0.30	0.14	-0.12
Ottawa	0.61	1.50	0.72	0.47	1.38	0.36	-0.14	-0.12	-0.36
Toronto	0.73	1.20	0.69	0.64	1.05	0.52	-0.09	-0.15	-0.17
Winnipeg	1.00	1.64	0.70	1.33	1.92	0.54	0.33	0.28	-0.16
Regina	1.01	1.93	0.66	1.33	2.77	0.43	0.32	0.84	-0.23
Calgary	0.99	1.51	0.69	1.20	1.64	0.59	0.21	0.13	-0.10
Vancouver	1.11	1.59	0.70	1.03	1.34	0.71	-0.08	-0.25	0.01

Source: Compiled from air passengers data in Statistics Canada, Catalogues 51-204 and 51-205, 1970, 1990.

As for the c's, they clearly indicate that the boundary effect is not diminishing, except for Halifax, Ottawa, Toronto, and Vancouver. This largely runs against the hypothesis of increasing North-South interaction, at the expense of East-West interaction. Most Eastern cities, particularly Maritime cities, showed a high increase. This is no surprise, considering the many losses of contacts that were noted earlier. Thus, in that regard, the four exceptions would appear as regional nodes of exterior communication. Might these cities be the leaders in an emerging North-South interaction network?

The next part intends to explore this question by looking specifically at the recent initiative of an air transportation firm which seems eager to tap the new business created by a more open market. Northwest Airlink appears to illustrate a new trend that has emerged since 1990, a trend not yet documented by official data.

The Advent of Short-link Transportation Firms

As seen earlier, the imposition of high tariffs at the time of the National Policy more or less isolated Maritime cities from important markets in New England. This contributed to the development of an important Canadian transportation industry, operating in concert with resource extraction industries. Times have changed, and Atlantic Canada now has important economic ties with New England. Of the $3.5 billion worth of exported goods from Atlantic Canada to the United States, 62 percent go to New England States. (Robb, 1993) This is an indication of the great potential that lies in intensifying North-South contact between these two regions.

A new 19-passenger direct daily flight service between Boston and Moncton, the first in 50 years, was inaugurated in May 1992. By introducing this flight, Northwest Airlink, a subsidiary of Northwest Airlines, is attempting to capitalize on close economic and cultural ties between New Brunswick and New England. (Allen, 1992) The schedule of this flight is clearly designed to accommodate business travellers. Arguably, this is a very small step, but the initiative was so successful that the aircrafts were replaced by others, offering twice as many seats, and the number of daily flights were increased from three to four. (*Times and Transcript*, 1993) The one hour and 20 minutes flight is a major improvement compared to the previous 5½ hours connection between Boston and Moncton via either Halifax, Saint John or even Montreal. (Allen, 1992) This initiative contributes to the growing importance of Moncton in the North American Northeast, and challenges Halifax's erstwhile role as the Maritimes' door to New England.

This example is a localized illustration of Northwest Airlink's intention to take advantage of new business travel patterns. Indeed, a map of the firm's continental flights clearly shows that a handful of Canadian cities are reached and "connected" to strategically selected anchor cities of the huge web of its parent company's continental flights. The North-South regional coverage is strong, with Boston linked to the Eastern Canadian cities; Detroit connecting with central Canadian centres; and Minneapolis, Portland, and Seattle serving the Prairies and Pacific regions (fig. 9).

Figure 9

Northwest Air Link Flights
"Linking" United States and Canadian Cities

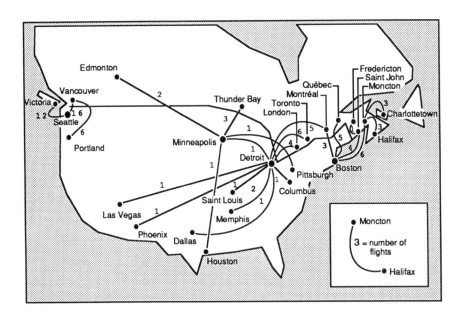

Air Atlantic (Canadian Airlines) and Air Nova (Air Canada) have reacted by intensifying their interaction with Boston, focusing on Halifax as their connection hub. For obvious reasons, Air Canada displays a "flight system" that is comparable to the observations made through the application of the gravitational model. While maintaining strong East-West interaction through Air Canada, many regional flights are scheduled by subsidiaries, which are tied to American destinations by a few "connectors," which act as interaction diffusers. Air BC connects western cities to Seattle and Portland; Ontario cities are linked to Cleveland, Hartford, Washington, and New York through Air Ontario; while

Air Alliance (Quebec) and Air Nova (mainly Atlantic Canada) rely on New York and Boston. Again, something that is evident in our preliminary conclusions and displayed in Air Nova's schedule is the regional role of Halifax as an interacting pole with the American Northeast.

Moreover, when looking more closely at Northwest Airlink's American air transportation hubs, a relation can be made with one of our preliminary conclusions above. A diffuse pattern of continental integration seems to decrease from East to West. By dividing the number of flights originating in Boston, Detroit, Minneapolis-Saint Paul, Portland, Oregon, and Seattle (notwithstanding the destination), by the number of destination cities, an index of destination specialization is obtained. A high value would mean a high destination specialization and a potential segmentation of markets, while a low value would illustrate a diffuse pattern. Boston displays an index value of 4.1, while Detroit and Minneapolis show 4.4, and Seattle and Portland have more restrictive scores of, respectively, 5.8 and 6.4. These findings seem compatible with the above results (fig. 10).

Figure 10

Important "Northwest Air Links" and Specialization Index of Destinations

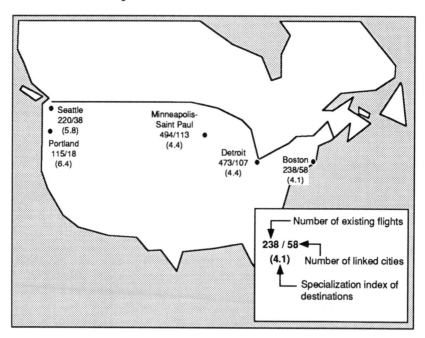

Railway transportation firms show a comparable evolution. Although it has played a vital role in the history and the development of Canada, the predominantly East-West railway network is being rationalized to be replaced gradually by a North-South one. The Amtrak network is a good example. More recently, there are a few cases where firms have bought strategically-located short railway lines. The advantage of such border-crossing short lines is twofold: they allow low operating costs, and it gives the opportunity to tap, and unite, two distinct markets. For instance, Guilford Transportation Industries, Inc. (GTI) is interested in acquiring the soon-to-be-abandoned Saint John-Sherbrooke line owned by CP Rail. (*Evening Times Globe*, 1993) According to the firm's president, this initiative aims to establish a "critical connection" to the United States, linking New Brunswick and New England markets, and opening Canadian and American markets. At first glance, it seems that Saint John, because of its proximity to the United States border, and the large capacity of its harbour, would benefit greatly from this new connection, attracting new activity to the port and enhancing its role as a point of entry to the North American market.

Conclusion: Interaction Patterns and Relation to the Three Shocks

This chapter has attempted to look at the patterns of air passenger interaction among Maritime cities, and compared them with those among Canadian cities, in a continental context. The main objective was to discover if the Canadian East-West field of interaction has been challenged by an emerging North-South one. A second objective was to explore the form this North-South field might take eventually, assuming it exists. Our main findings will now be related to the three shocks forming the object of this book, namely the coming of the information economy, the reduction in public spending in the region, and the globalization of the economy.

Our findings are relevant to the coming of the information economy. The interaction patterns looked at were mainly those of business travel, which involves the circulation of ideas and information. It appears clear that North-South interaction is becoming stronger, but that it is not yet replacing the still-dominant East-West pattern.

Generally, Canadian cities display patterns of diffuse North-South interaction, as opposed to constrained or channelled ones. Maritime cities show a similar pattern, and, in particular, show increasing selection of interaction with a handful of relatively-scattered but important American cities. Maritime cities tend to polarize their interaction with fewer - though strategic - cities like Boston, New York, Chicago and Los Angeles.

When comparing the interaction of Maritime cities with other Canadian cities, we find that the former tend to become marginalized, with the possible exception of Halifax, which still shows comparatively high interaction. This fact alone could be influential in an eventual reordering of Maritime cities' interaction - as, indeed, could be said of attraction of North-South interaction - through promotional agents like Northwest Airlink and GTI. To Maritime cities, Boston seems to balance the magnetism traditionally exerted by Montreal and Toronto.

These are facts indicated by air passenger data. Would other modes of interaction show the same pattern? For instance, Maritime regions are connected in a rather diffuse manner to American cities (e.g., Calais, Atlanta, Detroit, Chicago) through cable television service. What about electronic mail or telephone interaction, or television networks? Would it display a different pattern, or would it accentuate the actual one?

The reduction in public spending in the region is too recent a phenomenon to be reflected in the data. However, the recent advent of short-link companies could be seen as one anticipated reaction.

Finally, it is no surprise to notice a tendency towards continental integration in an era in which large economic blocs are formed through the increasing role of multinational firms and new trade arrangements such as NAFTA. As shown earlier, the interaction would operate in a rather diffuse manner, but two questions are of some concern. For Canada as a whole, the growing North-South interaction of the Pacific region is worrisome. Secondly, the apparent marginalization of Maritime cities is grounds for concern. Would the natural reaction be an intensification of southward interactions with Boston and New York? If so, how would Ottawa react to stronger Maritime trade links with the United States, and potential negative effects on Canadian transfer payments? It is possible that, in this way, a reduction in public spending could considerably weaken Canada economically and politically.

We are conscious that this analysis may not necessarily be shared by everyone. For instance, the New Brunswick Premier is said to spend much time in Toronto, trying tirelessly to attract new investors to New Brunswick. What is not said, however, is the origin of these targeted investors: are they Canadian or American? As ardent a federalist as a Maritime premier may be in trying specifically to attract Canadian firms, would this vision keep firms from looking South? A crucial question remains: How can the Maritime provinces maintain a viable economy in a continental context?

Finally, it could be argued that the use of air passengers data may bias the analysis. Indeed, it does among cities that are closely located, like Maritime cities in this study. However, the goals were set to measure interactions at a continental level, rather than a regional one. Nevertheless, observed interaction between Maritime cities is higher than that predicted by the gravity model. Obviously, the use of other types of interaction data (telecommunications, highway and rail transportation, electronic mail, etc.) could eventually complete the picture in further studies.

REFERENCES

Brunet, Roger, "Le déchiffrement du monde," in R. Brunet (dir.), *Géographie universelle*, tome 1, *Mondes nouveaux*, livre premier (Paris: Hachette/Reclus, 1990).

Claval, Paul, *La conquête de l'espace américain: Du mayflower à Disneyland* (Paris: Flammarion, 1989).

Coffey, W.J., M. Polèse, "Le déclin de l'empire montréalais: regard sur l'économie d'une métropole en mutation," *Recherches sociographiques*, 34(3) 417-437, 1993.

Evening Times Globe, (Saint John, N.B.), "U.S. Firm is Making Bid for Rail Line," 2 November, 1993.

Garreau, Joel, *The Nine Nations of America* (Boston: Houghton Mifflin, 1981).

Giddens, A., *Central Problems in Social Theory, Action, Structure and Contradiction in Social Analysis* (Berkeley and Los Angeles: University of California Press, 1979).

Globe and Mail, (Toronto), "The Feeling is Mutual," 23 November, 1993.

Goldenberg, S., *Histoire d'un empire: C.P.* (Montréal: Éditions de l'Homme, 1984).

Harris, R.C., "Regionalism and the Canadian Archipelago," in L.D. McCann, (dir.), *Heartland and Hinterland, A Geography of Canada*, 2d edition (Scarborough: Prentice Hall, 1987), pp. 533-559.

Innis, Harold, *Empire and Communications* (Toronto: University of Toronto Press, 1972).

Innis, Harold, *Essays in Canadian Economic History* (Toronto: University of Toronto Press, 1956).

Marshall, J., *The Structure of Urban Systems* (Toronto: University of Toronto Press, 1989).

McCann, L.D., *Heartland and Hinterland: A Geography of Canada*, 2d edition (Scarborough: Prentice-Hall, 1987).

Reclus, Élisée, *Nouvelle Géographie Universelle*, Tome XV, *Amérique boréale* (Paris: Hachette, 1890).

Times-Transcript, (Moncton, N.B.), "Moncton to Boston Air Link Launched," 20 May, 1992.

Times and Transcript, (Moncton, N.B.), "Northwest Airlink Increasing Flights, Staff," 20 April, 1993, p. 17.

Ullman, E.L., "The Role of Transportation and the Bases for Interaction," in W.L. Thomas, (dir.), *Man's Role in Changing the Face of the Earth* (Chicago: University of Chicago Press, 1956), pp. 862-880.

Vance, J.E., *The Merchant's World, The Geography of Wholesaling*, Englewood Cliffs (N.J.: Prentice-Hall, 1970).

Villeneuve, Paul, "Les métropoles canadiennes: ambivalences post-modernes," *Études canadiennes/Canadian Studies*, Revue interdisciplinaires des études canadiennes en France, 29, pp. 47-57, 1990.

Wilson, A.G., "Some New Forms of Spatial Interaction Models: A Review," *Transportation Research*, 9, pp. 167-179, 1975.

Wolfe, R.I., "Economic Development," in J. Warkentin (ed.), *Canada: A Geographical Interpretation* (Toronto: Methuen, 1968), pp. 187-228.

4

RESTRUCTURING WITHOUT TEARS
IN A FREE TRADE ENVIRONMENT

Benjamin Higgins

All over the world today former nation-states are breaking up, or threatening to break up, into regions. The splits are brought on by cultural, religious, linguistic, ethnic, social, political and economic conflicts. The countries involved are as diverse as Yugoslavia, Somalia, Cambodia and Canada. As Alvin Toffler puts it:

> As these (regional) disparities widen, they may well trigger an explosion of extremist movements demanding regional or local autonomy or actual secession. . . . In every nation some regions already regard themselves as economically cheated by the central authorities. (Toffler, 1990, p. 241)

The Maritime provinces, considered as a region, are not normally given to "extremist movements," but certainly Maritimers have felt "cheated by the central authorities" ever since Confederation. Will they feel cheated once again by the North American Free Trade Agreement? Product-mixes differ from region to region within the same country, especially a country as big as Canada. It is inevitable that free trade and the restructuring that free trade brings will have different effects among regions. If Quebec separates from the rest of Canada, or if it turns out that NAFTA has a harmful short-run impact on the Maritimes while benefitting other regions of Canada, it would not be inconceivable for a separatist movement to spring up in the Maritimes.

The long-run benefits of free trade are, of course, well known. Every region will specialize in the production of goods and services where it has a comparative advantage, leading to an optimal allocation of resources, apart from distortions resulting from the exercise of local monopoly and monopsony power. The desire for these benefits lies behind the world-wide movement towards free trade, as represented by GATT, the European Common Market, and NAFTA. Recent experience, however, in former socialist countries and industrialized capitalist countries alike, shows that "restructuring without tears" requires careful management of the degree to which and the sequence in which free trade is introduced in particular sectors and industries. All over the world we have seen floods of tears, heard screams of anguish, and watched governments tumble, because of restructuring imposed too precipitously and too indiscriminately. In some countries both inflation and unemployment have increased, and balance of payments crisis have arisen, through attempts to introduce free trade, and to restructure accordingly, almost literally overnight.

Let us imagine that the Maritimes constituted an independent country, and ask: "What would be the optimal process of restructuring for the Maritimes?" Then let us ask "What difference does it make that the Maritimes are part of Canada, and that Canada is a signatory to the Uruguay Round of GATT and to NAFTA?"

Towards the "Optimal Blend" of Market and Management

"Free trade" is part of a "free market." In reality, of course, no market is completely free. In any country there is some degree of government regulation, and some amount of planning at all levels of government. Countries like Canada, the United States, Western Europe, Japan and Australasia are described as "market economies," and sometimes as "free market economies," as opposed to the "centrally planned" or "command economies" of the former Soviet Union and similar socialist countries. The distinction, however, really refers to shades of grey rather than to a sharp contrast of black and white. It is important to remember that even a completely "free" market would not be the purely competitive market, which textbooks suppose will bring about an optimal allocation of resources. In the complete absence of government regulation and controls, planning, and public enterprises, what we would have is a collection of enterprises, organizations and individuals with varying degrees of monopoly power bringing about an almost haphazard allocation of resources. Such a market is bound to *mis*allocate resources to some degree.

However, a "free" market in this sense may yield "second best" results, and may in some circumstances bring rapid technological progress and economic growth. In the long run it brings better results than a command economy which "repeals the law of supply and demand" without putting a better calculus in its place. To achieve the best possible results, each country, on the basis of a thorough analysis of its circumstances, must choose its own "optimal blend" of leaving things to the market and managing of the economy. One thing is certain. No country in the world is going to have an efficient centrally planned economy in the near future, and no country is going to have a pure, totally free market economy either. To achieve efficiency, many if not most governments must make big governments less big, shrinking or scrapping bloated and inefficient government departments and privatizing badly managed public enterprises. But all countries are going to have some combination of market and management, a mix of decisions based on market signals and decisions based on considerations of equity and sympathy. Governments may not have wrongly intervened, but they may have intervened wrongly. In other words, government intervention as a principle may not have been proven a failure, but governments may have chosen ineffective policies, or implemented them inefficiently, or both.

Free trade may take place in a global market that is far from free. Even if the world economy is riddled with monopolies, it still pays each country in the long run to adjust to the conditions that exist now, or are expected to exist in the future. If a firm with a comfortable monopoly in the United States or Mexico can and will deliver its products to the Maritimes at prices well below those at which aggressively competing Maritime firms can afford to produce the same goods and services, and if this situation is not likely to change, an independent Maritimes should gradually phase out its own firms in those fields. However, the government of the independent Maritimes should phase out its enterprises only at the rate that it, or the private sector, can find alternative uses for the freed resources in endeavours in which the Maritimes has, or can develop, a competitive advantage.

The Spectre of Unemployment

The most serious danger associated with sudden shifts to free trade is that the short-run "restructuring" involved will take the form of increased unemployment. Unemployment is higher in the Maritimes than in any other region in Canada (except Newfoundland, which together with the Maritimes makes up Atlantic Canada). Any increase in unemployment would impose a heavy burden on the Maritimes economy. Free trade, like the free market, is often defended on grounds of "rational economics" and "efficiency." But there is nothing "rational" or "efficient" about unemployment. Unemployment of land, labour, or capital is the most inefficient use of resources that there is. A truly rational society would make the cost of employing another unit of any factor of production, for the entrepreneur, no higher than the social cost of *not* employing it to society as a whole. In the case of labour, for example, the social cost of unemployment may be calculated as the unemployment insurance benefits paid to the workers, plus the cost of retraining programs for the unemployed, plus [harder to quantify] the loss of skills entailed in long-run unemployment [and an associated opportunity cost]. A "rational" independent Maritimes government would accordingly offer to employers a wage subsidy equal to the sum of these avoided costs for each unemployed worker hired. The cash costs to the society would be unchanged, and the benefits to society would be the consequent increase in output, plus the improvement of morale, plus the acquisition or retention of skills, especially amongst young high school or college leavers, and amongst people over 50 where unemployment is highest. "Restructuring without tears" means restructuring without increased unemployment.[1]

"Rational" Restructuring Under NAFTA

An independent Maritimes could, if it wished, pursue a rational program of restructuring, planning removal of protection in terms of timing and sequence, keeping costs to entrepreneurs no higher than the social costs to the society as a whole, on the basis of a thorough analysis of the Maritimes and the various regions, sectors, and industries within it, in such a way as to achieve the long-run advantages of free trade with a minimum amount of short-run disturbance. In other words, it could select its own "optimal blend" of reliance in the market and management of the economy. But the Maritimes are not an independent country; they are part of a much larger and highly regionalized country, that is one of the three signatories of the North American Free Trade Agreement and also a signatory of GATT. How much difference does that fact make?

In the first place, a system of wage subsidies to keep the cost to the employer of taking on unemployed workers below the social cost of unemployment, and thus reducing the unemployment caused by free trade, would be totally impossible unless permission to utilize such schemes was written into the NAFTA and GATT agreements, and utilized by all three participants in NAFTA. As is well known, the American negotiators of the U.S.-Canada Free Trade Agreement made strong objections to the "subsidization" involved in Canada's regional development programs, and both before and after the agreement was signed, imposed countervailing duties on some products on that basis. (Higgins, 1990) Mexico may do the same.

The American economy is of course riddled with subsidies. However, most of them are administered by states or municipalities, and are designed to attract enterprises from other states or cities, enabling the federal government to maintain that the United States does not subsidize in a manner that distorts international trade. It is true that the state and municipal subsidies counterbalance each other to some extent, so far as location of industry is concerned, but they do give some enterprises an unfair advantage, and make it harder for Canadian enterprises to compete in American markets and easier for American enterprises to compete in Canadian markets. In addition, according to Alan Rugman and Andrew Anderson, the manner in which U.S. International Trade Commission (ITC) and the U.S. International Trade Administration (ITA) are administered is contrary to the General Agreement on Tariffs and Trade (GATT) Codes on Subsidies and Countervailing Duties and Anti-dumping Duties, to which the United States is signatory. (Rugman and Anderson, 1987; Higgins, 1990) There can be little doubt that NAFTA, the ITC, and ITA combined greatly inhibit the freedom of the Maritime provinces to pursue a truly rational system of restructuring. So long as all three are in effect, the Maritimes will have to go on accepting a "second best" policy for restructuring its economy.

Technological and Long-term Unemployment

Other forms of "adjustment" to the globalization of the economy, to the reductions in government expenditure, and to the "information revolution" (or, as some would have it, the "new industrial revolution") are the increase in long-term unemployment and in withdrawals from the labour force altogether. Both of these are marked trends in OECD countries in recent years. Some economists regard these two phenomena as inevitable, and treat the Non-Accelerating Inflation Rate of Unemployment (NAIRU) as "natural," and therefore somehow good. Others view the tendency for the NAIRU to increase in OECD countries with alarm, and seek ways of combatting it. In an article entitled "The Cursed Dole," the London *Economist* writes:

> Today's tolerance of unemployment would have astonished people in the 1960s. Despite having one worker in ten on the dole, many a government in Europe can now expect not only to survive, but to win re-election boasting of its economic prowess. Everywhere voters and politicians have grown used to unemployment that is indefensibly high. Yet there is no great mystery about why unemployment happens, or how to reduce it. The only mystery is why an avoidable misery has proved so politically tolerable. (*The Economist*, September 28th 1991, p. 16)

The NAIRU in many countries has become much too high, *The Economist* continues; it may be far above "full employment." The challenge to governments, therefore, is to bring the NAIRU down. This is mainly a matter of supply-side policies, not of Keynesian demand management. For one thing, unemployment benefits should stop after six months, as in Japan and the United States. "Open-ended entitlement to unemployment benefits is bad policy." At the same time, governments should help the unemployed to find work, as in Sweden, which has the best record on unemployment in Europe. Government should also provide high-quality training, and pay a wage subsidy to employers, again as in Sweden (and Australia); "and if all this fails, a guarantee of public employment." The net cost to the taxpayer, instead of paying unemployment benefits, "is small, at worst;" and the system improves morale and preserves skills. The system also includes scrapping all minimum wage laws, and curbing trade union power.

What is the "New Industrial Revolution?"

J. Blazejczak seeks to evaluate the "long-term effects of technological trends on the structure of employment." (Blazejczak, 1991, p. 594) He first asks, "what is the new technology?" He answers this question as follows:

> There is broad consensus on the following points:
>
> - The most important basic technology at present is commonly believed to be microelectronics;
>
> - Bio-technology will have an increasing impact, although it is expected to reach its full potential only after the year 2000, with advances in genetic engineering;
>
> - A key role for innovative solutions is attributed to new materials, the features of which can be designed with respect to specific applications;
>
> - Further technologies that are judged to be of basic importance are membrane and surface technology, lasers, new computers, software techniques and artificial intelligence.

He then adds an observation:

> - The economic importance of information will be further strengthened as new technologies allow better quality and more rapidly available information.

He then develops a three-dimensional technique for evaluation of new technology (sectors of the economy, fields of application of new technologies, and economic mechanisms) and applies it to changes in the sectoral structure of employment of Germany in the 1990s.

Richard Florida also tries to pin down the nature of the new technologies, but sums up the characteristics of all of them combined as "the new industrial revolution." (Florida, 1991, p. 559) He notes that there is still disagreement as to whether the next stage of capitalism will be characterized by "the rise of networks of small, flexible specialized firms" or "the return and continued dominance of big firms." (p. 560) However, he agrees that "what is new about the new industrial revolution is to be found in the rise of the new technologies of the microelectronics revolution (e.g. semiconductors, computers, software) and the new organizational forms that have emerged to harness them." (p. 560) In his view:

Moreover, at the core of the new industrial revolution lies a sweeping organizational transformation at the point of production. This reorganization I refer to as 'the new shop floor,' by which I mean the blurring of the distinctions between the factory floor and the R & D lab, as innovation becomes more continuous and the factory itself becomes a laboratory-like setting. . . . In doing so, the organizational forms of the new shop floor mobilize and harness the collective intelligence of the workers as a source of continuous improvement of products and processes, increased productivity and value creation. (pp. 560-1) . . . In the new industrial revolution, knowledge itself is increasingly important to production and to the further advance of technology and the productive forces. (p. 561)

He makes a distinction between old-fashioned Fordism, with its top-down management, and "Toyotism," with its emphasis on teamwork. He quotes Akio Morita, former chairman of Sony:

A company will get nowhere if all the thinking is left to management. Everybody in the company must contribute, and for the lower level employees their contribution must be more than just manual labour. We insist that all of our employees contribute their minds. (p. 567)

Florida maintains that the need to involve the knowledge and brains of the entire staff is well documented by what is currently happening in the field of manufacturing. "Although the microelectronic industry is still relatively young, it is the leading manufacturing employer in the U.S.A., with more than 2.6 million employees - three times as many workers as the automobile industry and nine times more than in steel fabrication." (p. 565)

In conclusion, Florida is full of praise for the new emphasis on teamwork:

The team is the mechanism through which workers are used to solve production problems and innovate. It becomes the source for adapting to production bottlenecks as workers use their own intelligence and knowledge to devise cooperative strategies to overcome such bottlenecks. The team is a simultaneous source of motivation, discipline and social control for team members, driving them to work harder and more collectively. (p. 570)

Does "New Industrial Revolution" = Technological Unemployment?

This description of the new technology, or the new industrial revolution, sounds like a beautiful new world, where workers, owners, and managers work together as members of a single, happy team, sharing in innovation and all contributing ideas, based on their intelligence and knowledge. It sounds like a prosperous, high-productivity world as well. There is just one drawback. To contribute their intelligence and knowledge, the workers must be intelligent and have some kind of advanced education or training. What happens to workers who have no such skills? The answer is simple: They join the swelling ranks of long-term unemployed, or drop out of the labour force altogether. It is true that some of the new technologies are so advanced that the machines do all the work on the basis of artificial intelligence, so that the machine-minders need not possess any advanced skills themselves. All the evidence suggests, however, that on balance, the new industrial revolution is leading to growing long-term unemployment or non-participation of unskilled or semi-skilled workers. Let us turn to a brief review of this evidence.

The United States

In a long paper prepared for the Brookings Institution, Chinhui Juhn, Kevin M. Murphy and Robert H. Topel ask "Why has the natural rate of unemployment increased over time?" (Juhn, Murphy and Topel, 1991) It is a study of "the evolution of male unemployment and nonparticipation in the U.S. labour force since 1967." (p. 75) They found that "both nonparticipation and unemployment contribute to a strong *secular increase* of nonworking time." (p. 77) Most of the secular increase in nonwork is accounted for by "an increase incidence of long jobless spells. Overall, nearly 80 percent of the long-term increase in nonwork is accounted for by spells lasting more than six months." (p. 77) "Based on observable indicators of skill like experience and education, it is well-known that unemployment is greater among less skilled individuals." (p. 79) Curiously, they found that rising unemployment has been associated with a long-term *decline* in sectoral mobility. One would think that rising unemployment would result in increased demand for retraining, and consequent increased sectoral mobility, a point to which we shall return below. Jobless men, especially those with long spells of nonwork, are much more likely to be single, and to rely on extended family for support. The number of jobless men has increased, and the wages they can command has fallen; but the real household income of jobless men has been more or less constant; since household incomes of working men has risen, the *relative* welfare of the jobless has declined.

The incidence of short spells of unemployment (less than 15 weeks) has remained nearly constant through time, but the higher incidence of long spells (more than six months) accounts for about two-thirds of the total increase in unemployment. The rising incidence of very long spells of unemployment also accounts for the rising rate of nonparticipation.

Nearly all of the long-term increase in the two jobless rates falls on less skilled individuals. For the least skilled workers, the jobless rate rose by nearly 16 percentage points between 1967-69 and 1987-89. The demand for labour has shifted towards more skilled workers. When unemployment rises, it rises more for unskilled workers. Inflexible wages are of little importance in the long run. Workers in the lowest decile of the wage distribution experienced a long-run rise in unemployment more than three times the average for the sample as a whole. Not only are nonworkers less skilled, but they are in categories in which wages have fallen over time. Employment and wages in different regions of the U.S. tend to rise or fall together.

In conclusion, the authors of this paper make the following points:

> We have shown that virtually all of the trend towards rising male joblessness in the United States is accounted for by the rising unemployment and nonparticipation of less skilled persons. For this group, increases in unemployed weeks are mainly attributable to an increase in the incidence of very long spells of nonwork. . . In many interpretations, the natural rate of unemployment is a fixed number towards which the labor market tends to gravitate. Our results challenge that view. . . . A long-run decline in the demand for various types of labor may increase the natural rate because the rewards to employment decline for marginal workers. Our results also imply that current unemployment rates have a far different meaning than comparable rates in the not-too-distant past.
>
> The composition of unemployment has shifted toward less skilled workers, who suffer comparatively long spells of joblessness and whose rewards from work have fallen sharply. In both respects, they resemble the growing class of men who have simply withdrawn from the labor market. . . . Our evidence shows that many workers with very low skills have either left the labor force completely or spent long periods without jobs. If joblessness itself generates declining market skills, either through depreciation of human capital or reduced on-the-job training, then the effects of reduced demand on work incentives will be reinforced. As a result, even an increase in demand for less skilled workers could not quickly reproduce the low jobless rates of the past. Past patterns of demand have altered the stock of human capital, rising future natural rates of unemployment and nonparticipation. (pp. 124-6)

The United Kingdom

Peter E. Hart, basing himself primarily on United Kingdom experience, maintains that there are several types of "structural" unemployment. (Hart, 1990) He begins his article with this warning:

> World markets are changing rapidly. If a small open economy such
> as the United Kingdom [or we might add, the Maritime provinces]
> does not adapt quickly enough to these changes, its firms will become
> uncompetitive and, if institutional rigidities prevent firms from
> adjusting, unemployment will persist. Such unemployment is said to
> be structural. It reflects a chronic disequilibrium in labour markets.
> (p. 213)

Structural unemployment is aggravated by segmentation, which makes sector-to-sector movement difficult, so that a general expansion of demand leads to increases in wages, prices, and imports rather than increased employment. Rigid policies to prevent inflation in some sectors only reduce output and employment in others. There are substantial differences in regional Philips (or trade-off) curves. Unemployment in some regions will reduce the rate of increase in earnings there without diminishing the inflationary tendencies in other regions. Thus "wage adjustment and labour mobility cannot be relied upon to correct regional imbalances in employment opportunities." (p. 215)

As early as 1930, John Maynard Keynes recognized the existence of technological unemployment, but thought it would be temporary. The micro-electronics revolution, however, by reducing the demand for unskilled and semi-skilled labour, has made technological unemployment chronic. There is a mismatch of skills and available jobs, which could be removed by adequate training and retraining programs, but "our training programs are *not* adequate and indeed have not been for a long time, and the result is that the necessary adjustments do not take place and the disequilibrium in the labour market persists." (p. 217) There is also a geographic mismatch. The variation in unemployment by regions increased from 0.8 to 2.9 percent in 1960 and 5.2 to 11.2 percent in 1988.

Three demographic shifts contribute to structural unemployment; increased female labour force participation; a growing proportion of young people; and an increasing number of elderly people. Women search less intensively for jobs; youths have higher turnover and take longer to find new jobs; elderly people have difficulty in acquiring new skills.

Employers may respond to a need for extra labour by hiring part-time workers who do not qualify for employers' pension contributions or holiday payments. Many of the long-term unemployed are "unemployable" as a result of chronic illness or disability, for which compensation is more generous than it was some decades ago. Such structural factors in current unemployment are important, "because they obstruct both neo-classical and Keynesian attempts to decrease aggregate unemployment." (pp. 226-7)

The Australian Unemployment Picture

In December 1993, the Commonwealth Government of Australia published a report of the Committee on Employment Opportunities, entitled *Restoring Full Employment: A Discussion Paper*. It contains an opening chapter providing a general survey of Labour Market Trends. The picture given by this chapter is similar to the unemployment picture in Canada, the United Kingdom, and the United States - and indeed, the picture in all OECD countries. During the 1980s Australia enjoyed the most rapid job growth of all OECD countries; but in the 1990s even strong output and employment growth failed to bring unemployment back to the levels achieved prior to the 1982-83 recession. Since 1983 Australian unemployment has been above the OECD average in every year but 1989, when it was about equal to the average. As in other countries, particularly disturbing was the growth of long-term unemployment:

> Since 1990, the number of long-term unemployed people (those unemployed for one year or more) have risen to unprecedented levels. By August 1993 over 35 percent (nearly 340,000) of those unemployed had been unemployed for two or more years. (p. 18)

The highest unemployment rate was in the 15 to 19 age group, and the numbers of unemployed were greatest in the 20 to 24 group. This latter group also had the highest rate of long-term unemployment. As in other countries, the rate of unemployment varied significantly with educational attainment. Only 6.2 percent of those with university degrees were unemployed, while 14.8 percent of those who failed to reach the highest level of secondary school were unemployed. Long-term unemployment also tended to diminish with the level of education attained. Over the past 20 years the dominant factor in growth of the labour force has been increased participation of women, particularly married women. This trend has been accompanied by a large increase in the number of casual and part-time jobs. This experience is shared by all OECD countries. In this connection, the report observes:

> This shift, however, does not appear to be directly associated with high unemployment for men. Countries with the highest participation rates for women have been those with the lowest rates of unemployment for men. (p. 39)

The Australian government recognizes that recovery from recession and accelerated economic growth may encourage enterprises to install new technologies, displacing lower-skilled workers. It may also encourage some drop-outs to return to the labour force. Thus the decline in unemployment may not match the increase in employment. One solution is to make sure that all members of the labour force have knowledge and skills that make them employable with the new technologies:

> The Commonwealth, State and Territory governments have sought to reform Australia's training system with an important objective being to improve our international competitiveness. Government initiatives include: more emphasis on making training relevant to the needs of industry; a greater focus on the outcomes of training - what an individual can do, rather than how long he or she has spent in the system; . . . (and) improved access to training for disadvantaged groups. (p. 76)

Demand for Retraining

An obvious solution for unemployment among the unskilled and semi-skilled is retraining. An econometric study of the demand for retraining in the United Kingdom, however, contains little good news. (H.L. Allen, B. McCormick, and R.J. O'Brian, 1991) Their findings were as follows:

> We have found that the demand for retraining amongst unemployed workers in a depressed region of the United Kingdom follows a pattern which is consistent with our framework. The probability of application: declines with age after 27 years; is greater where expected unemployment is greatest, namely, those leaving industries in long-term decline (engineering and shipbuilding) and least in industries in which unemployment is an equilibrium feature of the cyclical pattern of jobs in the industry (construction) in which turnover is high (services); is greater amongst those who are most distressed in unemployment in comparison with their last job; is less amongst union members; is greatest for workers with formal qualifications (O/A levels) and least amongst those with vocational training (City and Guilds/CSE/Apprenticeship). Thus it would appear that mid-career flexibility may be enhanced by formal qualifications and inhibited by earlier vocational training. (p. 201)

In other words, it appears that retraining is unlikely to be sought by two categories of workers for whom the incidence of unemployment is particularly high; young school leavers with neither formal qualifications nor experience, and older workers without much by way of formal education or higher-level skills.

What Can the Maritimes Do?

The world is going through a period of unprecedentedly rapid change. Any region that wants to keep up with the world must change rapidly, too. The

Maritimes is not a poor region by world standards. Only about ten of the world's richest countries have per capita incomes as high as those in the Maritimes. But the people of the Maritimes do not, on the whole, like rapid change. It is in this resistance to change that the danger lies.

If the Maritime provinces are to "restructure without tears," reducing rather than increasing unemployment in the process, they too will need to reform their education and training systems. Too much of the expertise of the Maritimes labour force is specific to natural-resource-based industries that are in decline, like coal mining, steel production, fishing and forestry and forest products. Such expertise is not transferable to the high-tech enterprises that are the core of "the new industrial revolution." Unfortunately, the unemployment that results from opening up a market to international competition is almost instantaneous, while building an education and training system suitable to "the new industrial revolution" takes time. Meanwhile, there is much to be done in the public sector of the Maritimes, particularly in offsetting damage to the environment, improvements to roads, railroads, ports, and airports, as well as development of schools, hospitals, parks and playgrounds. Such projects can provide employment while the transformation of the labour force is taking place, and will make the private sector more productive, and more attractive to investors, when completed.

Empty the Maritimes?

Some economists of extreme neoclassical persuasion would solve the problems of the Maritimes essentially by emptying them, encouraging emigration from the Maritimes to more dynamic regions within Canada, or elsewhere. Such a policy would constitute "restructuring" of a sort; but not of a sort that would appeal to the government of an independent Maritimes; and in recent years Atlantic Canada as a whole has actually experienced net immigration, although at the cost of high levels of unemployment. We are accordingly confronted once again with the vexing question: "Is it better to move people to jobs or jobs to people?" (Cf. Thomas Courchene and James Melvin, 1988)

People To Jobs or Jobs to People?

Neoclassical economists who criticize regional development programs on the grounds that they hamper the functioning of the market, and that accordingly a free market with flexible prices would have done a better job of reducing regional disparities, base their arguments on the following assumptions:

1. In a free market, with no artificial supports to wages and other prices, in regions where incomes and productivity are relatively low and unemployment relatively high, wages will fall.

2. In consequence, labour will migrate to more dynamic regions to obtain jobs at higher wage rates.

3. In addition, capital will be attracted to the disadvantaged regions by the lower wage rates, and the increased investment there will reduce employment, raise marginal value product, and ultimately raise incomes in the retarded regions.

Two quite separate kinds of question arise with regard to this sort of argument: Does it ever happen; and is it a good thing if it does? Let us deal with these questions in reverse order.

In the first place, let us be clear that there can be no concept of "efficiency" of performance of national and regional economies apart from its impact on human welfare. In any society, or any large group of people within it, there are many who attach great importance to staying where they are and doing what they are doing. Consequently, policies designed to permit them to do so cannot be dismissed out of hand as "impairing efficiency." There may indeed be a trade-off between what the government of Manitoba once called "the stay option," and other elements of social welfare. If so, this trade-off has to be appraised, before policy can be "efficiently" formulated. In many developing countries, in the province of Quebec, and in the Atlantic provinces, in Appalachia, in the Great Lakes region, there are a good many people who have a heartfelt desire not to move. It is nonsense to make people suffer needlessly, merely to satisfy some economists' special definition of "efficiency."

There is a difference between "mobility," in the sense of *willingness* to move, and actual movement. One of the studies of Canada's Royal Commission on Bilingualism and Biculturalism showed that the population of Quebec, especially the women, were extremely reluctant to move, even within Quebec. But the census data on migration showed that the proportion of the Quebec population moving to another place of residence was just as high as in the rest of the country. The juxtaposition of the two sets of data suggests that the pressure on people in Quebec to move was severe, and that there was a high social cost involved in actual movement.

There are other social costs involved in migration. The most obvious is that emigrants leave behind them housing, transport facilities, schools, hospitals, shopping centres, banks, factories, etc. which must also be provided for them at the other end of the line. In addition, we know that in all societies there are certain thresholds of population size at which certain types of economic activity appear or disappear. Studies made in various countries show that a movement of population out of lagging areas, if it is sufficient to exceed natural population growth and lead to an absolute decline in population, can become cumulative, leading not only to depopulation in terms of numbers, but to a decline in the average quality of the population in terms of education, training, and skills, and occupational structure. Anyone who has seen such areas - in east Texas, in western Virginia, in northern Minnesota, in Quebec's Cantons de l'Est, in the north and northeast of Brazil, or in west-central Australia - knows how grim they can be. We should not recommend solving the problems of depressed areas by emptying them, as an alternative to regional development, without knowing the costs; and *saving* these costs is one of the benefits of regional development.

A study undertaken for Public Works Canada showed that stability of regional economies is *positively* correlated with the rate of growth. The explanation for this relationship is provided in terms of interactions of cycles and trends, using a Hicks-style model of the trade cycle. This finding is crucial in deciding between a "move jobs to people" policy and a "move people to jobs" policy. Another consideration, of course, is that if unemployment is currently high everywhere in the country, moving from one region to another is no guarantee of finding a job. All of these factors must be taken into account, and measured as well as possible, in evaluating regional development programs which may have as one of their results holding people in the regions where they now are.

Let us now ask the other question: Does a free market with flexible prices guarantee elimination of regional gaps by factor movements? Obviously not. Labour does indeed move to jobs and higher incomes when the incentive is powerful enough. But rare indeed are the cases where the movement is sufficient to offset natural population growth and bring absolute declines in the population of large regions. In the United States, with its extraordinarily mobile population, there have been some decades in which the population of the two or three poorest States among the fifty fell; but in those decades those States remained poor, and the more recent increase of prosperity in them has been accompanied by immigration and population growth once more.

As for capital flowing to low-wage regions, there is little clear evidence that low wages by themselves are sufficient to attract enough capital to transform poor countries or regions into rich ones. The universal experience is that for repetitive jobs with a given technology, productivity of labour in developing countries like Indonesia, Thailand, and Malaysia, is as high as in the United States, while wages are a small fraction of the American level. In recent years there has been some flow of capital to take advantage of this situation, but it is a small proportion of total American investment in manufacturing. Many factors weigh more heavily than labour costs in investment decisions. As for technology being adapted to differences in cost and availability of labour, here a veritable hornet's nest of problems arises. There is a vast literature on choice of technology and "appropriate technology," but no clear conclusions emerge from it, except that most sophisticated enterprises adapt technology to scale of production, but not to relative costs of capital and labour. (Higgins, 1982, 1993)

What all this means is that in evaluating regional development programs in the past, and in making recommendations for the future, we cannot simply *assume* that in the absence of such programs free market forces would have brought about "adjustment," in the sense of eliminating unemployment, inflation, poverty, and inequalities.

Conclusion

"Restructuring" the Maritime's economy - without tears - by emptying it is neither an attractive nor a feasible solution. That being so, the solution must be sought in the improvement of the quality of its labour force, adapting it to "the new industrial revolution" and making sure that all of it is employable. Such a solution means not only *more* education and training, but *more of the right kind* of education and training. The people of the Maritimes have been justly proud of their educational system. By and large, the necessary framework for educational reform is already there. What is needed now, more than ever before, is the integration of the planning of education with manpower planning. This cannot be achieved by government alone. It requires a cooperative effort of academic institutions, employers' organizations, trade union leaders, and gov-ernments at all three levels.

Fitting the labour force for the kind of jobs available in "the new industrial revolution" is of course not the only, nor even the most important, objective of the education system in post-industrial societies; and the acquisition of the requisite skills is not only a matter of formal education. As David R. Howell and Edward N. Wolf put it:

> . . . most jobs require a multitude of different skills for adequate task performance, ranging from physical abilities, like eye-hand coordination, dexterity and strength, cognitive skills (analytic and synthetic reasoning, and numerical and verbal abilities) and interpersonal (supervisory, leadership) skills. Since widely varying levels of different kinds of school-based training are necessary to perform adequately the tasks that define each occupation, a single years-of-schooling measure would almost certainly provide a poor index of the relative skills, of, say, medical doctors, machinists, and stockbrokers. (Howell and Wolf, 1992, p. 128)

They proceed to an econometric study of skill formation and its change over time. Their results "raise doubts about the adequacy of years of schooling as a measure of workplace skills and TFP (total factor productivity) growth as an index of technical change." (Ibid.) There is, they say, "a growing consensus that computer-based technologies require lower levels of traditional shopfloor skills and higher levels of abstract and synthetic reasoning abilities." (p. 130) They find that a rise in the Capital Labour ratio, in itself, does *not* require more cognitive or motor skills, but does require more interpersonal or interactive skills, mainly because it leads to more management - labour confrontation. (p. 137) The growth in cognitive skills since 1970 is associated with technical and organizational change, production in large plants, and low or negative growth in capital intensity, industry employment and import penetration. (p. 141) It is also strongly complementary with the use of new technology. (p. 143) "Computer intensity, young capital stock, and high shares of engineers and computer specialists are all related positively for CS (cognitive skills) growth, with very strong effects for the latter two variables. . . . These findings have the rather obvious, but nonetheless important and often ignored, implications that effective policy initiatives must be grounded in research that adequately captures the diversity of skills in the real-world market place. . . . There needs to be more econometric research that recognizes explicitly the diversity of skills required in the modern workplace." (p. 144)

We might add, "and a great deal of other kinds of research as well:" to identify precisely what skills will be required in the Maritime provinces over the next two decades; to determine exactly the relationship of education and training of various sorts to the formation of those skills; and to assure that the educational system of the Maritimes fulfils its broader functions of instilling in its citizens culture, civilization, humanity, and discipline. This is an enormous task, and one that requires the cooperation of people in many fields of arts and science and many walks of life. If we want to make sure that the Maritimes "restructures" itself to the new global economy and society with as few tears as possible, we had better start on this task right now.

REFERENCES

Allen, H.L., B. McCormick and R.J. O'Brien, "Unemployment and the Demand for Retraining: An Econometric Analysis," *The Economic Journal* 102, March 1991, pp. 190-201.

Blazejczak, J., "Evaluation of Long-Term Effects of Technological Trends on the Structure of Employment," *Futures*, 23 July-August 1991, pp. 596-604.

Commonwealth of Australia, Committee on Employment Opportunities, *Restoring Full Employment: A Discussion Paper*, Canberra A.C.T., December 1993.

Courchene, Thomas J. and James B. Melvin, "A Neo-classical Approach to Regional Economics," in Benjamin Higgins and Donald J. Savoie, (eds.), *Regional Economic Development: Essays in Honour of François Perroux*, (Boston: Unwin Hyman, 1988), pp. 169-92.

Florida, Richard, "The New Industrial Revolution," *Futures*, 23 July-August 1991, pp. 559-76.

Hart, Peter E. "Types of Structural Unemployment in the United Kingdom," *International Labour Review*, vol. 129, no. 2, 1990, pp. 213-28.

Higgins, Benjamin, "Appropriate Technology: Does It Exist?" *Regional Development Dialogue*, vol. 3, no. 1, Spring 1982, pp. 158-202.

----------"Subsidies, Regional Development and the Canada-U.S. Free Trade Agreement," *Canadian Journal of Regional Science*, vol. XIII, no. 2/3, Summer/Autumn 1990, pp. 259-72.

----------"Technology for Development in the South Pacific," in Tony Marjoram, (ed.), *Minding the Machines: Technology for Development in the South Pacific*, (Melbourne and London: Australian Scholarly Publications and Intermediate Technology Publications, 1993).

Howell, David R. and Edward N. Wolf, "Technical change and the demand for skills by US industries," *Cambridge Journal of Economics*, 1992, no. 16, p. 127-46.

Juhn, Chinhui, Kevin M. Murphy and Robert H. Topel, "Why has the Natural Rate of Unemployment Increased Over Time?" (Washington, D.C.: *Brookings Papers on Economic Activity*, no. 2, 1991).

Rugman, Alan and Andrew Anderson, "A Fishy Business: The Abuse of American Trade Law in the Atlantic Groundfish Case of 1985-86," *Canadian Public Policy*, vol. 13, no. 2, 1987, pp. 152-64.

Savoie, Donald J. and Benjamin Higgins, "Towards a New Paradigm: Two Views?," in Donald J. Savoie and Irving Brecher (eds.), *Equity and Efficiency in Economic Development*, Montreal, McGill-Queen's University Press, 1992, pp. 394-420.

The Economist, "The Cursed Dole," no. 320, 28 September, 1991, p. 16-17.

Toffler, Alvin, *Powershift: Knowledge, Wealth, and Violence at the Edge of the 21st Century*, (New York: Bantam, 1990).

NOTE TO CHAPTER FOUR

1. Australia has such a scheme, administered by the Department of Employment, Education and Training, called Jobstart. Subsidies vary according to the duration of unemployment of the jobless and run up to $230 per week. The new workers are selected by the employers. Sweden also has such a scheme.

5

PUBLIC SECTOR ADJUSTMENTS AND THE MARITIME PROVINCES

Donald J. Savoie
Maurice Beaudin

The Maritime provinces have repeatedly been told in recent years that the federal government will be cutting back spending. Indeed, a central purpose of this collection of essays is to review the implications that globalization and reductions in government spending hold for the region. It is important to note that the two go hand in hand. To be sure, the serious fiscal situation confronting the federal government - where over 30 percent of tax revenues go to service the debt - puts enormous pressure on Ottawa to reduce spending. Still, globalization and regional trade agreements (i.e., the Canada/United States Free Trade Agreement and the North American Free Trade Agreement) impose a new discipline on government operations, on government's ability to introduce new measures, and even to continue existing programs. The new discipline will be strongly felt on the policy instruments long favoured by the federal government - fiscal, monetary, trade and redistributive policies.[1]

Globalization is also redefining the relationship various Canadian regions have with one another. The National Policy that was always at the core of every government's economic program for over a century is now history. The need to create strong East-West trade links, which inevitably favoured southern Ontario, is now much less important. As Ontario, Alberta and British Columbia - the "have" provinces - adjust to global economic forces, they may well question programs designed to maintain Canada's East-West links, whether these have taken the form of transfer payments to individuals, transfers to provincial governments, or of federal regional development programs. Ontario may well give priority to putting in place measures to undercut Michigan's cost structure, rather than to securing East-West links. As Canada's regions become inserted into the global economy differently, their links with the outside world will "become more important relative to their economic linkages within Canada."[2] In this sense, Canada becomes less able to act as the giant "mutual insurance company"[3] that former Premier Allan Blakeney once called it. We should never lose sight of the fact that the political impact of an equalization dollar that flows from Toronto to Ottawa to Fredericton and then back to Toronto is different from one that goes from Toronto to Ottawa to Fredericton and then to purchase goods produced outside of the country, let alone outside southern Ontario.

Added to the above is the ever-more-widely-held view that the public sector has grown too big and too inefficient. Even a long-time advocate of a greater role for government in society like John K. Galbraith now argues that: "It's more than the Liberal task to defend the system. It is also the task that the system be better administered. It is far more important now to improve the operation than enlarge and increase its scope. This must be the direction of our major effort."[4]

Public choice literature, which applies economic thinking and theory to government operations became the new fashion in the 1980s. This literature, which is highly critical of the public sector, had an impact far beyond the halls of academe. Margaret Thatcher made it required reading for senior government officials during her stay at 10 Downing Street.[5] The result is that there is a move throughout the Western world to have "government by markets," or, failing that, to remodel government according to market and business concepts.[6]

Canada has not escaped this trend. Brian Mulroney tried and to some extent succeeded in privatizing a number of crown corporations and in contracting out government activities. The new Chrétien government appears to be walking down the same road. The newly-appointed minister responsible for Public Service Renewal declared in his first major speech that: "Over time, governments collectively have promised more than they could deliver and delivered more than they can afford." He added: "Too many citizens have fallen into the habit of turning to government to solve problems that should be addressed in other ways."[7]

The new government's thinking is clear - the federal government went too far in establishing the welfare state and the role of government must be reeled back in. There is a view widely held in government circles that a number of public policies over the past forty years or so have disrupted the ties between effort and reward and have created economic disincentives to work, thrift and entrepreneurship.

Given all this, it is evident the federal government will be busy over the next ten years redefining its role in society and restoring the balance of its accounts. Again, there is a widely-held view in government circles that potential revenue has already been pretty well tapped. Federal tax revenues have increased to 18 percent of Gross Domestic Product (GDP) in 1991 from 15 percent in 1981. When all governments are included, the proportion of tax revenues to GDP has gone from 31 percent in 1981 to 39 percent today - a figure well above both the OECD average and the record of Canada's major competitors - the United States and Japan.[8]

The hostility that greeted the introduction of the Goods and Services Tax (GST) illustrated a growing problem for advanced welfare states - a tax revolt feeding a growing underground economy. Constant increases in existing taxes and the introduction of new ones have made it very expensive to be honest. Society's stock of honesty has fallen as a result.

Ottawa's new direction - reducing the role of the federal government in society and repairing its balance sheet without imposing new taxes - poses important challenges for the three Maritime provinces. How can the region make the transition from its dependence on the public sector, notably on the federal government? This begs the question: How dependent is the economy of the Maritime provinces on the federal government?

Federal Government Spending in the Region

Direct spending on goods and services by all levels of government amounted to over $9 billion in the three Maritime provinces in 1991, equivalent to more than one-quarter of GDP. Federal spending was 36 percent of this total, and provincial spending a further one-third. The remainder was split between local governments and hospitals.

There is no denying that the key player in generating a high level of public spending is the federal government. The following points tell the story well:[9]

- Provincial governments in the three Maritime provinces depend heavily on federal transfers. About 40 percent of provincial revenues in New Brunswick and Nova Scotia are in the form of federal transfers. The figure is higher still for Prince Edward Island (44 percent). This compares with 30 percent for Quebec, 15 percent for Ontario, 25 percent for Saskatchewan and 11 percent for British Columbia.

- The percentage of total personal income derived from federal government transfers is substantially higher in the region than elsewhere. The national average is about 15 percent. However, in the case of Prince Edward Island, about 23 percent of total personal income is derived from transfer payments or one-and-a-half times as high as the national average. The proportion stands at about 20 percent in both Nova Scotia and New Brunswick. The comparable figures are 16 percent in Quebec, 11 percent in Ontario, and 13 percent in Alberta.

- Federal transfers have enabled the three Maritime provinces to close the gap on a number of fronts. The per capita fiscal capacity of the ten provinces - or at least the ability of provincial governments to spend - now falls within a narrow range, a much narrower range than existed as recently as in 1960 (about 15 percent either side of the national average).

- Increased provincial expenditures have yielded better public services. Between 1962 and 1988, the three Maritime provinces moved considerably closer to the national average in health and education spending.[10]

Federal government spending in the region takes various forms. Besides transfer payments to the provinces and to individuals, the federal government buys goods and services, operates offices and military installations, and provides for a variety of programs in most sectors.

It is possible to secure a regional breakdown of federal spending under the above headings by consulting the Public Accounts and Statistics Canada. The regional breakdown of federal government spending under the various headings points to a consistent pattern for the Maritime provinces: on a per capita basis, the region leads other regions on all fronts. A calculation of spending less inflows (i.e., revenues generated by the regions) reveals that Prince Edward Island received (1990-91) $2,745 per person more in federal spending than the Island generated in revenues for the federal Treasury. The comparable figure for New Brunswick was $1,828, and $998 for Nova Scotia. The figures for some non-Maritime provinces include $1,828 for Saskatchewan, $984 for Manitoba and $405 for Quebec. Ontario, Alberta and British Columbia, meanwhile, contributed more to the federal Treasury than their provincial governments and their citizens received from it.

Defence activities account for an important part of Ottawa's expenditure budget, and Nova Scotia and New Brunswick have both received an important share. Table 1 shows that even in absolute terms (rather than on a per capita basis) Nova Scotia and New Brunswick rank fourth and fifth in the share of defence spending. In terms of employment, the naval base in Halifax is the second largest Canadian military base anywhere.

When Defence expenditures are presented on a per capita basis, one sees that Nova Scotia and New Brunswick are strongly favoured over other provinces (see table 2).

Federal transfers to individuals as a percentage of per capita income are also substantially higher in the three Maritime provinces than in any other regions excluding, of course, Newfoundland and Labrador. Maritimers benefit more, for example, from the Unemployment Insurance program than do other Canadians. Indeed, many more from the region draw from the program every year than do other Canadians - by the late 1980s, for example, about eight percent of the population of the Maritime provinces received unemployment insurance payments, compared to only 3.8 percent of Albertans and 2.5 percent of Ontarians. The Unemployment Insurance program accounted for 46 percent of transfers to individuals in 1990-91. The cost of the program amounts to over $17 billion annually, with Maritimers and Atlantic Canadians securing by far the most benefits from it per capita. Newfoundland and Labrador benefitted to the tune of $1,410 per person, Prince Edward Island $1,193 and New Brunswick $905. This compares with $444 for Ontario, $391 for Alberta and $303 for Saskatchewan. It is also important to bear in mind that because of the region's demographic composition, more Maritimers consistently qualify for old age security supplements and family allowances than other Canadians.

Table 1

Defence Expenditures by Province
Millions of Dollars, 1989-90

Province	Expenditures	Percentage
Ontario	$4,108.2	36.2
Quebec	1,607.0	14.2
British Columbia	1,862.2	12.0
Nova Scotia	893.2	7.9
New Brunswick	845.5*	7.5
Alberta	621.7	5.5
Manitoba	470.5	4.1
Newfoundland	108.1	0.9
Saskatchewan	87.9	0.8
Prince Edward Island	47.4	0.4
Canada	10,152.7	89.5
Foreign	1,198.9	10.6
TOTAL	11,351.6	100.1

* Includes $576.6 million from the frigate program. Without the frigate program, however, New Brunswick would drop from fifth to seventh position.

Source: Officials with the Department of National Defence.

Table 2

Department of National Defence
Per Capita Expenditures by Province
1988/89

	*	**
Newfoundland	183	182
Prince Edward Island	395	392
Nova Scotia	1,087	1,012
New Brunswick	4,299	374
Quebec	170	124
Ontario	373	250
Manitoba	432	282
Saskatchewan	90	90
Alberta	257	227
British Columbia	230	205
Northwest Territories	26	25
Yukon	56	36
CANADA	413	

* Includes 1987/88 contracts
** Excludes contracts

Source: Department of National Defence.

This dependence on the federal government in one form or another explains the large trade deficit with the rest of Canada.[11] Atlantic Canada as a whole now has a trade deficit of nearly $6 billion with other regions of Canada.

Though the details of the situation may surprise some observers, the above in general terms is well known to many students of Canadian politics and economics. (See, for example, table 3 for a detailed breakdown of federal transfers to all Canadian provinces and territories for 1992-93, and figure 1 for a breakdown of provincial revenues by source.) It is also well known that the federal government has already begun to introduce cuts in transfer payments to the provinces and to individuals. In the case of New Brunswick, for example, Ottawa contributed 45.1 percent of provincial spending in health care in 1986-87. By 1990-91, the final figure is likely to come in at 37.1 percent. The comparable figures for Nova Scotia are 44.5 percent in 1986-87 and 40.5 percent in 1990-91. In addition, in recent years the Unemployment Insurance program has been tightened, regional development programs have been cut back, and a "clawback" provision has been instituted in federal transfers to individuals, notably in old age security and family allowance payments.

Public Sector Employment in the Maritime Provinces

What is probably less well known, but no less important, is the degree to which the Maritime region relies on the public sector for both employment and earned income. During fiscal year 1990-91 the three Maritime provinces alone had 152,269 public sector employees. Put differently, with 6.5 percent of the Canadian population, the region had nearly 10 percent of total public sector jobs and 11 percent of federal government jobs. Put differently again, the public sector accounted for 21 percent of the total labour force in 1990 and generated 26.6 percent of earned income in the region. One can easily appreciate the importance of the public sector to the region's economy when one compares those figures to the national average, where the public sector accounts for only 12.2 percent of total employment and generates only 14.3 percent of earned income.[12]

Federal government employment in the region accounts for 38.7 percent of all public sector employment, compared with 34.7 percent at the national level. Broken down by province, Nova Scotia relies the most on federal government employment, with 48.2 percent; followed by Prince Edward Island, at 39.6 percent; and New Brunswick, at 28.6 percent, some six percentage points below the national level. Indeed, the New Brunswick rate is much lower than Ontario's (37 percent), Manitoba is 39 percent and those of British Columbia and Quebec (32 percent).[13]

Public sector employment generated $4,9 billion in salaries in 1990-91 in the Maritime region. Federal government departments, agencies and crown corporations accounted for 46.2 percent of the total, though they accounted for

Table 3

The National Finances 1992

Estimated Federal Payments to the Provinces, Territories, and Municipalities 1992-93*

Cash Transfers (millions of $)

	Nfld.	PEI	NS	NB	Que.	Ont.	Man.	Sask.	Alta.	BC	NWT	Yukon	TOTAL
General Purpose Transfers													
Equalization	953.0	202.0	1,001.0	928.0	3,935.0	-	997.0	565.0	-	-	-	-	8,561.0
Statutory subsidies	9.8	0.8	2.4	1.9	4.8	6.2	2.3	2.3	3.9	2.6	-	-	37.0
Reciprocal taxation	-	-	-	-	0.3	-	-	-	-	-	-	-	0.3
Public utilities income tax transfer	10.0	3.0	-	-	26.0	76.0	5.0	0.2	148.9	10.0	0.2	0.7	280.0
Youth allowance recovery	-	-	-	-	-426.0	-	-	-	-	-	-	-	-426.0
Territorial financial agreements	-	-	-	-	-	-	-	-	-	-	822.2	223.3	1,045.5
Grants in lieu of property taxes	4.5	1.6	15.5	13.2	85.6	171.9	16.2	9.5	19.0	34.2	4.2	1.7	377.3
Total general purpose cash transfers	977.3	207.4	1,018.9	943.1	3,625.9	254.1	1,000.5	577.0	171.8	46.5	826.6	225.7	9,875.1
Established programs financing													
Insured health services	157.6	35.6	247.9	199.7	1,067.0	2,339.4	301.7	272.1	703.0	870.1	13.2	7.5	6,215.0
Post-secondary education	53.1	12.0	83.4	67.2	245.8	726.7	101.6	91.6	236.3	288.3	4.2	2.5	1,912.6
Total established programs financing	210.7	47.6	331.4	266.8	1,312.8	3,066.1	403.3	363.7	939.3	1,158.4	17.3	10.1	8,127.6

Table 3...

	Nfld.	PEI	NS	NB	Que.	Ont.	Man.	Sask.	Alta.	BC	NWT	Yukon	TOTAL
Cash Transfers (millions of $)													
Specific purpose transfers													
Canada assistance plan	135.0	32.2	230.0	214.0	1,615.0	2,242.3	260.0	183.0	599.9	799.7	22.0	7.8	6,341.9
Other health and welfare	6.6	0.4	9.7	5.6	17.3	83.7	6.5	10.1	24.2	30.3	54.7	6.4	255.5
Gross revenue insurance program	-	1.6	0.6	0.7	48.0	64.6	90.6	302.1	135.8	3.1	-	-	647.1
Bilingualism in education	4.0	2.0	6.7	23.5	86.9	71.6	9.8	16.2	11.0	11.4	0.9	0.8	246.6
Services to young offenders	4.8	1.9	5.9	4.6	29.5	62.1	5.7	7.1	14.8	17.1	3.6	1.1	158.2
Justice	1.7	0.2	3.3	1.7	16.7	42.6	4.2	2.6	7.7	10.2	2.1	0.6	93.6
Transportation	54.9	2.7	13.9	6.7	27.5	7.6	3.7	1.3	1.9	22.7	1.7	1.3	145.9
Other	11.4	3.5	7.3	4.7	214.0	12.3	14.8	9.9	8.6	6.1	14.6	9.3	316.5
Total specific purpose cash transfers	218.4	44.5	277.4	263.3	2,054.9	2,597.8	395.3	532.3	803.9	900.6	99.6	27.3	8,205.3
Total Cash Tranfers	1,406.4	299.5	1,627.7	1,473.2	6,993.6	5,908.0	1,799.1	1,473.0	1,915.0	2,105.8	943.5	263.1	26,208.0

*Excludes tax transfers

Source: The National Finances, 1992.

Figure 1

Provincial Revenues by Source

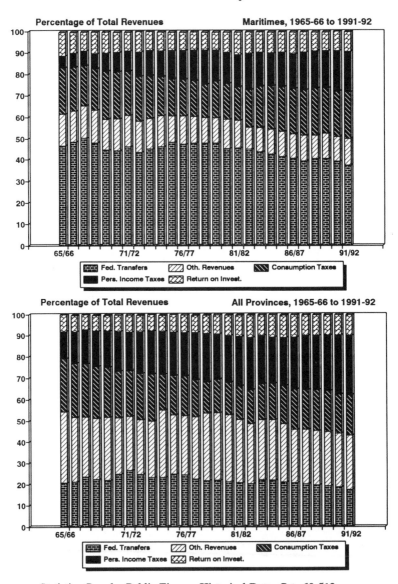

Source: Statistics Canada, Public Finance Historical Data, Cat. 68-512.

Figure 2

Public Sector Employment

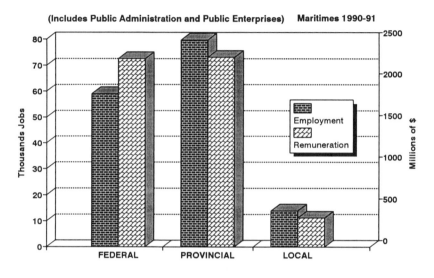

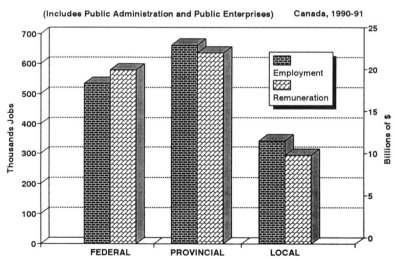

Source: Statistics Canada.

only 38.7 percent of total public sector employment. Federal employment in the region pays a great deal more than other public sector employment. The average federal job pays $38,417 a year, compared to $28,744 for provincial government jobs and $25,079 at the municipal level. Still, public sector salaries in the region exceed by a wide margin the region's total average salary, which stood at $23,283 in 1991 (see fig. 2).[14]

It is also important to note that the average salary in the Maritime region stood at only 83 percent of the national average in 1991. However, for the public sector as a whole the average annual salary stood at 92.2 percent of the national average, and in the case of federal government employment it stood at 99 percent.[15]

Another way to look at the importance of public sector employment in the Maritime provinces is to review its importance to GDP. Statistics Canada now publishes annually provincial GDP figures by industry or category.[16] It is possible to group together several categories - federal, provincial and municipal governments, including education and health care - to gain an appreciation of the importance of the public sector to provincial GDP. Table 4 below shows that public sector employment constitutes a far larger share of provincial GDP (25.5 percent in the Maritimes) than it does at the national level (16.1 percent).

Table 4

Public Sector and Provincial GDP in 1990

	Public Administration and Defence	Health and Education*	Public Sector
Prince Edward Island	14.4	15.1	29.5
Nova Scotia	14.0	13.1	27.1
New Brunswick	10.6	12.0	22.6
Maritimes	12.7	12.8	25.5
Canada	3.7	9.5	16.1

* For 1987

Source: Statistics Canada, Catalogue 15-203.

It is also important to stress that federal government employment in the Maritimes is largely concentrated in urban centres. Indeed, nearly 75 percent of all federal public service jobs are found in five urban centres. Table 5 shows that Halifax alone has nearly 10,000 federal public service jobs.

Table 5

Federal Public Servants and Urban Centres

Urban Centre	Number of Public Servants
Halifax	9,898
Charlottetown	1,679
Fredericton	785
Moncton	2,651
Saint John	926
TOTAL	15,939

Source: Statistics Canada, Treasury Board Secretariat, and Public Service Commission Annual Report, 1992.

Given the importance of federal public sector employment in terms of job numbers, salaries and impact on the region's urban economies, it is important to present breakdown of jobs by department, particularly in that some federal departments are more vulnerable to spending cuts than others. For example, it is unlikely that Ottawa would or could launch extensive job cuts in correctional services or national revenue. Prisons need to operate and parole board officials are needed to ensure a smooth functioning of the penal system. Similarly, tax auditors are required to manage the country's income tax system, a responsibility that belongs to the federal government. We also know that every federal tax auditor generates additional tax collection several times his or her salary.

It is also clear, however, that other federal departments are particularly vulnerable to spending restraints. Events taking place throughout the world in the last ten years have led the government of Canada to rethink its military strategy, to look at closing down some military bases, and to realign others. We also know that the total cost of operating military bases is high - \$4.5 billion in 1992-93. Officials with the Department of National Defence suggest that the first military installations to be eliminated are single-function bases located far from large urban centres (i.e., away from Toronto, Ottawa, Winnipeg). This raised specific concern for the Maritime provinces (notably Nova Scotia) which have had a number of single function military installations. Other departments that could be vulnerable to a new round of spending cuts include Transport Canada (because of a reliance on privatization, and increasing reliance on trucking, which falls under provincial jurisdiction) and the Department of Fisheries and Oceans (the collapse of the groundfish sector will put pressure on the department to reduce the number of its employees).

A review of the size of federal government departments reveals that the region has a large number of jobs in "vulnerable" departments. The four largest departments in terms of employment in the region are Defence, Transport Canada, Human Resources and Development and Fisheries and Oceans (see table 6).

Looking at Recent Trends

Public sector employment as a whole grew by 5,085 jobs between 1986-87 and 1990-91. It is important to note, however, that government restraints began to take hold when the recession started to bite in 1990. It is also important to note that some 5,852 federal public service jobs were lost - 9 percent of the public sector job total - during the same period. The rate of federal job losses in the Maritime region equals the role of federal job losses at the national level (9.5 percent). Still, the total wage loss to the region amounted to \$225 million in current dollars for the fiscal year 1990-91. A large portion of these job losses came in federal crown corporations (for example, the CN shops closure in Moncton).

During the period from 1986 to 1991, provincial government employment grew by 8,367 jobs (up 11.8 percent) and municipal sector employment by 2,568 jobs (up 22.7 percent). The region led the nation in terms of job growth at the provincial and municipal level. For the nation as a whole, provincial government employment grew by only 1.4 percent, and municipal employment by 12.8 percent. The result is that in the three Maritime provinces the provincial and local levels generated 61 percent of total public sector employment in 1991, compared with 56 percent in 1986; and they accounted for 54 percent of total public service income in 1991, compared with 50 percent in 1986.[17]

Equally important is the geographic location of federal government jobs, in contrast with provincial and municipal jobs. As we saw earlier, federal public

Table 6

Federal Government Employment by Department and Agency
1991

	P.E.I.	N.S.	N.B.	Maritimes	Total %
National Defence (public servants)	46	5,575	1,125	6,746	30.4
Transport	214	1,423	972	2,609	11.7
Human Resources and Development	186	821	1,285	2,292	10.3
Fisheries and Oceans	50	1,167	481	1,698	7.6
Correctional Service	3	349	686	1,038	4.7
Veterans Affairs	797	163	58	1,018	4.6
Environment	61	703	165	929	4.2
Agriculture	192	227	358	777	3.5
Supply and Services	12	290	451	753	3.4
National Revenue (customs and excise)	17	377	346	740	3.3
Public Works	33	479	184	696	3.1
National Revenue (taxation)	59	351	261	671	3.0
Health and Welfare	26	225	98	349	1.6
Royal Canadian Mounted Police (public servants)	25	146	103	274	1.2
ACOA	24	64	164	252	1.1
Forestry	5	17	144	166	0.7
Energy, Mines and Resources	1	142	2	145	0.7
Multiculturalism and Citizenship	0	129	0	129	0.6
Indian and Northern Affairs	0	119	5	124	0.6
Other Services	117	385	309	811	3.7
TOTAL	1,868	13,152	7,197	22,217	100.0

Source: Statistics Canada, Treasury Board Secretariat, and Public Service Commission Annual Report, 1992.

service work is concentrated in the five largest urban centres in the region. These jobs strengthen the region's urban structure in that they are well paid, stable and professional. By definition, provincial and in particular municipal employment is less concentrated, and spread out in various provincial capitals, regional centres, and municipalities. The negative implications of present trends continuing are clear for the region's larger urban centres.

In addition, municipal government are a "creature" of provincial governments and, as we saw earlier, the three Maritime provincial governments are highly dependent on federal government financial resources. Future growth in provincial and municipal jobs is unlikely, given the pervasive role federal dollars have played in the past. Federal austerity will deter such growth, if not dictate shrinkage, in the future.

Looking Ahead

Several sectors in the Maritime economy face major adjustment issues. Restructuring in the fishery, new developments in rail transportation and in the pulp and paper industry are just some of the important challenges ahead. The Atlantic Canada Opportunities Agency (ACOA) estimates that 30,600 jobs will be lost in the three Maritime provinces over the next few years. Hardest hit will be Nova Scotia, with an estimated 22,700 jobs in several key sectors expected to be lost. The number for New Brunswick is 6,700; for Prince Edward Island, 1,200.[18]

The region will not be able to rely, as it has for thirty years, on the federal government and federal crown corporations to create new jobs or to pump up the local economy through transfer payments, whether to the provinces or to individuals. Indeed, for reasons discussed earlier in this chapter, it is reasonable to expect that we will soon add the federal government to sectors such as the fishery and the pulp and paper industry that already are going through significant downward adjustments.

The region, at least before the era of generous federal transfers, was built on a culture of self-sufficiency, independence and innovation. We know that dependency on transfer payments diminishes individual self-respect, inhibits social and economic development and relieves from individuals and communities the primary responsibility for their economic well-being. The region needs to return to its "roots," its "old ways." We need to encourage attitudinal change and self-employment. The region needs to focus its efforts on what it does well, to make up for expected job losses. We need to concentrate our energy, skills and whatever financial resources are available to develop and promote the region's agri-food products, consumer products, fish and seafood, forest products, medical and health care products, and tourism. The region's five largest urban centres will have to play a key role in preparing the region to compete in a highly competitive global economy. Recent and future federal government job losses mean that the region and its communities - geographic, professional and entrepreneurial - will have to be creative, mutually supportive, and confident, to ensure that they can deliver on what will no doubt be high expectations.

NOTES TO CHAPTER FIVE

1. See, for example, Thomas J. Courchene, "Global Competitiveness and the Canadian Federation," paper prepared for the University of Toronto Conference on Global Competition and Canadian Federalism, 15 September 1990, mimeo.

2. See Donald J. Savoie and Ralph Winter, (eds.), *The Maritime Provinces: Looking to the Future*, (Moncton: Canadian Institute for Research on Regional Development, 1993), chapters 1 and 12.

3. Richard Simeon, "Thinking About Constitutional Future: A Framework," paper prepared for the C.D. Howe Institute, December 1990, mimeo, p. 12.

4. Quoted in *Dimension Magazine*, (Moncton, N.B.), Winter 1986, p. 13.

5. See, for example, Donald J. Savoie, *Thatcher, Reagan, Mulroney: In Search of a New Bureaucracy*, (Pittsburgh: University of Pittsburgh Press, 1994).

6. See Peter Self, *Government by the Market*, (Colorado: Westview Press, 1993).

7. Notes for an address by Honourable Marcel Massé, minister responsible for Public Service Renewal to the National Conference on Government Relations, 1 December 1993, mimeo, p. 2.

8. See, for example, Donald J. Savoie, "Les déficits et la dette: le point de vue de l'administration publique," in L. Denis Desautels, (ed.), *Les déficits et la dette,* (Ottawa: Bureau du vérificateur général du Canada, 1993).

9. See Donald J. Savoie, *ACOA and the Upcoming Adjustment Decade*, presentation to the Management Committee of the Atlantic Canada Opportunities Agency, December 1993, mimeo.

10. See Donald J. Savoie, *Regional Economic Development: Canada's Search for Solutions*, (Toronto: University of Toronto Press, 1992), chapter 8.

11. Savoie and Winter (eds.) *The Maritime Provinces*, chapter 9, p. 226.

12. See Statistics Canada, *Public Sector Employment and Remuneration 1990-91*, Catalogue 72-209, October 1991.

13. Ibid.

14. Ibid.

15. Ibid.

16. Ibid.

17. Ibid.

18. Consultations with senior officials with the Atlantic Canada Opportunities Agency, December 1993.

6

HIGH-TECH IN SMALL TOWNS

Dorothy Downing

Small towns now have exceptional new possibilities in light of the new economy's communication facilities, high-tech opportunities, the trend towards diverse and *decentralized* economies, and the replacement of centralized mass production with the "flex firm" able to turn out highly varied, customized products in short runs and small batches. The increasing number and variety of organizational units, new wealth creation systems both *local* and global, combine with powerful technologies to make it possible to do *locally* what previously could be done economically only on a national scale.

The fact that these changes are spawning many smaller organizational units, and that today's technologies offer rapid means of communication, opens up opportunity for entrepreneurs who dislike pollution, and the pressure of city life, to move into beautiful rural settings and also take advantage of less-expensive overhead. Surveys reflect that new patterns of population movement are already emerging. For decades, there has been a pattern of rural dwellers moving to the cities of the Maritimes; recently the tide has turned, and there has been a slight increase of people moving *into* small towns over those moving *out* of the small towns.

This chapter presents interviews with ten entrepreneurs who *have* moved into small town settings. The questions asked why the entrepreneurs had made the move, their views on the adequacy of small town facilities and technical support for business, the adequacy of small town amenities, and what they would still like to have in business and technical terms, as well as in everyday living and quality of life. Unbidden by questions from the interviewer, the entrepreneurs also offered ideas for job creation, on the role of government in helping entrepreneurs, and on teamwork in the workplace.

One of the basic factors supporting the belief in the prospects for growth in high-tech business in small towns is that the Maritimes have so much to offer in terms of magnificent scenery, recreational, and cultural opportunities valued by potential entrepreneurs. Great store is set on the attractions of the Maritime traditions and the values they embody, and the warmth of the traditional architecture with its touch of magic. Since so much of this legacy is in the small towns, some brief descriptions are included in this study.

New Brunswick

Dark, dramatic and moody, the stupendous Bay of Fundy penetrates to end in gentle shoals in New Brunswick; at the head of one of its branches is the town of Sackville, situated at the edge of the Tantramar Marshes.

Sackville

The town is a gracious, and long-established one, close to the borders of Nova Scotia - an area famous for its enormous flocks of passing water fowl and sea birds. There is an air of excellence about the town. Dominating Sackville physically and culturally is Mount Allison, a first rate liberal arts university. Its campus includes some fine collegiate architecture; it hosts symphony orchestras, touring theatre groups and, as well, its music and drama departments present musical evenings and plays.

On a quiet, tree-lined residential street two blocks from the centre of town is Hawk Communications, occupying several attractive traditional houses. The company specializes in marketing communications, including advertising, publishing, public relations, graphic design, and it provides strategic, creative and marketing direction for client communication programmes.

David Hawkins, founder of the company, originally left Montreal to go to Mount Allison. "I had been working in Montreal for seven years," said Hawkins, "and I was stressed out. So the thought was that I would go back to university. I really had to start over, I had no interest in Montreal any longer, or in any city in fact. I was among the people who were leaving traditional urban environments in the seventies in favour of the more conservative environment of the small towns and rural communities."

However, Hawkins was shocked as he became aware of the extent to which the Maritimes were being artificially sustained by the federal government support system. He became convinced that things *could* be achieved in the Maritimes independently. "When my wife and I started the company, it was really a personal political statement," said Hawkins. "We handled no government business whatsoever for the first few years. We took no grants of any sort. We really set out to prove, I guess, as much to ourselves as anyone else, that this could be done. We started the company in 1978 with no capital, absolutely zero. The bank would not finance us for quite a period of time. We had two Visa cards and a Mastercard. We financed the company with those: we ran them right up, until they were taken away from us, because that was the only way to get capital to carry on. But by the time they took the cards away from us, we had enough cash flow and enough receivables to take care of ourselves.

"A powerful reason why we started the business was that it was a means of creating jobs for ourselves (more suitable than the ones we had) and creating jobs for other people was 'top of mind,' also," Hawkins said. "I feel strongly that unemployment relates very closely to the whole issue of economic development. We think *we* are in the economic development business, because we are mainly a marketing communications company, as opposed to a more narrowly focused advertising agency. Market communications *includes* advertising, but it goes far beyond that. When we provide strategic marketing direction or other services, we help our clients achieve more than they would without us, to become stronger and bigger, and thereby create more stable employment for more people. One could say that all business contributes to economic development, and we are in the marketing communications slice of the economic development pie.

"The Hawk thematic is 'The Power of Teamwork'," said Hawkins. "I believe individuals and individual effort are extremely important. However, we must work together with a sense of *community* and *partnership*. We must serve our clients, each other, and work in concert with our clients and suppliers, associates and their families, in the context of [an] over-all community." In fact, Hawkins has done a great deal to help his community.

When asked if the technological resources in Sackville were adequate, Hawkins said: "Our company, without question, has the most advanced computer and graphic technology available within our industry. We are not impeded by our location. Sure, some of the resource people we need to operate may be in Montreal, Toronto or New York. But that has not proven to be a whole lot of a problem for us. We are close to an excellent airport, and are just an hour and a bit from Montreal by plane, two hours from Boston, two hours and a bit from New York. If anything, we feel advantaged by our place on the map. We have cultural resources here; Mount Allison offers us theatre and music; we are just a thirty-five-minute drive from Moncton, and two hours or so from Halifax. We often go to Halifax, Fredericton or Saint John to see a movie, go out to supper and then come home.

"I guess if Sackville were not a university community, it is unlikely that I would have come here initially, or that I would have stayed here. At the same time, while some of our dear close friends are indeed university people, they are no closer and no dearer than our friends in the rest of the community. I know this is a community that protects me and [one] that I protect. We have a certain kind of closeness here because there are only five or six thousand people, a certain kind of safety, a certain kind of sociability and civility. Overall, I think these are major plusses."

The East Coast of New Brunswick

On the East Coast of New Brunswick near Lamèque, is the beautiful wooden church of Sainte-Cécile, famous for its perfect acoustics; an international baroque festival is held there every year. The interior of the church is entirely painted with pastel designs. In fact, Maritimers often like to paint their churches and houses with evocative combinations of colours. The East Coast is an important area of the fishing industry. On the Acadian Peninsula, the Acadian fishermen have been using high-tech for years. From the larger ports, such as Lamèque, Caraquet and Shippagan, $2 million fishing boats set off to fish in the Gulf of St. Lawrence, with their radar and sonar systems in duplicate - if an electronic piece of equipment were to fail it would be too costly in time lost from fishing to return to port for a replacement. Further south are the towns of Cap-Pelé and Shediac. Shediac is the self-styled "lobster capital of the world." Cap-Pelé is a hub of the shellfish packing industry.

Cap-Pelé

Cap-Pelé is a breezy seaside town with low red cliffs and sandy beaches. The houses along the shore often stand isolated on windswept lawns interspersed by the *boucanières*, painted in carnival colours. These are the old Acadian smokehouses in which fish is still smoked by a centuries-old process. In fact, Cap-Pelé is one of the hubs of the fishing industry; apart from the *boucanières*, are the packers, including Cape Bald Packers, and Beauséjour Seafoods, owned by Joseph Landry. He also owns Downeast Plastics, a company which, among other things, makes boxes for packing fish and rigid insulation.

Joseph Landry left Cap-Pelé in 1937 when he was fifteen years old to work in construction in Halifax, and in Goose Bay, Labrador and Newfoundland. He came home ten years later when he had word from his brother and his partner "Uncle Pat" that their fish plant in Cap-Pelé had burned down.

His brother told him that Uncle Pat wanted to see him. "I knew what they wanted. They offered me a partnership to rebuild," said Landry. "I said to myself, they want me to do the work and they want my money. Sure enough they did. After working at 0.45, 0.60, 0.75 cents and a dollar an hour, I had saved up $8,000, so I had enough money to pay my share, and I was ready to work.

"We started building the first week of Lent. Then you had Fat Tuesday, Ash Wednesday, out of the working week, and then not much work was done in Holy Week. But on Easter Monday, the factory was ready, and we packed 250 cases of sardines.

"In 1958, I bought the rest of the shares of Cape Bald Packers; my brother had bought a plant in Georgetown, P.E.I.; Uncle Pat had said he wanted to retire (he was 75). That same day that I bought his shares, he rented an old factory, he took my supply of lobster, my work force, and I was left with a building but no organization. I had been doing all the work, they had been running the business. So I was left with no contacts, no supplies and no crew.

"It was not very fair, but I was stubborn. It only took me ten years to build the company back. In 1990, the company of Cormier LeBlanc went bankrupt. Cormier LeBlanc was the company that Uncle Pat (he was not my uncle) had formed when he sold his shares to me: I bought Cormier LeBlanc to have access to the ocean salt water.

"Downeast Plastics came about because a guy who was making buoys for the fishermen out of polystyrene went bankrupt. We bought some of the equipment and formed Downeast Plastics which had a hard time too. We reorganized the company by having meetings once, and sometimes, twice a week. We appointed a young man as acting sales manager and two of my sons, Victor, as production manager, and Denis, who assisted him."

Could it be described as high-tech? "That depends. Once you know something, it's easy. My sons had been brought up amongst machinery all their lives. They have never worked at other places; they were not interested in college. They all went for industrial courses. I think they have gained as much knowledge as in a city - probably different knowledge. Our technology is as good as at any other plant, and we have a quality control program that is second to none. They are doing better and better all the time.

"Facilities? We are very much self-contained. In our plastic plant, we have a machine shop. All the equipment is built by our own people; I designed it. I have an electrician's license and a stationary engineer's license, and I did a lot of studying, I bought trade books, and I have taken courses all my life.

"In 1990, I had a bad year. I was in a consortium selling herring to the Russians; they backed out of the deal and I lost $600,000. Then, I lost two container-loads of canned crab because the enamel lining in the cans was defective. I lost three-quarters of a million dollars. We sued the makers of the cans; the case is still open. Then a firm in Boston which owed me money for lobster went bankrupt, and I lost another $200,000; that case is still open. Finally I had provided equipment for some fishermen to fish lobster, but the catch of lobster went down, the fishermen were not able to pay me back and we lost $250,000, which just about cleaned us out of our capital.

"Yes, it was a let-down, but it was nothing important. I saw my banker, and said: 'You know, at my age I have to make it back.' We arranged everything, and then all we had to do was make money. That was when we bought Cormier LeBlanc. All in all, I still had my health, my reputation, my contacts, my customers in England, France, the U.S., Japan and Canada. Those are things you can't burn, you can't lose."

Shediac

Shediac is a light-hearted seaside town with many facets. It is a fishing port; it is also a summer resort with handsome homes along the bay and the river. Because it is so attractive, Shediac is also a dormitory town; many people live in Shediac and commute twenty minutes to work in Moncton.

There are some lovely traditional white frame houses, such as the elegant Georgian-style Shediac Hotel, and the beautiful Victorian mansion that is home of the gourmet restaurant *Chez Françoise*. The Maritimes seem to have escaped the more florid Victorian modes, maybe because they built so much in wood, and perhaps because there is a lot of good taste in the Maritimes; they incline towards fantasy rather than pretention. In nearby Moncton, for instance, there are many Victorian houses, some of them featuring turrets, they do not look pretentious, but rather gracious. One is often reminded of a friendly castle in a storybook.

Armand Belliveau has established his company, Glenwood Kitchen, in Shediac. When he came up from Massachusetts in 1973 he was in fact coming home. "I was born in Kent County, New Brunswick, and when I was a teenager, my family moved to Massachusetts. I moved back here in 1973 with my brother, to sell kitchen cabinets in the Maritimes for an American company. We were distributing when we first started, and changed to production when the exchange rate changed from Canadian money being worth more than American money (between 1975-1978) to the reverse. We now sell to distributors around the Maritimes.

"Six years ago we started a new shop in Massachusetts. It is managed by one of my brothers. So right now, we cut the wood here and send all the pieces to Massachusetts for assembly. But in future, we will assemble more here. We are finding it too expensive to produce in Massachusetts. Too many rules.

"Since we started, we have made five extensions to our building. We now have computerized machines." Could he operate as well in Shediac as in a big city? "We have better workers here, not necessarily better technicians, but more reliable than in Ontario or the United States. The bigger the city, the more independent they are. We feel we have good workers, more loyal. Absenteeism is not a problem. Maybe if I want something fast, it might take a day or two longer than if I were in Toronto. But I don't feel that it is a major problem.

"Prices are a lot lower here. A house would be a third of the price here, compared to what it would cost in Toronto or Boston. But it was a purely business decision to come. I don't care where I am. Wherever I am, it is home. It is the best place until I move."

Prince Edward Island

Driving off the ferry and onto Prince Edward Island, one takes the highway to Charlottetown through Anne of Green Gables' storybook countryside, with its clearly drawn contours, pure colours, and its towns with colourfully painted churches and houses.

Charlottetown

Donald Deacon's house is on a quiet street only a few blocks from the centre of Charlottetown, yet it was possible to park right in front of his salt-box house, complete with window boxes full of brilliant flowers, and a yacht at anchorage at the end of the street.

Donald Deacon has a venture capital business. He decided to establish here for three reasons. "First of all, I guess, it's because this is where my mother's family started in the 1700s, so there are a lot of relatives in the Maritimes and I always liked that. Secondly, one of our sons came down twenty years ago. And thirdly, I spent five years in the armed forces with a bunch of Cape Bretoners, and I was really impressed by their resourcefulness, and their loyalty to each other.

"I recognized that they were a very real resource for successful production; they were incredible. We were always the first on action, with the least problems. Because of these Cape Bretoners, I always thought that Atlantic Canada did not need to be the end of the world as far as productivity was concerned. I thought the big thing would be to come down here to help things work, to enable them to become productive.

"I planned to retire in 1980 from the family firm in Toronto (S.H. Deacon, and Hodgson Inc.) and set up a venture capital business. We were backed by some of the large institutions, and we had several million dollars to invest in the area, but a lot of things went wrong. "The 200-mile fishing bonanza, which seemed to be a great one did not turn out that way," said Deacon. "The Hibernia is an offshore oil project that looked like a good bet has given costly evidence that megaprojects are not the solution to Atlantic Canada's future. Where we have had some success has been in small ventures where we have provided value added employment, and production for niches in the market place, and in going far beyond the Atlantic markets to sell.

"To my mind, the latter solution is essential for us to emphasize in Atlantic Canada. We are not going to find solutions suddenly by a huge infrastructure. It is by our skills at developing markets elsewhere. We are on the sea with access to boat transportation; there are many opportunities, and high-tech helps you to communicate with anyone. I can talk to London, Calgary and Washington quite easily, so I can sit here in Charlottetown and have a high quality of life, and I don't have to spend two hours a day commuting to work.

"The advantages go far beyond commuting time. The cost of living in this part of the country is, I would say, at least 30 percent lower than a similar quality of life in Central Canada. The other night we went to the theatre in Victoria, to see as good a play as I have seen anywhere, with a cast of four. It cost $8 a ticket. Live theatre is important, and these are the things we can have on the Island, and that we can do well. We have our own symphony here, which has improved tremendously with the help of our director Brian Ellard, who comes over from the Department of Music at Mount Allison University. All these things, to my mind, provide for a quality of life which is very attractive.

"I think we have special opportunities for simple things. We had a play called Strike at Putney Green Church. It was written by a local lady, and it was a marvellous show. But when they tried to turn it into a fancy musical for the Confederation Centre, it did not do well. This reflects the problems in our business efforts. We make the mistake of trying to emulate New York and Toronto. We focus our attention on what other parts of the country have done to be successful, yet we can do our own thing very well."

The Industrial Park

Regis Duffy's multi-million dollar firm, Diagnostic Chemicals, is housed in the West Royalty Industrial Park on the outskirts of Charlottetown.

"I'm a local product," said Dr. Duffy. "I was born in Kinkora, P.E.I., I live in Charlottetown now and enjoy it. As chemistry professor at the University of P.E.I., I used to run a summer school for students in research projects, and the problem was funding. We ran an ad looking for funding in the pesticide field; the ad drew a blank, but someone in New Jersey contacted us about a chemical we could manufacture. So we started manufacturing, using the university labs. We then became aware that there was a whole field in which chemicals were involved in the analysis of blood, and that the field was rather large.

"We moved off the campus and formed a company in 1972. We worked in a garage in downtown Charlottetown, then we moved out here to the industrial park, which gave us a very good deal. They built the building for us, financed it and leased it back to us at very attractive rates. So that was a great start. If you can keep your capital light at the beginning of your business career that is very desirable. It worked for us.

"For what I do, we have what we need here. There used to be a time when local services were important in terms of machine shops and such. It's not nearly so important today; the equipment is so specialized that it is impossible, even if you are in Montreal, to service much of it on a local basis. Very often, fixing something means replacing a motor.

"*Research* is important; we spend half a million on research every year, and *marketing* is also very important. Eighty percent of our work is exported to Mexico, Taiwan, Europe, Hong Kong and the United States. The U.S. market is the largest and most sophisticated in the world. People in most small European markets would love to be living in P.E.I. because it is so close to Boston. Marketing is where it starts and stops and marketing is difficult for small companies." Could the government play a role? "Government people are not marketing people, but a government can maybe finance some of a small company's marketing efforts; ACOA pays for some of the people *we* put in place to go out to Europe to look around.

"In any case, all this new information flow offers us wonderful new opportunities we can find for ourselves." Dr. Duffy picked up a piece of paper from his desk. "This piece of paper came from a small company in Holland. It is a literature search on new patents that have been published. They simply give you a hundred new ideas of how to make something. Now the Holland service is in the scientific field but there are probably all kinds of other opportunities that could be accessed today by searching through the literature. A company like this could be set up in Charlottetown, and it could be selling services like this all over the world.

"So we must look for all these new opportunities that are all around us. And the government - I think that all they can do is provide a positive business environment as they did for me. Yup, what they did for me was just perfect."

Nova Scotia

In Nova Scotia, one begins to see the bewitched houses. When the British Empire Loyalists brought their New England architecture up to the Maritimes, it changed a little. Some dormer windows of the Cape Cod cottages slid down from where they had been situated in the centre of the roofline to the edge of the roof. In doing so, they elongated themselves so that they became long narrow triangles the shape of a witch's hat creating a distinctly magical look. The same effect occurs when Maritimers paint their Victorian houses with unusual combinations of vivid colours. Springhill's taste in colour runs to the more conservative; they usually paint their occasional Victorian whimsies with a mixture of pastel colours.

Springhill

Springhill is built on a high hill. At its crest, tranquil houses are set among old, spreading trees and have marvellous views over the Nova Scotia woods and hills. Towards the bottom of the hill, David Surrette has his company: Surrette Batteries, Ltd. His father came up first from the United States. Later Surrette joined him, and eventually decided to accept Springhill as his home.

"I like small town living," explained Surrette. "I think the quality of life is better for my family. As for facilities, the electronic age has come - faxes and modems make things much simpler, and high-tech sure comes into play.

"Today anyone in manufacturing who is going to survive basically has to undergo a complete change into the new technologies. Today we are producing more with less. We are not working harder but smarter. And to accomplish that, some other changes had to take place. We got involved in profit-sharing; all employees are involved, and get a copy of our statement once a month. There's nothing secret; we ask them not to spread it around the community, but they have access to all the financial data. We're into Total Quality Management: everyone participates in problem solving, decision making, and so on."

So then, is it more like a team? "Absolutely. I'm the technical person, but I make very few decisions. I am called in at meetings, I contribute some expertise, but as a participant. I'm not there as one who says we will or will not do it. Major things do come up when I do make the decision, but most of them are made by management or people on the floor.

"Now if I were with an industrial commission to develop industry in a small town or community, I would go with people who have a lot of commitment to the community - they're not going to take off and go south of the border because things are cheaper down there. Five years ago, 15 plants were producing acid batteries in this area. Now it's down to four, because many of these plants were multinationals and it was more economical to go south of the border. In small towns you don't have the turnover of people when you get into problems like Canada is facing today, we all have a big stake in what we are doing, and we stay.

"Moreover, in small towns operating costs are lower, and we get a lot of help from the community. If we need something all of a sudden - we need an air compressor and there is nothing here that will help - there's no problem. Call the foundry, and they'll send one down. But then, by the same token, we cooperate with them. We are all very protective of what we have here."

Cape Breton Island

Cape Breton Island is one of the most beautiful areas in Nova Scotia. Between its highlands run the great Bras d'Or Lakes - huge glittering arms of sea water, moderating the temperature of the land surrounding them. The University College of Cape Breton is one of the most important institutions on the Island. It provides a centre of technological excellence as well as of cultural life. It is located at Cossitt Lake on the outskirts of Sydney for ease of access for people in all the communities of Cape Breton County. It is deeply involved with the business life of Cape Breton.

T.S.I. Sensor Incorporated, for example, is established within the university itself and its project engineer, Jan Peter De Souza lives nearby in Sydney. "There were three primary reasons for establishing T.S.I. Sensor down here," De Souza explained. "The first was to get involved with the Canada Space Agency Program, which was under-represented by companies in the Atlantic provinces; the Hibernia project was just gearing up. Also, there was the opportunity of assistance from ACOA through ECBC who were willing to help high-tech companies get established. Moreover, there was the chance of locating on the campus which has good facilities. The CAD-CAM computers were a plus; there was no need to procure any expensive equipment - we could just lease or borrow."

Anything else needed in the way of facilities? "We are pretty well set up. It's the best CAD-CAM centre east of Montreal, even better than at the Technical University in Nova Scotia in Halifax. We have enough for what we do, but there is not a great deal of support from the local area itself. We are ordering a lot of electronics, usually from distributors through Toronto. . . There is no direct distributor here. The closest source you might find for some of the things we need is in Halifax, but it's very limited. There are quite a few companies here who would welcome a distributor."

De Souza was glad to get back home to the Maritimes after ten months training in Toronto for his job at T.S.I. Sensor. "If you want to buy a home in Toronto and start a family, you can't possibly do it unless you are both working and making good money; it would mean a quarter of a million dollars for a home; how can you even think about saving? And back here we can do more outdoor sport. I do a lot of mountain biking. You have to go so far out of Toronto to get away from it all. Everybody's following you. There are always people around, whereas in the Maritimes, you can go and get lost in the wilderness very easily."

North Sydney

North Sydney is a small port with an industrial park where Lolek Morawiecki has his company: National Work Clothing. He lives in Big Bras d'Or, a rural region on Big Bras d'Or Lake. He came down from Toronto because of a job opportunity. "The opportunity came up for me to start a rainwear factory for a gentleman here," said Lolek Morawiecki. "We ran the company for him for nine years, and then in 1990 we bought it from him.

"You couldn't get me back to Ontario with a team of horses. We live out in the country - on the water, salt water, it's great. The people are great. When we first arrived our neighbours came down to welcome us. The schools are great. The children have lots to do. You don't need to worry where they are, and you know what's going on in the big cities! It's a great life-style, I'd recommend it to anybody."

Can the business be run as well as in Toronto? "We can do everything. We have a fax, the telephone, and a computer hooked up with our partner. The overhead is less. The people are hard workers. We've been here ten years now and we've never had to let anyone go because they couldn't do the job properly. Once you train people they catch on quickly; they work hard, and there's very little absenteeism.

"The company hasn't needed outside experts to develop systems or products. Help, if needed, is available: There are people who have let us know they are available. University graduates and students are supplied to us at very nominal fees. There is no shortage of technical training, no shortage of academic training; it's all here, it's all available. I think that someone looking to start a business who would come down here, spend a month to meet the people, see what facilities are available - they would come permanently. He would find financial assistance available; ACOA helped me. I have nothing but good things to say about them. Any questions were answered properly, problems were ironed out, they gave us all the help they could.

"I would like to see the government bring down people interested in starting a business, bring them here to see what we have. I'm not looking for General Motors, people who would hire a thousand, people like that don't stay for long. I've seen people start small, and they grow and they stay. I know that I made a decision on the spot. We had flown down to meet with the gentleman I worked for initially, and we had real estate people take us around, and when we saw the house, with 50 acres which overlooked Big Bras d'Or, we said yes, we'll buy it, without even getting inside the house to see it.

"I have everything I want; I have good people working for me; the family enjoys it here. Why should I want to go back to Toronto?"

The Nova Scotian South Shore

On the South Shore of Nova Scotia one hears not-so-ghostly echoes of Yo Ho Ho and a Bottle of Rum on the cobbled waterfront of Halifax: in the Rum Runners' Bar in Lunenberg; and the old port of Yarmouth. The echoes are not entirely imaginary, because many of the old trading families are still there, still trading, still exporting and doubtless still drinking a tot of rum or such in the evenings.

As well as the old ports, there are the more decorous summer resort towns, which are growing in part because they are attractive and close to Halifax. More and more people live there all year round, including the occasional high-tech entrepreneur along with his modem, personal computer, and his company.

Chester

Chester is an attractive, traditional, extremely well-heeled village of 1,400 year-round residents along with a large summer population which comes down to its summer homes, scattered over the lawns of the hill rising behind the village, or hidden away in the woods. David Hilchey, general manager of Reinforced Plastics Limited lives here. The company itself is located in Mahone Bay.

Mahone Bay

One approaches Mahone Bay along a narrow country road thick with trees on each side. Suddenly the trees fall away and, with a shock, one is confronted with the expanse of Mahone Bay; on its far side, hovering above the water like a small enchanted city in a book of fairy tales, the town itself. Three exquisite churches, and at least one bewitched house are lined up along the bay, along with light-hearted summer homes including a lovely Victorian fantasy in muted greens and yellows. Up on one of the side streets is Reinforced Plastics.

David Hilchey was brought up in Truro, Nova Scotia. He acquired a degree in geology and physics at Dalhousie University. Then job opportunities took him away from the Maritimes to other parts of Canada, including Calgary and Toronto. But he still subscribed to the *Chronicle Herald* (Halifax), and nursed hopes of coming back. Finally, an opening became available at Reinforced Plastics, and so he came home.

"Reinforced Plastics makes fibre-glass piping," explained David Hilchey. "It is a speciality corrosion-and-abrasion resistant piping used by Dupont, Kodak, and people like that. We also manufacture abrasion-resistant piping that carries limestone slurries. One-third of our business is in Canada, one third in the United States, and one third overseas. We have 160 people working here. Sales run around twelve million."

More and more, Hilchey is directing research outside of his own facility. At one time, people at the firm used to do all themselves, but they were always making do because they could not afford all the equipment. Now they use consulting firms and they link with some universities on special projects. "We are also fortunate that in Halifax there is an advanced materials engineering centre, the technical centre of the University of Nova Scotia, and the Nova Scotia Research Foundation. They have a machine worth $300,000 we could not hope to acquire."

Hilchey also needs university graduates who are generalists with very good foundations for doing in-house research. "Composites need a great deal of research when you get into some fairly sophisticated aspects of composites, and you need a lot more than you can get in books. A lot of it comes from years of research right here and what we do outside. Generally speaking, an organization usually accumulates a body of knowledge and it grows incrementally, little by little, and if we do it fast enough, we stay ahead of the people in Finland or Washington State where our competitors are.

"At the same time, it breaks my heart that you have wonderfully bright young people graduating from university who can't find work. They come in here, and I've even suggested to them to simply go out and volunteer somewhere to work for three months. It's amazing how many people can make themselves invaluable. I would go along with it if someone were remotely useful to us. What can we lose? Except I wouldn't relish telling him later that I couldn't use him. True, but at least he would go away with some valuable work experience that he could put on his *curriculum vitae*, and if he has proven himself able and dedicated, he'll take a reference with him.

"I think employers down here want to hire people. I think we all have a sense of responsibility that we should employ as many people as we can, which is probably not a rational business objective, but we are all members of the community."

Yarmouth

Yarmouth is an old historic port situated in South Western Nova Scotia. It remains a substantial, gracious town, with some handsome old Victorian mansions. On its outskirts is Tristar Industries. Its president is Keith Condon.

"Once we were in the ship building business in this area and the ships were sailed by very entrepreneurial people," Condon said. "They sailed the world, trading furs, lumber and whatever from Nova Scotia, for goods including sugar and particularly rum, so we've had this export fever since Day One." A lot of families from the early days are still here and many of them are still in the export business.

"Tristar Industries grew from the special vehicles division of a local car dealership which started manufacturing ambulances and grew. There were further spin-offs: Since Tristar makes ambulances for export throughout the world, and because the health field needs communication facilities, the firm added that business as a sideline in its Nova Scotia market; it sells computers, cellular phones, and faxes.

"People ask us why we aren't in Halifax or Toronto," Condon says, "it's because this is home. And quite frankly, any logistic of penalty for dealing from Yarmouth, as opposed to dealing from Halifax, is insignificant. In fact, Yarmouth has a great location as far as we are concerned. We are on the eastern seaboard - a very good place for export in the world market. Yarmouth is also the gateway to the United States. Two ferries operate in the summer. We have an airport with daily flights to Boston. From an exporter's point of view, to be able to jump on a plane and be in Boston in an hour, and in Halifax in 45 minutes, is a plus. From there you can be anywhere in very short order.

"Moreover, the overhead is less; the workforce is very accessible. There is a very large transient workforce in this area, including skilled people. For example, when we get into some of larger contracts, and hire as many as forty people, we find that half of them have worked for us before, so the learning curve is somewhat shorter.

"We pretty well make our own facilities. Here we have our own CAD-CAM system, and our own operator, and we have an engineer on staff. But as far as people being available, we are not far from the university system in Halifax, and up the French shore, and then there are the community colleges."

When asked whether companies were more democratic these days, more of a team, Condon replied, "Well, there certainly is a structure, but we have a very unusual policy here: basically, our factories belong to our customers, so when we bring people in from Europe, for example, to build a fleet of vehicles, we always invite at least two people from the management area of that fleet - the people who engage in design and operation. We sit down with the computer, and in the boardroom with our technical people, and we make sure that what they expect is what they are going to get, and we put it on paper." Actually, what he is doing is including his clients in his team.

"We all work very closely with them. They mingle with our workforce (we're all on the same level here). That can be a bit dangerous at times when you have your customers looking over the shoulders of your people, but on the other hand, if we can't meet the demands of the customer in an honest and open way, we'll never keep them as a customer. In fact we develop solid, long lasting friendships regardless of how the business goes. And there's a lot of evening - I won't say partying - cultural exchange is the best way to put it," he said. *...Yo ho ho..ho...ho....ho.....!*

I think that what you have really been telling me is about the people and values that the Maritimes have to offer? "No question about it."

Why don't more business people move down here? "I'm very irritated about this. People from Toronto tend to think we're all backwoods and mickey mouse in this area. I've heard the same words used in my own boardroom from people that we've actually hired: 'Oh - you can't put Nova Scotia on the stationery, because if people see you are from Nova Scotia they won't do business with you.' *I've heard people say this!* And I've got a real problem with that. Nova Scotia is the flag we wave, and I've done business with bigger places than Toronto. It's not that everyone in Toronto is like that, but generally speaking, in the business world, people want to be with the big address. So they can be with the big address. Us? We'll just do the big business!"

The Amenities of the Small Towns

There was a general consensus among the entrepreneurs interviewed that the amenities of their small towns were adequate, save for a few mild qualifications concerning the limitations of very small towns.

Education

"I'm very happy with Nova Scotia's system of education in general, and I'm very happy with our own schools in Yarmouth," commented Keith Condon. David Hilchey was particularly pleased with the new high school in Chester. "It's a good school. I'm on the board." "The schools are great," said Lolek Morawiecki, speaking of those at Bras d'Or. "Our children had spent three years in schools in Ontario, and we found that when they got here they were a little behind. We think the system here is at least equal to the system in Ontario, if not better."

In one of the smaller towns - Springhill - David Surrette considered the school system adequate, said that the range of courses might be less than would be available in a larger town, but he was satisfied so long as his children saw something of the rest of Canada and beyond.

Security

Security was considered to be generally very good, with very little crime.

Hospitals

In general, the hospital services were considered satisfactory. There were fewer services in the very small towns, but they were available nearby. In three of the smaller towns, hospital service was scanty. There was a small hospital in Springhill, but serious cases had to go to Halifax. Cap-Pelé does not have a hospital, but two major hospitals are available in Moncton, a thirty-five-minute drive away, and a clinic is available in Shediac, a twenty-minute drive away. In Chester, hospitals were about thirty miles away, but they had local clinics and an ambulance.

In Sackville, there is a regional hospital with a day surgery program. Specialists, including surgeons, come to Sackville from Moncton on specific days. People come into the hospital from the area encompassing Memramcook to Cape Tormentine. As well, Moncton hospitals send some of their day surgical cases to Sackville.

Recreation

Recreation was considered very satisfactory, and cultural needs appeared to be fulfilled, especially for towns near a university. Of Yarmouth, Condon said: "In terms of theatre, there's probably never enough around, but our recreation centre is very active in amateur theatre, and they do bring in some professional groups now and then." Once again, the very small towns are limited in that regard. Springhill has a lively high school theatre group. Chester, one of the smallest towns, has a very lively little theatre.

David Hilchey sums up life in Chester. "It has everything I need in a community: a rink for the kids, an 18-hole golf course, a swimming pool; we have soccer, gymnastics, tennis and sailing lessons. The kids are busy all summer. I love Halifax. It is a marvellous city, and it's nice to have it forty miles away. We used to think that we were going to be there every weekend, and now if I went in once every two months I would be surprised, and that would be to go to the symphony two or three times a year. We see the local theatre in Chester, and the Chester brass band - which is internationally known - they are always winning prizes. We play bridge with some friends, and we don't really need Halifax."

Conclusions

The answers to our key questions have come back clear and positive: a modern high-tech company can operate successfully in a small town with the help of today's communications, and usually with lower operating costs and a reliable workforce. The list of mild business complaints was even less than in the case of the social amenities: Jan Peter De Souza needed an electronic distributor in Cape Breton; David Hilchey sometimes had difficulty persuading technical people to come to Nova Scotia.

Although our entrepreneurs recognize that you cannot expect an opera house in a small town (although one wonders, when one considers Mount Allison) they have made a choice for the quality of life the small towns offer. The general consensus is that the amenities of small towns in the Maritimes are satisfactory, and may even, in some cases, be above the average.

The enormous importance of the universities' role in the personal life and business life of the entrepreneurs emerges again and again, not only in terms of education, but as centres of excellence in terms of equipment and expertise. They also make an invaluable contribution to the cultural and social life of the surrounding communities. A similar value attaches to the cities, and the small towns of the Maritimes usually have the advantage of nearness to cities.

The unbidden issues also had positive ideas and answers.

The Entrepreneurial View on Unemployment

Refreshingly, our entrepreneurs approached unemployment from a grass-roots level, placing responsibility squarely on their own shoulders. Says *Condon*: "My answer is to go find the business and bring it home." *Duffy* advises looking for the opportunities all around us, particularly the opportunities latent in the high-tech field; he produces a concrete example in the information circular he had received from Holland, created through the use of high-tech, and could be emulated and applied to any number of information areas. *Hilchey* suggests three months voluntary work as a door opener for beginning workers. *De Souza* points to a highly possible opportunity: that Cape Breton needs an electronic distributor. *Condon*, with his spin-offs, demonstrates the importance of keeping one's eyes open. *Hawkins* tacitly suggests creating jobs for oneself, as he did, or jobs for others, and regards it as his mission to help his clients create jobs. *Deacon* went down to Charlottetown with venture capital to get things going. *Morawiecki* suggests the government bringing down ten entrepreneurs to take a look at the Maritimes.

The Role of Government

The entrepreneurs favour seed capital, judicious loans and grants for specific start-up purposes. It is better for the government to pay for a marketing scout selected by the entrepreneur, advises Regis Duffy, rather than establishing government bureaucracies and having them make such choices. Duffy says the government can provide a positive business environment, as it did for him with help, such as a good rental deal from the industrial park, and paying for marketing scouts.

Teamwork in the Workplace

There has always been a disturbing aspect of the new technologies in that they create unemployment, yet one can see, even in this short study, that apart from making operations more efficient, they are also demolishing hierarchies, and creating a more educative, creative and egalitarian workplace. David Surrette specifically points out that for him, changing over to the new technologies led to other changes, including profit-sharing and quality management, with his people participating in problem-solving and decision-making. Hawkins also stressed the importance of teamwork; Condon included his clients in his team.

Furthermore, high-tech is also having spread effects. For example, a cluster of communications companies has formed in Sackville. The Tribune Press and Hawk Communications have been joined there by Simpson Gilbert Advertising Communications, and Chromascan Atlantic, a company which prepares colour separations for printing and advertising, and which services the three other companies.

Taken as a whole, there was a wonderful vitality throughout the interviews, an entrepreneurial determination to get the Maritimes on the move. The entrepreneurs offer us an enormously dynamic and positive picture. They have confronted the three shocks: they have responded to the public spending cuts with job creation; they are operating in the global economy successfully, using new technologies to advantage. They offer us a concept of our small towns as caring, responsible, protective and enjoyable communities, and show how our businesses can adapt to the new economy. They demonstrate what Deacon advises: build small ventures rather than megaprojects, produce for niches in the marketplace, and sell the product far beyond the Atlantic markets.

PART II

THE MARITIME URBAN SYSTEM:
A NECKLACE OF CITIES, NOT ALL OF THEM PEARLS

7

HALIFAX, THE MARITIMES' METROPOLIS:
A FRAGILE EQUILIBRIUM

Benjamin Higgins

> Halifax remained much the same. It had always
> looked an old town. It had a genius for looking
> old and for acting as though nothing could
> possibly happen to surprise it.
>
> Halifax, more than most towns, seemed gov-
> erned by a fate she neither made nor understood,
> for it was her birthright to serve the English in
> times of war and to sleep neglected when there
> was peace.
>
> They lived in Halifax in an anomalous perma-
> nency, unreconciled to be Americans or even
> Canadians, content for the moment to let their
> status drift with events, convinced that in being
> Nova Scotians, they possessed a peculiar cause
> for satisfaction, an excellence which no one had
> ever troubled to define because no one outside
> the province believed it existed, and everyone
> inside took it for granted.
>
> Hugh MacLennan, *Barometer Rising*

Of all Canadian metropolitan centres, Halifax provides the best illustration of the
Veblen-Ayres theory of development. Thorstein Veblen and Clarence Ayres, each
the leading Institutionalist of his own generation, believed that economic
development or underdevelopment depended on the outcome of a race; not a race
between technological progress and diminishing returns in agriculture, as the
Classical school would have it, but a race between technological progress and
obstacles to it: tradition, customs, beliefs, ceremonies, values, irrational fears,
and other aspects of culture inimical to change. Since World War II, Halifax has
had its share of technological progress, entrepreneurship, and innovation. Yet its
continued progress has been periodically delayed by a remarkable tenacity in
clinging to the old order. The continuing prominence of the military in both the

society and the economy; the fact that many Haligonians regard their educational institutions primarily as devourers of land and taxes; the dependence on transfer payments; the strong ties to the "Boston States" and a tendency to think of Ottawa as a foreign capital, devoted to the interests of Ontario and Quebec; the mistrust and suspicion of outsiders; the almost equal mistrust and suspicion of each other; these attitudes have prevented Halifax from being the dynamic growth pole that it should be.

The plan of this chapter is as follows. We begin our story of Halifax's recent development with a "snapshot" of the city's economic and social situation in 1970, provided by Voluntary Planning's "Encounter on the Urban Environment" in that year. We then jump twenty-one years to 1991, and provide a second snapshot provided by another Voluntary Planning encounter, The Encounter on the Nova Scotia Economy. A comparison of the two "snapshots" reveals remarkable, and puzzling, similarities between the two. Had nothing happened to Halifax in the two intervening decades? To answer this question, and provide a statistical picture of recent trends, we look first at Census data for 1981 and 1991. To bring the story up-to-date, we make use of Employment and Immigration Canada's *Local Labour Market Review* for Metro Halifax June-December 1993. From these various sets of facts, we next endeavour to assemble a new picture of where Halifax is and where it is going. Finally, with this picture before us, we ask two questions. (1) Does it really matter to the other cities in the Maritimes urban structure what happens to Halifax? and (2) Is Halifax *the* development pole for the Maritimes? The answers we give may be surprising to some readers, irritating to others; but some, at least, will give a sigh of relief.

Halifax in Crisis: February 1970

In the week of February 22nd to 28th 1970, an extraordinary event took place in Halifax, Nova Scotia. The Nova Scotia Voluntary Planning Board, supported by the Nova Scotia Cabinet Committee on Planning, staged an encounter on the urban environment. What actually took place was a public, intensively and extensively publicized, airing of the economic, social, and political ills of Halifax-Dartmouth, Nova Scotia, and the whole Atlantic region. Attention was focused on Halifax-Dartmouth as the major metropolitan centre of that region.

The format of Encounter Week was as follows. A team of twelve persons was assembled, each a leader in his particular field. The fields were diverse: an American sociologist; an American tourism-recreation expert; a Canadian development economist; a Canadian industrial executive; an American urban development expert; a Canadian trade union leader; an English environmentalist; a Canadian professor of journalism; an American urban management expert; a Canadian transport economist; an American urban economist; a black civil rights worker from New York. Disparate as this group was, they proved to have been astutely chosen so as to strike sparks off each other, and off the various groups that they "encountered."

The team, which inevitably became known as "the Twelve Apostles" in the media before the week was half gone, worked an eighteen-hour day or more throughout the week. The daily schedule was: 6:30 A.M., wake-up call; 7:00 A.M., breakfast meeting of team and organizers; 8:00 A.M., first "encounter." The team met at approximately one-hour intervals during the day, representatives of particular groups in the Halifax, and Nova Scotia community, such as federal government officials; provincial government officials and politicians; municipal and county government officials and politicians; trade union leaders; financiers and industrialists; the media; the armed forces; educators at all three levels; farmers and fishermen; welfare workers and people on welfare; and churches.

At 6:00 P.M., there was a cocktail discussion of the day's events; at 7:00 P.M., a dinner meeting to organize the evening's television show; at 8:00 P.M., a televised open meeting, labelled "On the Town," to express reactions to the day's encounters, answer questions from the live audience (which reached 3,000 people by the end of the week, while the TV audience ran to hundreds of thousands, the most popular show on the air in the Atlantic region). At 11:00 P.M., there was a team meeting (with many nightcaps) until early morning, to evaluate the day and prepare for the next. When the week was over, the organizers confessed that part of their strategy had been to wear the team to a frazzle, so that it would lose inhibitions, become irascible and voice gut-reactions without premeditation. The organizers knew what they were doing.

The encounters were organized with an ingenuity that bordered on the fiendish. For example, when we visited the Volvo plant, the organizers made sure that we were driven through the black ghetto in its neighbourhood. Then when we went into the plant, which operated with teams for each car on an open floor rather than an assembly line, it was immediately apparent that there was not a single black employee in the plant. This discrimination became the principal theme of that evening's telecast. When we met with the welfare officers and recipients, we were taken to a tumble-down church in a slum area. They did not say: "Now we are going to show you some slums:" it was not necessary to say anything. On the long table behind which the "Twelve Apostles" sat, facing the audience during the meeting, were carafes of water and glasses. After the last evening's meeting we were all parched, and drank a lot of water. When the meeting was over we all wanted a bathroom, but the church had none. However, across the street was an open door leading to a toilet with a single naked light globe burning. We went in one by one - and saw the appalling conditions under which several families were living in a single house. The whole thing was staged by the organizers.

The organizers wanted to administer a shock treatment to the team. They succeeded. The team was shocked by what they saw and heard and they said so, in individual encounters, in the evening television shows, and in interviews with the media. Among the things that shocked them were the widespread poverty and unemployment; the appalling slums; the beggars in the streets and the mendicant mentality of a society obtaining three quarters of its income from subsidies and other transfer payments; the inadequacy and haphazard management of the welfare system; the intensity of racial discrimination and conflict; the inadequacy of the primary and secondary school systems and the indifference to, and even resentment of, the excellence of the universities. As Joe Scanlon, Director of Carleton University's School of Journalism, put it in the final televised session of the encounter, the team "spent several years in Halifax in February 1970."

Problems and Prospects: Halifax, Nova Scotia, and the Atlantic Provinces

Let us look more closely at the reactions of members of the team to what they had learned during the encounter, as expressed during the wind-up session.[1] The chairman of that session was Dennis McDermott, then Canadian Regional Director of the United Auto Workers, one of the most influential trade union leaders in the country, and later Canada's ambassador to Ireland. Perhaps because he wanted to begin the session with an overview, he called first upon the author of this chapter. I endeavoured to provide a thumbnail sketch of the whole economic, social and political situation of the region, as it had been in the past, as it was in 1970, and as it might be in future.

> To an economist, Nova Scotia provides a familiar enough pattern, a relatively rich and progressive economy, converted in a rather short period into a relatively poor and stagnant one. As we all know, 150 years ago the Maritimes was the most economically advanced region in Canada, not very different from New England to the South. But in the mid-19th century, the economy based on fish, forests, coal and superb wooden sailing ships gave way to Confederation and the deliberate policy of shifting the axis of trade from North-South to East-West. The shift of the center of population to the West didn't help. All this is common knowledge. But what is perhaps less widely and deeply understood is that a prosperous economy which bogs down produces a society in which individuals and groups are frustrated, aspirations cannot be fulfilled and the once unified society splinters into interest groups, each fighting to keep what it has and trying to get a little bit more.

Wilbur Thompson, then Chairman of the Department of Economics at Wayne State University and a world renowned urban economist, picked up the theme of the role of Halifax in the Atlantic economy and the prospects for future development of both. He saw only a small role for manufacturing in the future of the Halifax-Dartmouth region. Able-bodied males with limited education, seeking employment in manufacturing, would be well advised to go elsewhere.

It will take time for Halifax to become a great city, a competitor in the world system of cities. In the intermediate stage, Halifax must become increasingly a regional capital.

David Kirkbride was vice-president of Canadian Industries Limited, one of Canada's largest multinational corporations. His picture of the state of the Atlantic provinces economy was not very different from that of the economists on the team, but interestingly enough, he was more insistent than they on the need for planning at all levels, including the private sector. The team had encountered, among business organizations and leaders, attitudes and practices which were not conducive to the good of the community as a whole.

Town Planning

Two members of the team dealt more specifically with the town planning aspects of the development of the Atlantic region. Edward Logue, then president and chief executive officer of the New York Urban Development Corporation, began by saying that any urban community must have goals and policies, but these would not differ much from one part of North America to another, and do not get us very far. His question was: "How can we improve the lot of those that have not enough without penalizing overmuch those who are comfortable with the system as it is?" If people in the region are talking about social progress for the underprivileged by redividing the pie rather than by making the pie grow, they are really talking about revolution: and the Atlantic society was not ready for revolution.

Dr. Logue went on to stress the dangers of relying too heavily on tourism, saying that unless the society is a strong one to begin with, it can lead to disgruntled and corrupt people. He also emphasized the need for an overall regional development agency with authority as well as responsibility for planning and implementation. He mentioned Stockholm and Boston as models from which lessons could be learned.

Dr. Frank Steggert, then director of the Urban Observatory and professor of Management at the Georgia State University, grouped his summary remarks under the headings of apathy, organization, problem solving, and voluntarism. What looks like apathy, he said, often reflects a feeling among the people of a community that the benefits they are receiving from public goods and collective services are less than their individual contribution to the costs. Some people appear apathetic because they feel powerless, distant, and ineffectual. A few seem apathetic because they are well satisfied with their share of the benefits. In the Halifax community he found a mixture of the three.

Sectoral Problems

Two of the "Apostles" confined their remarks to problems in particular sectors of the Atlantic economy related to their own fields of specialization. Dr. Konrad Studnichi-Gizbert, fellow of McLaughlin College of York University, is a specialist in transport economics. He began by praising "God's Gift" to Halifax, "the marvellous position of a marvellous port." Unfortunately, he continued, over the years, "Quite a bit of overall nonsense has been committed" with respect to the port, mainly in the form of "neglecting the inter-relationships." The highway system was underdeveloped. The internal transport system of the city of Halifax-Dartmouth was inefficient. Transport must be planned together with industry, housing, welfare services, and everything else. As it was, transport was a bottleneck.

Dr. Clare Gunn, professor of Tourism and Recreation Development at Texas A & M University, quoted a report showing that outlays for tourism and recreation constitute the largest single input to the economies of coastal counties in the United States. Tourist interest in the Atlantic region was at a high level. If the people of Nova Scotia really wanted tourist trade, they must give it "a more positive total commitment." Tourism requires a concerted effort on the part of many people. Protection of the heritage and improved physical environment are important. Expensive tourist complexes should be built. There is insufficient awareness of the need to build up an entire tourism system for the whole Atlantic region.

Quality of the Society

Dr. Scott Greer, professor of Sociology at Northwestern University, concentrated his final statement on the quality of the Atlantic provinces society. He prefaced his remarks by saying:

> What can one say that is responsible and not dishonest, after being deluged for 19 hours a day with data, personalities, social groups, processes, of this small but charming provincial society? I think that I will start off by saying that you are part of the débris of the British Empire. I do not think that is anything that I would be ashamed of; it was a great empire and one of the very few in human history that liquidated itself in a fairly honorable fashion.

Halifax-Dartmouth had some assets: the concentration of the military establishment, ship-building, offshore oil, the education centre for eastern English-speaking Canada, the medical centre for eastern English-speaking Canada, essentially a government town. But in the process of dismembering the British Empire there were social costs. Canada is a large-scale and very rich society he said, but found it a very spotty, very uneven society, an inheritance from the British Empire. In the process of social change many people are hurt. But it should not be the weakest, most helpless groups in society that pay the costs of economic growth, as was then the case.

The Socio-political Environment

Dr. Martin Rein came to Encounter from the Centre for Environment Studies in London, England. His final statement, however, showed him to be more concerned for the social and political environment of the Atlantic society than for its physical environment. He began with a strong statement:

> It does seem to me that you have here a political culture which tends to inspire indifference, caution, and, to some extent, fear as well. . . (The) economy and culture each reinforce each other to produce this political culture. You have an economy of scarcity. The occupations which are strongest in this community - medicine, your bureaucratic government and the military - all reinforce this sense of hierarchy. It seems to me that this political culture is reinforced by a very powerful ideology which I think could be roughly summarized as *Welfare as a Burden.*

In the context of the political culture Rein described, the notion of welfare as a burden reinforces the caution and indifference of the community. It was high time to re-examine the entire subsidy system. Such a study would probably show that the major beneficiaries are the middle and upper income groups and not the poor, and might yield more solid knowledge of the incentive effects of various kinds of subsidy.

Racial Relations and Religion

The black civil rights leader on the team was the Reverend Lucius Walker, executive director of the Interreligious Foundation for Community Organization of New York. Naturally enough, Walker devoted his summary remarks to racial relations and the role of religious institutions in the community. The Halifax-Dartmouth community reminded him forcefully of the deep South of the United States; he confessed that he had referred to it at some points as "Halifax, Mississippi," and added, "Like the deep South, it's characterized by depression, repression, and oppression." Where the black community has seemed offensive to the values and attitudes of the larger community, he continued, it has been disrupted socially, economically, and psychologically, as in the case of Africville (a black squatter settlement which was bulldozed into non-existence by the Halifax government). There was need for some kind of retribution.

Communications and the Media

During the week, the media came under heavy fire from the team for being too narrowly based, too exclusively representative of the views of the conservative upper income groups, and too limited in coverage of world events. But in his final statement, Professor Joe Scanlon said: "I know of no other community which has devoted as much public affairs programming to something such as Encounter." The very heat of the debate during Encounter Week showed that the community had a capacity for communication.

The Trade Union Movement

As chairman of the final session, Dennis McDermott reserved his remarks to the end. As a trade union leader, he confined those remarks to the labour movement. It was his understanding that his task was to look at labour as it relates to expanding industry. That turned out to be a short, uninteresting, academic exercise, he said, because there was so little expansion of industry. With unemployment so high, he continued, there should be a plentiful supply of labour once industry did start to expand; but that turned out not to be the case, because so high a percentage of the unemployed turned out to be unemployable. This fact points to the importance of training and upgrading programs. And related to all the other economic and social problems was the "very obvious desperate housing shortage."

Halifax, Nova Scotia, the Atlantic Region, 1970: A Snapshot

The Encounter Team did not arrive in Halifax in February 1970 already expert on the economy, society, and polity of the metropolis, the province, and the region. They were not afforded the opportunity for leisurely and scholarly study. Their appraisal of the city, the province, and the region was, as it was meant to be, impressionistic. But coming from such a group, with training and experiences elsewhere that provided them with a capacity for comparative analysis of the basis of the vivid and detailed picture that was unfolded before them, and having no axes to grind, the strong reactions voiced by the group carried deep significance. Considering the diversity of their professional backgrounds, the degree of unanimity achieved within one week remains impressive. All agreed that the current picture was grim, but also that there were glimmers of hopes for the future.

Turning to the economy, the Atlantic region was worse than underdeveloped, they found it decadent, the result of a former leading region being transformed in a rather short time into a lagging one. The resource and technology base of its former relative prosperity was gone. There was a potential for mass exodus from the region. There was unwarranted smugness about the educational system, which was not well designed for the region's needs, and too little appreciation of the role of good universities in economic development. The housing situation was critical. The transport system was inadequate, there was unawareness of the requirements for a lively tourist industry. There was need for more and better planning and for fewer planners. Planning and policy mistakes have been made with regard to industrial growth, the container port, and housing. Unemployment was high, many of the unemployed were unemployable, and facilities for training, retraining, and upgrading were inadequate. It was doubtful whether Halifax could ever regain its position as a leading manufacturing centre, and manufacturing was no longer a leading sector in economic growth. The whole picture was "messy." All in all, it was not a snapshot on which one would base an optimistic prognosis.

In 1970, Halifax and the Atlantic region seemed to be in a Slough of Despond from which they might never escape. Now it seems that Halifax did escape, but that it is in danger of sliding back into the slough.

Halifax at the Crossroads: The 1990s and Beyond

In May of 1991, Halifax's Voluntary Planning Association organized another "Encounter." This time it concentrated on the Nova Scotia economy. In preparation for this second encounter, Voluntary Planning released in March 1991 a 33-page paper entitled *Our Province, Our Future, Our Choice: a Consultation Paper for a Nova Scotia Economic Strategy*. This paper was used as "the focus of discussion" for "public consultation meetings" in ten regions of Nova Scotia. In July 1991, Voluntary Planning published a "brief summary" (22 pages) of these discussions under the title *Report on the Public Consultation Process: Encounter on the Nova Scotia Economy*.

The first of these documents opens with a brief statement outlining "The Challenge of Change." It is worth reporting the first pages of this statement in full, since it gives the flavour of the whole report.

"Nova Scotia is at a critical crossroads in its economic history. The world is changing rapidly and inevitably:

-   Traditional international political and trading alliances are shifting;

-   Trade barriers - inter-provincial as well as international - are falling;

-   Global advances in technology are altering the way products are made and marketed, and the ways in which business itself is conducted;

-   Big is no longer synonymous with "better" when it comes to business;

- Everyone - from heads of state, to heads of corporations, to heads of households - has become aware that economics and environment are inter-connected and that we must preserve and enhance our environment in order to be successful economically.

Those changes create opportunities. But Nova Scotia faces enormous difficulties too. Some problems - like the current recession - are temporary; others involve significant structural, long-term changes in our economy."[2]

The report is a statement of good intentions (and we all know what road is paved with those), rather than a concrete plan or program for the reconstruction of the Nova Scotia - and thus the Halifax-Dartmouth - economy. It states that the strategy must be private-sector driven, outward-looking, stress value-added, technologically-advanced, performance-oriented, environmentally-sustainable, and regionally-sensitive. "Our goal," it proclaims, "is to build an economy that is based on *competitive* success so we will be able to sell more goods and services in the market place. . . Nova Scotians must increase the amount and diversity of the province's economic activity."[3]

For so innocuous a document, the reactions of the public, as summarized in the May report, were surprisingly strong. For someone who was a member of the first Encounter Team, they engender an overwhelming sense of *déjà vu*. Nova Scotians seem to have the same worries and problems, and much the same suggestions for improvement, as they did twenty-five years ago.

The report continues by saying that: "No one disagreed with the paper's assertion that Nova Scotia has a serious problem. The majority of people felt the paper understated the problem." Interestingly, the report states that "private sector was invariably interpreted to mean 'big business'. This interpretation also held extremely negative connotations of smokestacks, loss of control over our natural resources and environment, and exploitation of workers. Nova Scotians do not entirely trust business and industry."[4] These attitudes suggest that the concentration of ownership and power in the private sector has not diminished much in twenty years. Consequently, instead of regarding the "private sector" as the generator of economic and social progress, the people of Nova Scotia regard it as a threat to the environment and the creator of inequalities of wealth and income - just as they did when the first encounter was organized. But this mistrust of private enterprise does not incline Nova Scotians to socialism: "Nova Scotians are disillusioned with politicians and do not trust government (regardless of political affiliation)." Do they mistrust everybody?[5]

Is Halifax Developing?

"Development" may be defined as growth of income and employment, as a result of technological progress, and structural change which involves a transfer of land, labour and capital from less productive to more productive uses. Has

Halifax been developing in this sense? Let us look first at the changes that have taken place in Halifax between the census years 1981 and 1991 in these respects.[6]

Income

Halifax is not a "poor city." In 1991, employment income in Halifax was 100.6 percent of the Canadian average. Of all urban centres in the Atlantic provinces, only Fredericton and the small town of Kentville, Nova Scotia, had a higher rate of growth of employment income between 1981 and 1991. (Halifax, 91.4 percent, Fredericton, 92.4 percent, Kentville, 105.1 percent) Since the growth of Halifax exceeded that of all centres in Nova Scotia, it is safe to assume that the growth of per capita gross domestic product and personal income per capita was also higher in Halifax than in the province as a whole. Growth of per capita GDP was higher in Nova Scotia in all years but three between 1981 and 1991 than in Canada, in most years susbstantially; thus growth of per capita income was higher in Halifax than in Canada during the decade. Growth of personal income per capita was also higher in Nova Scotia than in Canada in all years but two, in some years substantially; thus per capita personal income grew faster in Halifax than the Canadian average. Moreover, employment income grew in all sectors of the Halifax economy during the decade.

However, these figures reflect the mediocre performance of the Canadian economy rather than the spectacular performance of the Halifax one. Most of the growth of per capita income resulted from inflation. The growth of real employment income (at 1981 prices) was only 14.3 percent in the entire decade, an average of a little more than one percent per year. At that rate of growth, it would take two generations for per capita income to double.

Employment

The Halifax labour force grew by 22.3 percent during the decade, compared to 18.1 percent for Canada and 16.1 percent for the Atlantic region. The labour forces of Bathurst, N.B., Charlottetown, P.E.I., Kentville, N.S., Moncton, N.B, and St. John's, Nfld, all grew more rapidly than Halifax, and Fredericton nearly as fast. (66.6, 36.6, 24.3, 24.1, 22.4 and 22.2 percent respectively.) Thus it does not appear that during the decade Halifax "was the locomotive pulling all the other cars along," as used to be said of São Paulo and all the other Brazilian cities in the 1960s and 1970s. The fast-growing sectors were business and other services, health, construction, and hotels and restaurants; but all sectors - even manufacturing - showed some growth.

Structural Change

The income figures provide some evidence of technological progress and rising productivity in the Halifax economy. This growth factor, however, does not seem to have been bolstered by structural change. Four sectors of the Halifax economy had incomes a little above the Canadian average for the sector: Public administration (107.3 percent of the Canadian average), primary production, (103.7 percent), hotels and restaurants, (100.2 percent), and education (100.2 percent). In absolute terms, the high-income sectors were public administration, education, transportation, construction, Finance Insurance, and Real estate (FIRE), in that order. All of these sectors had average incomes between $26,000 and $31,500. All of these high-income sectors, except construction and public administration, experienced declines in their shares of total employment between 1981 and 1991; construction increased only from 5.2 to 5.4 percent, and public administration only from 10.5 to 11.8 percent. The declines were not great: the biggest was in the public administration sector - with the highest incomes of all - from 17.9 to 15.8 percent.

The structural change was therefore rather slight; but most of it was in the wrong direction. The trade sector suffered a decline from 18.1 percent of total employment to 17 percent. This sector had the second-lowest average income, $17,781; its shrinkage might therefore be considered a favourable sign. On the other hand, the poorest sector, hotels and restaurants, with average income of only $10,070, experienced a slight increase in share of total employment. On the whole, then, the picture of structural change in Halifax during the decade is one of stagnation rather than serious decline: it certainly is not a picture of vigorous development. It should also be noted that whereas the relative shrinkage of the manufacturing sector and relative expansion of the services sector is generally regarded as a sign of healthy development, this is not true for Halifax, since incomes in manufacturing are almost 50 percent higher than in services, and incomes in the service sector of Halifax are only 89.9 percent of the Canadian average.

Let us now turn to more recent figures.

The More Recent Employment Picture

The more recent figures show the recession of the 1990s brought stagnation or decline to Halifax. Year-end Labour Force Survey data indicate that average total employment fell from 157,600 in 1989 to 155,400 in 1993. The only sector showing improvement was community, business, and personal services. Fortunately for Halifax, this sector is much the biggest employer in the region; employment increased from 61,300 in 1989 to 67,100 in 1993. Finance, insurance, and real estate, a moderately important employer, held its own at

11,000. All other sectors declined. The biggest drop was in manufacturing, from 12,600 to 9,700, followed by transportation, communications and utilities, which fell from 16,400 to 13,900. Construction also suffered a substantial drop, from 8,600 to 6,400. The other two sectors, trade and public administration, experienced relatively modest declines in employment (see fig. 1).[7]

Unemployment increased during 1993, from 10 to 11.1 percent, or from 17,000 to 19,300. Employment actually increased by 1,700 in 1993, but the labour force rose by 4,000 as a result of a rise in the participation rate by 1.3 to 68.4 percent, after two years of decline.

It is always difficult to separate cyclical movements from changes in trend; but in the case of Halifax the only difference between the movements from 1992 to 1993, and the movements from 1989 to 1993, is that the trade sector, which is the second biggest employer, registered a modest increase in employment from 1992 to 1993, compared to the modest reduction for the longer period (table 1). The December 1993 *Local Labour Market Review* is fairly optimistic where retail trade is concerned, but presents a mixed picture for wholesale trade. It states, "Perceptions about the recovery of retail trade have been supported by survey results. A survey by Deloitte and Touche indicates 70 percent of retailers believe their sales are going to increase this year over the previous year. Optimism was less pronounced among department stores with only 60 percent anticipating a slight increase of 2 to 4 percent. On the consumer side, another survey indicates that only 20 percent of consumers felt that they would spend more this year than they did in the previous year. On the other hand, 50 percent felt that they would spend about the same" (p. 23).

While Halifax is clearly caught up in a long-run trend towards becoming a services centre rather than a manufacturing centre, the experience regarding employment in the sub-sectors of the community, business, and personal services sector is very mixed. For example, budgetary restraints have reduced employment in the education and health fields. Since the future prosperity of Halifax depends so much on the upgrading of its labour force, the restraints on education are most unfortunate. As may be seen from table 1, the number of primary and secondary schools in Nova Scotia has actually declined since 1987-88, as well as the number of full-time students, and the number of full-time teachers at the primary and secondary levels. At the tertiary level, two non-university institutions have been lost, while at the university level the number of full-time teachers has not kept pace with enrolments, resulting in a rise in student-professor ratios, and a possible decline in the quality of education.

According to the December 1993 *Local Labour Market Review*, further cuts in education budgets are to come: "The province plans to cut more than 10 percent from its education budget over the next four years as part of its deficit reduction legislation. The Dartmouth City School Board said it may have to lay off as many as 85 teachers due to funding cuts. They said that there were few alternatives, since teachers' salaries make up 87 percent of expenses." (p. 30)

Figure 1

Employment by Industry Sector
Halifax County - 1989-1993

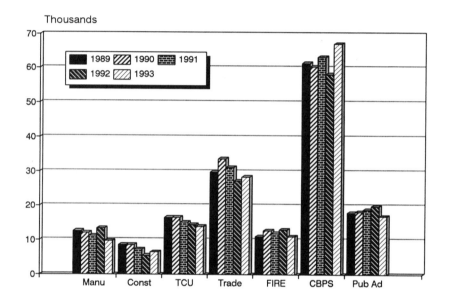

Source: Statistics Canada.

	Manu	Const	TCU	Trade	FIRE	CBPS	Public
1989	12.6	8.5	16.4	29.9	11	61.3	17.9
1990	12	8.5	16.5	33.6	12.7	60.3	18.1
1991	11.1	7.2	15	31.2	11.9	63.2	18.8
1992	13.4	5.4	14.4	27.2	13	58.1	19.8
1993	9.7	6.4	13.9	28.4	11	67.1	16.8

Legend:

Manu - Manufacturing
Const - Construction
TCU - Transportation, Communication
and Utilities

Trade - Wholesale and Retail Trade
FIRE - Finance, Insurance & Real Estate
CBPS - Community, Business & Personal Services
Public - Public Administration

Table 1

Employed Labour Force by Industry Division
Halifax County - Annual Averages 1992 & 1993

Industry	Number Employed in 1993	Number Employed in 1992	Absolute Change* 1992-1993	Percent Change* 1992-1993
Agriculture	0**	0**	***	***
Other Primary Industries	0**	2,100	***	***
Manufacturing	9,700	13,400	-3,700	-27.6
Construction	6,400	5,400	1,000	18.5
Transportation, Communication & Utilities	13,900	14,400	-500	-3.5
Trade	28,400	27,200	1,200	4.4
Finance, Insurance & Real Estate	11,000	13,000	-2,000	-15.4
Community Business & Personnel Services	67,100	58,100	9,000	15.5
Public Administration	16,800	19,800	-3,000	-15.2
Total	155,400	153,700	1,700	1.1

Source: Statistics Canada, Labour Force Survey, Three Month Moving Average Data.

* Calculated by the LMI Unit
** Statistics Canada does not publish numbers less than 2000 in their monthly data
*** Cannot be calculated

A similar situation prevails in the health field. With the aging of the population, the demand for health services is increasing, but hospitals are reducing staff through attrition, retirement packages, and layoffs. It is projected that in Nova Scotia as a whole, employment in hospitals will fall by 1,000 by 1999. Since Metropolitan Halifax employs a large proportion of provincial hospital personnel (18,775 people in health and welfare services in 1991), the brunt of these cuts is likely to be felt in Halifax. The Victoria General Hospital plans to reduce its operating budget by $850,000, eliminating 36 surgical and 29 medical beds, having already closed 56 beds in December 1993, and 15 more in April 1994, laying off 157 workers. Similar cuts are planned by other Metro Halifax hospitals. The Pharmacare program for senior citizens has also reduced its budget.

Like most Nova Scotia cities, Halifax has high hopes for tourism. According to the projections of the *Canadian Occupational Projection System*, the accommodation and food services sector in the province is likely to show strong growth to 1999. Meanwhile, hotel occupancy rates, and hotel employment, fell in 1992 but recovered slightly in 1993. The Halifax Hilton laid off 150 full-time and 100 part-time employees. The management has stated that it would rehire the 250 employees and create an additional 400 new jobs if it is granted a license for a casino.

In 1993, public administration was the third largest sector in terms of employment, accounting for 10.8 percent of total employment in Halifax County. At 16,800 employment was below that of 1985, and well below the 1992 peak of 19,800. Employment fell at the federal, provincial, and municipal levels, and is expected to fall more in the next few years. According to the Labour Force Survey definition, public administration does not include the armed forces; these too suffered reductions in personnel. The December 1993 *Local Labour Market Review* estimates that "as a result of the February 22, 1994 federal government budget, as many as 1,000 military and civilian jobs could be lost in Nova Scotia over the next four years, with three bases or stations closing and a fourth being downgraded." (p. 37) Provincial government employment in Nova Scotia is expected to be reduced by some 1,000 by 1999, and municipal administration employment by 800.

Next in line was the transportation, communications and utilities sector, with 13,900 employees, down from a peak of 16,500 in 1990, but slightly more than the 13,400 in 1985. According to the December 1993 *Local Labour Market Review*, "The forecast for this sector . . . is pessimistic. Declines in employment are expected throughout the transportation sector, with the most positive area being the Port of Halifax, where a strengthening of the competitive position is expected to make employment levels relatively stable. The communications sector is also expected to show some decline. The television and radio industries are expected to face stagnant markets and increased automation, particularly in the radio industry. Employment with the telecommunications carriers, such as Maritime Tel & Tel, will decline as they face an increasingly competitive industry. Canada Post is expected to continue to rationalize operations and reduce employment levels. Utilities, such as Nova Scotia Power Incorporated (NSPI) will have to deal with stagnant markets and employee rationalization." (p. 17)

Employment in the finance, insurance, and real estate sector was higher in 1993 than in 1985, but substantially below its peak in 1992, and at its lowest level since 1989. Banking remains relatively strong in Halifax. Canada's two largest banks, the Royal Bank of Canada and the Canadian Imperial Bank of Commerce, both had significant cuts in worldwide employment, which they say is due to greater efficiency and automation rather than a drop in profits. The Royal Bank will cut 4,100 jobs in Canada alone during 1994, but maintains that Atlantic Canada will remain relatively unaffected, since the region is one of the bank's most profitable areas. The Toronto Dominion Bank opened a treasury office in Halifax in October 1993.

Restructuring is also taking place in the insurance industry. One of Canada's largest companies plans to discharge 700 employees. Residential housing presents a mixed picture. The average price of houses is up by 8 to 10 percent, but sales have fallen off at the upper end of the market and the vacancy rate for apartments has increased slightly over 1992. Additions to total office space in 1992 were only 14.5 percent of the average of additions over the previous five years.

In 1993, manufacturing accounted for only 6.2 percent of total employment in Halifax County. Employment is less than in 1985, and substantially below the peak of 13,400 in 1992, dropping 27.6 percent to 9,700. By far the biggest employer was the transportation equipment industry, followed by printing, publishing and allied industries, electrical and electronic industries, and fabricated metal products industries. No other industry accounts for as much as 7 percent of total manufacturing employment. Among food and beverage industries, Moosehead closed its Dartmouth plant, but Olands Breweries signed an agreement to produce beer for the Cuban government and raised its capacity accordingly. The plastics industry accounted for only 2.5 percent of total manufacturing, but is forecasted to grow slowly to 1999 and more rapidly thereafter.

Construction employment fell marginally between 1985 and 1993, from 7,400 to 6,400, after reaching a peak of 9,300 in 1989. The number of housing starts declined 12 percent from 1992 to 1993. Non-residential construction also declined, the biggest drop taking place in institutional and government construction, from 29.8 to 22.5 million dollars. The December 1993 *Local Labour Market Review* states that "There are a number of construction projects planned in the environmental field, though many of the projects appear uncertain." (p. 16) These include a 118 million dollars garbage incinerator for the Metropolitan Authority, for which a definite site has not been selected; and a 398 million dollars Halifax Harbour Clean-Up.

Employment in agriculture is not reported for Halifax County, being less than 2,000, but in Nova Scotia as a whole, there was a decline of 5.4 percent for the year, following a drop of 21.5 percent the year before. It is unlikely that Halifax did not share in this decline. To add to the troubles of the forestry industry, the pinewood nematode was found in two recent shipments to Britain and, as a result, the European Community will stop importing Canadian lumber that is not heat treated. Nova Scotian employment is expected to fall between 1993 and 1999. The pulp and paper industry is particularly depressed, and is expected to remain so. The troubled fishing industry will lose still more jobs as a result of further reductions in groundfish quotas in 1993, which are expected to be further reduced, especially for cod. The mining industry as a whole is expected to be relatively stable, but coal mining is expected to decline slowly. The use of prefabricated steel and pipes by Halifax-Dartmouth Industries Ltd., in its construction of coastal defence vessels, will reduce employment by some 600 jobs.

The Economic Development Task Force

In August 1993, the City Council of Halifax appointed an Economic Development Task Force, consisting of one Admiral of the Atlantic Forces, one Professor of Economics from Dalhousie University, and eight representatives of the business and financial community. Their mandate was broad: "to identify ways to enhance the City's economy and thus, improve the quality of life." In their twenty-five page report, *Economic Development Action Plan for the City of Halifax*, the task force stressed the need for stronger ties between the city and its region and the world. They concluded "that Halifax can be a strong and vital 'world city' at the centre of the Atlantic region if it is prepared to take charge of its own destiny and understand the urgent need for a coordinated and strong economic development force." (p. 1)

With this end in view, they made a number of interrelated recommendations: the creation of an Economic Development Unit to coordinate all development efforts of the city; the creation of five "Champion Teams to study the needs in particular sectors, such as transportation, downtown Halifax, tourism, culture, and research for development; the establishment of a Technology Exposition Centre; and finally, they recommended in effect that the city's universities "wake up," and realize their full potential for promoting economic development in the city and the region. The universities, they say "can be engines for economic growth in terms of the emerging knowledge-based economy, in terms of research and development, in terms of cultural and intellectual stimulation, and in terms of international connections and exposures. We believe this full potential for economic growth is being largely missed because the universities are somewhat insular and isolated from the economic community, from each other, and from the City." (p. 24)

It will be interesting to see how many of the task force recommendations to the city are implemented. Meanwhile, the very fact that the task force was appointed by the city council, and the fact that they wrote such a candid, strongly worded, and sensible report, are encouraging signs of change.

Conclusion

As already stated, it is hard to distinguish trends from cyclical factors. The whole industrialized world is in recession, and Halifax is no exception. What we see in Halifax is a very mixed picture, with advances here and declines there, with some improvements in the application of science and technology, some improvements in productivity and skills, but adding up to essential stagnation in quantitative terms. In the decade 1981 to 1991, the population increased from 293,011 to 336,000, just over 10 percent, less than one percent a year compounded. Since the natural rate of population growth was presumably above one percent, these figures suggest a small net emigration over the decade, hardly the mark of a booming metropolis. With unemployment running at 11.1 percent in 1993, Halifax was better off than Nova Scotia as a whole (with unemployment around 14 percent); but, once again, hardly presenting a picture of a booming metropolis.

Does Halifax Matter?

Does it matter to the rest of the Maritime provinces what happens to Halifax? Twenty years ago, I would have regarded such a question as absurd. At that time I wrote a paper for one of the advance conferences held in Moncton, New Brunswick, for the *Habitat* conference in Vancouver in 1970. In it I argued - still being much under the influence of Perroux's growth pole doctrine - that in order for the Maritimes to have a strong urban system, it was necessary to have a vigorous Metropolitan Halifax of at least 500,000 people, to serve as *the* growth pole for the whole urban hierarchy, in order to have a Saint John and Moncton of 250,000 each, and so on down the line, more or less according to the rank-size rule. Today, with the information revolution and other technological changes, I am not so sure. As Dorothy Downing's paper in this volume shows, in today's world it is possible to have high-tech industry and sophisticated services in very small towns, even villages. Being close enough to Halifax to attend occasional concerts or live theatre may be more important than the generation of spread effects from Halifax to smaller centres. Halifax's "central place" functions may be more significant than its "growth pole" role. As a central place, Halifax - or Moncton - may be big enough for most purposes. The real "growth poles" for an enterprise in Sackville may not be Halifax at all, but rather Boston, New York, Montreal, Toronto, even London or Paris. Halifax has its charms, and people may be glad to drive the relatively short distance from other Maritime cities to enjoy them. But I no longer believe that the growth of Halifax is the *sine qua non* of a prosperous Maritime urban system.

It is a good thing that it is not. There is nothing in the Halifax picture that convinces me that it will enjoy rapid growth in the near future, and much to indicate to me that it will not, especially the Paretian *residues* mentioned by Hugh MacLennan in the passages from *Barometer Rising* that begin this chapter.

Halifax: Development Pole of the Maritimes?

As the only city that could possibly be considered a "metropolis" of the Maritimes, it is natural enough that some people should consider Halifax as the "development pole" of the Maritimes as well, and to pin their hopes of healthy growth of the entire Maritime urban system on the growth of Halifax. To do so, however, is to fall prey to what I have called elsewhere, "Boudeville revisionism."[8] As formulated by François Perroux, the originator of the growth pole (*pôle de croissance*) or development pole concept, it was part of a much broader and much more complex general theory, in which growth poles are concentrations of "propulsive industries" in space, generating spread effects in the form of "fields of force" to a global "economic space." Perroux was quite emphatic that he was not talking about "banal" or geographic space, let alone about increases in income and employment in the peripheral region of some urban centre selected as a "growth pole." There is no telling *a priori* where the spread effects will be felt; they may not be in the same country as the one where the propulsive industries are located. Perroux's treatment of how growth poles are formed and function is highly abstract and theoretical. Consider this distinction between growth poles and development poles, made in his last publication on the subject: "The growth pole is a set that has the capacity to induce the growth of another set; the pole of development is a set that has the capacity to engender a dialectic of economic and social structures whose effect is to increase the complexity of the whole and to expand its multidimensional return."[9]

Obviously, such a general theory is non-operational. So Jacques Boudeville and other economists charged with practical planning simply replaced it with another theory, and one that Perroux had explicitly rejected, namely that a growth pole or development pole (they dropped the distinction between the two) is an urban centre generating spread effects to its own peripheral region. Once this happy doctrine is accepted, planners can imagine that by pushing or pulling new enterprises into urban centres of retarded regions, it is possible to reduce regional disparities, decentralize urbanization and industrialization, and accelerate national development all at once.

The only trouble with this simplified version of development pole theory is that, these days, it is nearly always wrong. When Perroux first introduced his concept in 1950, many industries were natural-resource based, and cities grew up in regions where the natural resources were found. In such urban centres, the simple theory of growth poles might have been applicable, but today the propulsive industries in major urban centres are based, not on natural resources, but on human resources. Planners found that it was indeed possible, although not easy, to lure new enterprises into urban centres selected as "growth poles." But in most cases the hoped-for and expected spread effects in the rest of the region did not appear. How much of the inputs of materials and equipment used in the Volvo plant in Halifax is purchased from plants in other parts of the Maritime provinces? The Volvo plant no doubt led to a slight increase in the population of Halifax itself, and so to an increase in demand for retail establishments, banking services, transportation, and the like, in Halifax itself. But these are not what is normally meant by "spread effects."

It is, of course, important that Halifax be *there*, in order to meet the demands of people in its peripheral region for live theatre, music, sophisticated shopping, spectator sports, night life, museums, university education, and specialized health services - just as it is important that Boston, New York, Montreal and Toronto be *there* for those affluent people who like to make occasional visits to larger cities in order to enjoy the same things at a still higher level. But it is not necessary that Halifax should *grow* in order that smaller urban centres in the Maritime hierarchy should grow. The spectacular growth of Moncton during the last decade or so has little to do with "spread effects" of investment made in Halifax. Indeed, it may well be that there are more "spread effects" *from* Moncton *to* Halifax than there are the other way around. The advantages of having a fine seaport are considerably less today than they were a century ago. Given another century, or even half a century, the advantages of its central location in the Maritimes, its bilingual entrepreneurs and its bilingual labour force, may well make Moncton, not Halifax, *the* metropolis of the Maritimes. Growth of Halifax would be good for the entire Maritime economy; but it is no longer the *sine qua non* of the growth of the Maritime economy.

As the metropolis of the Maritimes, with an economy highly dependent on global trade, government spending, and information, it was inevitable that Halifax should be particularly vulnerable to the three shocks described by the editors in their Introduction to this volume - almost as vulnerable as it was to the shock of the tremendous explosion that is the centrepiece of Hugh McClelland's novel, *Barometer Rising*. But Halifax survived even that disaster. In his chapter on Saint John, George De Benedetti suggests that its very strengths are at the same time the source of its weaknesses. With Halifax the situation is reversed; the very weaknesses of the Haligonians are at the same time the source of their strength: their refusal to be surprised whatever happens; their flexibility in responding to a fate not of their own making, and which, indeed, they do not fully understand; and their complacency and quiet confidence in their own excellence; these attributes of the Haligonians also enable them to take shocks in their stride. We can be confident that whatever happens to Halifax in the decades to come, it will still be *there*.

NOTES TO CHAPTER SEVEN

1. Voluntary Planning Association, *Transcript of Final Session of the Encounter on the Environment*, (Halifax, 1970).

2. *Our Province, Our Future, Our Choice: A Consultation Paper for a Nova Scotia Economic Strategy*, (Halifax: Voluntary Planning, March 1991), p. 1.

3. Ibid., p. 5.

4. *Report on the Public Consultation Process; Encounter on the Nova Scotia Economy*, 22 May to 30 May 1991, p. 1.

5. Ibid., p. 8.

6. The figures for 1981 and 1991 are all taken from Statistics Canada, Special data, Custom Products Services, Advisory Service, December 1993.

7. The figures for 1985 to 1993 are taken from Employment and Immigration Canada, Metropolitan Halifax Canada Employment Centre, *Local Labour Market Review*, July-December 1993.

8. Benjamin Higgins and Donald J. Savoie, *Theories of Regional Development and Their Application* (New Brunswick, N.J.: Transaction Press at Rutgers University, 1994).

9. François Perroux, "The pole of development's new place in a general theory of economic activity," Chapter 2 of *Regional Economic Development: Essays in Honour of François Perroux*, edited by Benjamin Higgins and Donald J. Savoie, (Boston: Unwin Hyman, 1988).

8

SYDNEY: THE DEVASTATION OF A NINETEENTH CENTURY INDUSTRIAL HEARTLAND

Benjamin Higgins

"Industrial Cape Breton" or Metropolitan Sydney, is an example of the most recalcitrant kind of region to be found in Canada or, indeed, anywhere in the world: a once-thriving industrial city and home to Canada's largest private employer; but whose major industries (coal and steel) are now in obvious decline, and whose high-tech industries and sophisticated services are so small in scale and so slow to expand that they cannot prevent total employment from falling and unemployment from growing. The result of this declining economy is net emigration that exceeds natural population growth, so that total population, too, is diminishing. And emigrants are mostly young and relatively well-educated.

Gordon DeWolf describes Cape Breton on the eve of World War I as "the industrial heartland of Nova Scotia, producing steel and rails for a rapidly expanding nation, held together economically by two railroads stretching four thousand miles from Atlantic to Pacific." (DeWolf, 1988, p. 254) The Dominion Steel and Coal Company was then exceeded only by the federal government in total number of employees. The future of Cape Breton and its centre of concentrated industrialization looked bright. It wasn't.

The railway boom ended in 1914, and the steel plants suffered. The Sydney Mines steel plant closed, and coal production averaged only 3.9 million long tons per year between the wars, compared to a peak of 5.5 million in 1915. John Mellor describes the conditions as of 1925: "Time was running out. Thousands of men, women, and children were now in the last stages of malnutrition and sickness. Scores of little children had already succumbed, as witnessed by the pathetic daily processions of miners' families carrying white coffins on their shoulders." (Mellor, 1983, p. 289) For the next forty years DOSCO struggled to keep going, but in 1965 it announced that it was closing its mines, threatening the miners with the loss of 6,500 jobs.

What had happened, and whose fault was it? In retrospect, we can see the decline of the Cape Breton and Sydney economies as the fault of no one, or as the fault of the entire Cape Breton and Sydney society, depending on how you want to look at it. Elsewhere, I have described the Cape Breton economy as being "cursed with rich natural resources." (Higgins, 1993, pp. 133-134) I go on to explain:

In the period since World War II, Canadian development has been hampered by the heritage of rich natural resources and a vast hinterland. Countries without those things, like Singapore, Hong Kong, South Korea, Taiwan, Japan, Switzerland and Norway, Finland and Sweden have no choice but to follow the human-resource route to development, making economic and social progress on the basis of knowledge-intensive enterprises. Countries and regions choosing the natural-resource route, encouraging resource-intensive "smokestack industries," tend to get stuck on that muddy road. The quantum leap to development based on knowledge, information, and science is delayed far too long, and the country or region falls farther and farther behind the ones who have already made that leap. Within Canada, no region has been more hampered by addiction to its "rich natural resources," and a hinterland that was always vast relative to its population, than Cape Breton.

From 1915 to the present day, Cape Breton and its primate city, Sydney, have struggled to keep steel and coal alive, instead of making the difficult but necessary "quantum leap" from natural-resource-based development to human-resource-based development. In that endeavour they have been aided and abetted by both the federal and the provincial governments; probably no region of comparable size has received more technical and capital assistance than Cape Breton, during the period since 1965. Not only have these efforts failed to maintain the coal and steel industries at anything like their former scale, but they have replicated the former pattern of Cape Breton development. Even during its period of prosperity, most of the capital, entrepreneurship, and management has come from outside the Island; Cape Breton has provided only the natural resources and the labour; and the traditional industries that these efforts were designed to maintain did not train their workers in skills that were transferable.

Still, by world standards, Cape Breton and Sydney are hardly poverty-stricken. In 1987 Cape Breton had a per capita income ahead of all but the twelve richest industrialized countries - exceeding the average incomes of the United Kingdom, the Netherlands, Austria and Belgium. But unemployment (almost 30 percent) is high and young people are leaving. Disparities in household income are excessive. Business stagnation and a lack of opportunities, together with relatively low standards of public services and amenities, lead to "a certain drabness of everyday life that often accompanies *relatively* low incomes." (Higgins, 1993, p. 130) A society that generates 30 percent unemployment, and concentrates much of it in its youth, will, as Adam Smith said, be "melancholy," even if average incomes are quite respectable. And, as is well known, economic decay can easily become cumulative. There are certain thresholds of population where, successively, certain kinds of economic activity tend to disappear from any region. Moreover, those that disappear tend to be the ones that generate relatively high incomes, so that *per capita* incomes tend to fall for the region as a whole, even as total population shrinks. Suppose that Cape Breton's population fell to the few tens of thousands who could be supported by natural resource-based industry alone: farming, fishing, forestry and mining; plus a few people making a living by selling Cape Breton's magnificent scenery to tourists; and the services needed to support these. In that case, the University College of Cape Breton might disappear, for lack of the quantity and quality of population to support such an institution. That would be the ultimate disaster for Cape Breton.

Yet, the law of cumulative causation can work both ways. If in the next few years enough high-tech industries and sophisticated services are created in Cape Breton to increase employment and to hold on the Island its younger and more educated people, a process of cumulative expansion may set in. Cape Breton today is poised on a very sharp knife-edge; it could go either way. To assure cumulative expansion rather than cumulative decline, astute policy will be needed at all three levels of government.

Before dealing with the future, however, let us review briefly the natural resource-based development of the past that brought Cape Breton, and Metro Sydney, to its present predicament.

Coal

Coal mining on individual leases began about 1800. In 1826 George IV granted the coal mines of Nova Scotia to his brother, the Duke of York, apparently to help him meet his debts to his jeweller. The following year the duke leased the mines and minerals of Nova Scotia to a British consortium, the General Mining Association (GMA), for 60 years. Both the Nova Scotia government and Nova Scotia private interests were outraged by the arrangement of the Duke of York's ownership and the GMA's monopoly of mining of Nova Scotia coal, and in 1854 the duke's heirs gave up their claims to the mines in return for a substantial payment. The GMA retained rights in Cape Breton, but abandoned claims elsewhere in Nova Scotia. Other companies too began mining in Cape Breton, many of them American. This fact, together with the Reciprocity Treaty of 1854, resulted in substantial increases in exports to the Untied States. The Cape Breton coal industry as a whole expanded rapidly.

Gordon DeWolf writes: "By 1915, nearly 12.5 thousand miners were employed. Towns in Cape Breton, such as North Sydney and Sydney Mines on the north side of Sydney Harbour and Glace Bay, New Waterford and Dominion on the south side of the Harbour took on all the characteristics of company towns." (DeWolf 1988, p. 254) But in the story of the first century of Cape Breton's major industry, we see something else as well. From the very beginning middle-to-large scale development depended on capital, entrepreneurship, technology, and even management from outside the region. The decisions that determined the fate of the great majority of native Cape Bretoners were not made by themselves or even by other Cape Bretoners, but by people in Halifax, other metropolitan centres of Canada, Great Britain and the United States. Not only have Cape Bretoners been denied access to entrepreneurial and managerial skills; they have not even had the opportunity to acquire a wide range of technical skills. Least of all have they been given the opportunity to learn *transferable* skills.

Steel

An American entrepreneur named H.M. Whitney was interested in Cape Breton coal, and in 1893 persuaded the Nova Scotia government that it could be most efficiently exploited by a single large company. His Dominion Coal Company was chartered in that same year, and set about expanding Cape Breton coal production for export to Boston and central Canada. Recognizing the limitations of these markets, he decided to establish a steel industry within the region, using Newfoundland iron. The Nova Scotia Steel Company was established in 1895 with this objective in view, and four years later the Dominion Iron and Steel Company with Whitney as president. In 1913 a new Dominion Coal Company was formed by amalgamating eight companies on the south side of Sydney Harbour, while the Nova Scotia Steel and Coal Company (Scotia) was established on the north side. The steel companies relied heavily on rails for their markets, and profited from the railway construction boom. But this boom ended in 1914. The steel mill at Sydney Mines closed, and coal production fell accordingly. Both Scotia and DOMCO were in trouble, and in 1920 they were taken over by a British holding company, the British Empire Steel Corporation (BESCO). Ten years later this company was reorganized as the Dominion Steel and Coal Corporation (DOSCO).

It is virtually impossible to exaggerate the importance of such companies within an economy and society as small as Cape Breton's. The image of Cape Breton as a coal and steel region, and little else, was transformed into a belief that Cape Breton's future, as well, depended on these industries to the virtual exclusion of all else, a belief that solidified into a conviction as durable and impenetrable as steel itself.

The Decline of the Industrial Heartland

Ideally, the transition to a human-resources-and-knowledge pattern of development would have started in Cape Breton soon after its natural-resources-and-knowhow economy began to decline, on the eve of World War I. This decline was followed by unemployment, hardship, and unrest among the miners. The next three decades brought little improvement. Coal and steel remained Cape Breton's principal employers, accounting together for over 20 percent of total employment; but both industries were in trouble, and Cape Breton was no longer Nova Scotia's industrial heartland. The announcement in 1965 that the Dominion Steel and Coal Company would close its mines, threw both the federal and provincial governments into shock. The federal government set up a royal commission, with Dr. J.K. Donald as chairman. The commission recommended phasing out the coal mines, eliminating them altogether by 1981, and creating alternative employment in new industries. The commission proposed setting up two crown corporations, one for each of these rather different tasks. Instead, a single corporation was established, the Cape Breton Development Corporation (DEVCO) with two divisions.

DEVCO: The Cape Breton Economy in Intensive Care - or in a Nursing Home?

DEVCO came to epitomize the last gasps in the struggle to maintain the Cape Breton economy by keeping the steel and coal industries going. But it also marked the beginning of efforts to develop the region by generating employment outside these industries, especially in sophisticated services and in smaller-scale, higher-tech, manufacturing enterprises. The corporation's task was greatly complicated by DOSCO's announcement of the closure of their Sydney Steel plant, the second biggest employer in the region, after the coal fields themselves. The federal government drew the line at helping the steel industry too. The Nova Scotia government took it over, but on a provisional basis, that ensured a state of semi-permanent uncertainty for almost three decades.

In the early years the Industrial Development Division (IDD) pursued the then-fashionable policy of providing incentives to lure "footloose industries" to the region. Tom Kent, President of DEVCO from 1971 to 1977, has little praise for these efforts. "In practice," he says, "the looseness was chiefly in the financial arrangements and, despite the buoyancy at that time in the national economy, most of the attracted enterprises quickly became expensive failures." (Kent, 1988, p. 87) For the coal mines themselves, the basic strategy was to phase them out. Systematic reduction of output and employment in the coal mines may have been less disruptive than sudden closure would have been; but it was nonetheless, extremely demoralizing.

Kent had a different idea: rather than phase out the coal industry, modernize it. His 1972 plan for DEVCO still entailed cutting the work force in the mines by 40 percent or more, but it did call for raising the value of production, both by improving the quality of the coal produced and by modernizing mining techniques. This expansion would be justified by the installation of a coal-fired Nova Scotia Power Corporation plant at Lingan, and by upgrading the Sydney Steel plant. The first part of this scheme - the power plant and modernized coal production - went well. The second part - steel - did not. In large measure, Kent suggests, DEVCO's hopes for a rejuvenated steel industry were blasted because DEVCO had no control over the steel industry, and because neither the Nova Scotia nor the federal government moved quickly or imaginatively enough to establish a modern steel plant before it became unprofitable to do so.

DEVCO did have some successes in smaller-scale, less capital-intensive, and more attuned-to-the-present enterprises. One of these was in tourism, and especially the "bed and breakfast" tourist homes. Another was fish farming, with results that Kent describes as "mixed." Salmon farming was a commercial success, but trout farming ran into problems of disease, poaching, and marketing, and oyster farms did not justify DEVCO's investment.

In appraising DEVCO's performance as a whole, Tom Kent says:

> For only a brief period in the mid-seventies was there any net improvement in the Cape Breton economy. Predominantly, DEVCO has been running hard in order that Cape Breton should not slip further back.

Given its terms of reference, its organization, and its historical setting, there was no way that DEVCO could escape the concern for natural-resource-based development. Inevitably, most of the time and energy of its staff were directed towards coal, and towards steel and electric power as saviours of the coal industry. After that they did what they could (and tried some things they could not) in the fields of fishing, forestry, and farming. DEVCO, in short, was foredoomed to failure.

The Strait of Canso

During the 1970s and early 1980s efforts were also made to industrialize the Strait of Canso, with the deepwater harbour at Port Hawkesbury as the key factor. In the early years of the DREE operation (1968-1972), infrastructure was provided in the Strait of Canso area under the Special Areas program. Similar efforts were made under a Strait of Canso Industrial Development Agreement of 1974, and a Strait of Canso Industrial Development Agency was set up to promote industrial development. These efforts had some results, but few of them were lasting. Most successful was Stora Industries Limited, a Swedish-owned pulp and paper mill employing 1,000 people in the mill and another 1,000 in the forests. A generating station built by the Nova Scotia Power Corporation, originally oil-fired and later converted to coal, is still operating. The heavy water plant constructed by Canadian General Electric, and later taken over by Atomic Energy Canada, closed in 1985. (A similar plant in Glace Bay suffered the same fate.) A shipyard was expanded under the program but has also gone out of operation since. The core of the Canso development was to have been a petro-chemical complex, but it never came into existence.

For four centuries development of Cape Breton was based upon exploitation of natural resources, and for almost two of these centuries this development has centred around coal and steel. Inevitably, the creation of a coal-and-steel economy has created a coal-and-steel society as well. The very success of this economy and this society from 1800 to World War I implanted many Paretian *residues* in the inhabitants of the Island. Since its relative prosperity came mainly from coal and steel, it is only natural for many people to have come to think of prosperity based on these industries as a natural state of affairs in Cape Breton, for the future as well as the past, and to be fearful of the uncertainties attached to untried alternative routes to a high standard of living. Such a climate has not been one to nurture innovative entrepreneurship. If new sets of attitudes and values are to be inculcated, and new products and technologies introduced, the region must have institutions with the capacity to nurture the necessary socio-cultural transformation in the Cape Breton society as a whole, not just among a few entrepreneurs.

Enterprise Cape Breton (ECB) and Enterprise Cape Breton Corporation (ECBC)

In 1987 the Industrial Development Division of DEVCO was separated from the coal mining operations, and became an autonomous federal crown corporation called the Enterprise Cape Breton Corporation. Its mandate was to promote industrial development *other than* coal and steel, in Cape Breton and the portion of mainland Nova Scotia - across the causeway from Port Hawkesbury, around the town of Mulgrave. Enterprise Cape Breton was established in 1985, by the federal government, with an almost identical mandate: "to develop a modern, diversified, resilient economy in the Strait of Canso area." In 1987 ECB was transferred to the newly-created Atlantic Canada Opportunities Agency (ACOA), becoming in effect an agency of ACOA for its region of responsibility. ECB and ECBC worked closely together - they even occupied adjacent floors of the same office building in downtown Sydney. But it obviously didn't require two agencies to do one job. In 1992 both agencies were scrapped and their personnel joined in the Sydney office of ACOA, in the same building, and doing essentially the same job that the two agencies had done together before.

The three agencies have had a mixed record. A recession in Nova Scotia, combined with Cape Breton's own unfavourable trends, added up to depression in Cape Breton. Hence, a good many of the new enterprises supported by them failed. There were, however, some successes, in a wide variety of fields.

Perhaps their most useful contribution to Cape Breton development, however, was their support of UCCB and a major planning exercise designed to produce an integrated development plan for the region.

Where is Sydney headed? In trying to answer this question, we shall use more or less the same devices that we used for Halifax, except that in the Sydney case, we do not have "snapshots" provided by two "Encounters," twenty years apart. We first look at Census data for 1981 and 1991, to get a picture of trends during that decade. (Statistics Canada, December 1993) Then to get a picture of more recent trends, we examine two publications of the Metro Halifax Canada Employment Center (CEC): the *Area Profile* of March 1994, and the *Industry Profile: Manufacturing* of April 1994. We then endeavour to interpret these data. Finally, as indications of the dynamics of the Cape Breton society, we look at two promising and distinctly Cape Breton institutions, New Dawn and the University College of Cape Breton - and make up our mind.

Sydney: Signs of Decay

In contrast to the relative stagnation of Halifax, Sydney shows clear signs of decline. Real employment income rose only 6.7 percent in the entire decade 1981-1991. In 1991 per capita incomes were slightly below the average for Atlantic Canada, and 79.6 percent of the Canadian average. Both the population and the labour force declined. Only two sectors had incomes above the Canadian average: Primary production (mostly coal - 120.45 percent) and education (103.8 percent). The first of these was declining in terms of share of total employment and the second was stagnant. As in Halifax, the lowest incomes were earned in the hotels and restaurants sector, which showed some expansion in share of total employment. Business and other services, which had the second lowest income, also slightly increased its share of total employment. Much the biggest decline in share of total employment came in manufacturing, from 14.79 to 8.84 percent.

All sectors showed a decline in the size of the labour force except hotels and restaurants (+20.53 percent), public administration, (+16.96 percent) and business and other services, which had negligible increase of 0.12 percent. Again, the biggest loss of labour force was in manufacturing, 42.69 percent, followed by transportation with a loss of 22.3 percent. Neither of these sectors, however, have particularly high incomes. The highest incomes were earned in the education sector ($29,708 in 1991), followed by primary production ($24,486), transportation ($24,417) and finance, insurance, and real estate ($23,142). All these sectors lost labour force between 1981 and 1991. The trade sector was virtually stagnant.

It is interesting to note that the overall loss of 4.08 percent of labour force was made up of a loss of 13.5 percent of males and a gain of 10.5 percent of females. The importance of the trade and finance, insurance, and real estate sectors in total employment would help to explain this phenomenon, those being sectors that employ large numbers of females.

More Recent Trends

More recent data show no reversal of these discouraging trends; if anything, they show a further worsening of the economic situation in Metro Sydney, and for Cape Breton in general. The unemployment rate for the Island increased from 21.5 percent in 1992 to 25.7 percent in 1993. Unemployment was particularly high among young people aged 15 to 24. It reached an average level of 41.5 percent in 1993. As a consequence the labour force participation rate has fallen to 50.2 percent, composed of 56.6 percent for males and 44.0 percent for females. These rates are substantially below those for Nova Scotia as a whole: 67 percent for males, 52.2 percent for females, average 59.8 percent.

Employment is heavily concentrated in three sectors, which together account for about two thirds of the total. As in Halifax, much the biggest sector is community, business, and personal services, with 42.1 percent of total employment; followed by trade with 18 percent and transportation, communication and other utilities with about 8.1 percent. As may be seen from table 1, the only sector in which employment increased from 1990 to 1993 was Community, Business, and Personal Services (CBPS), and that only by 0.5 percent. Much the biggest decline took place in "other primary," consisting of fishing, forestry, and mining. Most of this decline was in mining. The second biggest drop was in construction, although manufacturing was close behind. The fall in employment in the trade sector is attributed mainly to the recession, although the decline in population is a contributing factor. According to the March 1994 *Area Profile* of the Canada Employment Centre's Metro Sydney office, "Several nationally run retail chain stores and small locally-owned businesses have had to close their doors this past year." (p. 9) With regard to construction, the *Area Profile* states, "the construction industry on Cape Breton Island has suffered recently and the Industrial Cape Breton Area is no exception. The industry will likely face further decreases in employment when the Cape Breton Regional Hospital is completed early in 1994. Although the Scotia Synfuels project remains a topic of discussion, tangible projects in the planning stage fall within the small to medium range." (p. 9)

DEVCO remains the biggest single employer in the Sydney area, although it is operating only two mines, the Phalen colliery, which began operations in 1987, and the Prince mine. These mines employ about 2,300 people and have been producing about four million tonnes a year, which is expected to fall to 3.4 million tonnes in 1993-94. About sixty percent of this production goes to the Nova Scotia Power Corporation on contract, and much of the rest to Brazil, Denmark, and Mexico.

Table 1

Employment by Industrial Sector
Economic Region 210
Cape Breton Island
(3 Month Moving Average Estimates)

Industries	1990	1991	1992	1993	Actual Change 1990-93	% Change 1990-93
Other primary*	6,300	6,400	4,600	3,400	-2,900	-46.0
Manufacturing	4,500	3,800	3,200	3,300	-1,200	-26.7
Construction	3,200	2,800	3,600	2,300	-900	-28.1
Transportation, Communication, Utilities	4,600	4,200	4,900	3,700	-900	-19.6
Retail & Wholesale Trade	10,000	9,500	9,600	8,600	-1,400	-14.0
Finance, Insurance, and Real Estate	-	-	-	-	-	-
Community, Personal, Business Services	19,000	17,400	17,700	19,100	+100	+0.5
Public Administration	3,600	4,400	3,100	3,500	-100	-2.8
Total	53,100	50,100	48,700	45,400	-7,700	-14.5

Source: Sydney Metro CEC *Area Profile*, March 1994.

* excludes agriculture

Figure 1

Employment by Industry Sector
Cape Breton Island 1991-1993
(3 Month Moving Average)

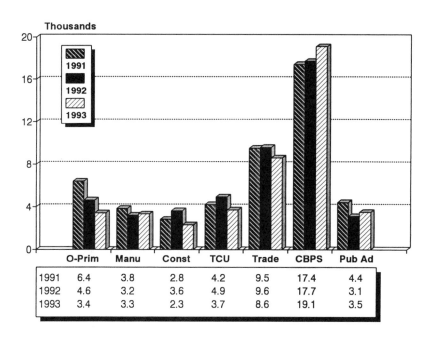

	O-Prim	Manu	Const	TCU	Trade	CBPS	Pub Ad
1991	6.4	3.8	2.8	4.2	9.5	17.4	4.4
1992	4.6	3.2	3.6	4.9	9.6	17.7	3.1
1993	3.4	3.3	2.3	3.7	8.6	19.1	3.5

Legend:

O-Prim	-	*Other primary*	*Manu* -	*Manufacturing*
Const	-	*Construction*	*Trade* -	*Wholesale and Retail Trade*
TCU	-	*Transportation, Communication and Utilities*	*CBPS* -	*Community, Business & Personal Services*
Pub Ad	-	*Public administration*		

Source: Statistics Canada.

Regarding fishing, the *Area Profile* says:

> Much of the fishing industry collapsed in 1993 as cod quotas were reduced or suspended province-wide to protect Atlantic Canada groundfish stock. Compounding this problem is the ripple effect in the fish-processing sector. A 190 million dollar federal aid package is assisting unemployed fishery workers. (p. 7)

In their discussion of manufacturing, the Sydney Employment Centre returns to this point. Fish-processing in the area, they say "has been devastated by the recent closure of the cod fishery." National Sea Products, described as an "industry giant," have been forced to close their plants at North Sydney and Louisbourg, eliminating approximately 700 jobs in the Sydney Metro area.

SYSCO's work force has declined further in the past two years, but is expected to stabilize at about 775 persons. The steel company has recently reached an agreement to supply rails to Mimmetals of China, one of the world's biggest trading companies, which purchases for China's rapidly growing railway system. The Metro Sydney CEC reports that while the sub-sector consisting of manufacturing transportation equipment has declined in recent years, a hopeful sign is the creation of two new high-tech firms. Cape Breton Precision Components, a subsidiary of Magna International Inc., manufactures automobile parts. The I.M.P. Group has a contract with Spar Aerospace to provide housings for space station equipment. A small but promising industry is the production of plastics. Cape Breton Plastic was started in 1989 to produce plastic bottles for beverages, but has recently created Trans Atlantic Preforms, which is exporting its products to the rest of Canada and to the world market. Copol International is producing polypropylene film for use in packaging. Micronav is manufacturing microwave landing systems equipment for airports in Canada and overseas. The company has been awarded a four-and-a-half year, $83 million contract, by the federal government.

Population

The CEC *Area Profile* also provides figures of population growth and decline, which are a good indicator of the general economic and social health of the Metro Sydney region. Total population increased from 1941 to 1961, from 82,079 to 90,590. It fell to 80,323 in 1981, 76,191 in 1986, and 72,388 in 1991. Moreover, the age groups below 30 all experienced declines between 1986 and 1991, the most severe declines occurring in the age groups between 15 and 29. Lack of employment opportunities are certainly part of the explanation of this emigration of young people.

Appraisal

In interpreting these figures, we must try to answer two questions, which are closely related to each other: which of the changes represent long run trends, and which reflect the recession or other temporary factors? and which ones are peculiar to Cape Breton, and which ones are common to all regions of Nova Scotia, the Maritimes, or Canada as a whole? These are difficult questions, and answering them requires gazing into a reliable crystal ball; but something can be said.

First of all, the decline in manufacturing employment in recent years has been felt all over North America, and is likely to continue. It reflects a process of general structural change in industrialized countries. However, the decline in steel production, and the related fall in employment in coal mining, are peculiar to Cape Breton. They are the product of long run trends, not of temporary recession. The collapse of the fish-processing industry of course affects other Maritime regions than Cape Breton, but there is little comfort in that fact, and it is also a trend that is unlikely to be reversed in the near future. The drop in employment in public administration is partly a result of widespread government fiscal difficulties, but also of a widespread disappointment in, and distaste for "Big Government," which is also unlikely to disappear in the near future. Rationalization can be expected to continue in the transportation, communication and utilities sector. Trade, and finance, insurance, and real estate can be expected to pick up with recovery from the recession. Community, business, and personal services will continue to dominate the employment scene.

Such sectors as business services and finance, insurance, and real estate can grow if there are new businesses to serve, or if such services can be exported from the Island. Cape Breton is not favourably located geographically for the export of services, but if highly sophisticated and highly specialized services can be developed it may be possible. It is worth a try.

There is little hope for today's large employers in manufacturing. Neither seafood nor steel looks promising. However, there are some promising new ventures in relatively small and very high-tech manufacturing. The "base-industry-export multiplier" theory has its limitations, as I have explained elsewhere. (Higgins and Savoie, 1994) It is not really a *general* theory of regional development. But there can be no doubt that a regional economy as small as Cape Breton must develop a number of competitive export industries if it is to prosper. Cape Breton's traditional natural-resource-based industries seem to have passed their peak of production and employment. Future growth of Sydney and Cape Breton therefore will depend on human-resource-based enterprises.

There are some hopeful signs. As Dorothy Downing's chapter in this volume shows, throughout the Maritime provinces there is a surge of indigenous entrepreneurship in relatively small towns, creating new high-tech manufacturing and sophisticated services; and a new willingness - even eagerness - for "hotshot" entrepreneurs to settle in small towns. Metro Sydney is fortunate in having within it the University College of Cape Breton, which not only provides scientific, technical, and engineering skills, but has demonstrated considerable entrepreneurial and managerial talent as well. The trick is to identify "niches" which Cape Breton enterprises can fill. In this regard, Donald J. Savoie writes:

> . . . the University College of Cape Breton's CADCAM (computer assisted design, computer assisted manufacturing) development and training capacity, in combination with the Cape Breton Mould and Magna facilities could become such a niche. It could be used not only to develop marketable export products but also as an attraction in aggressively selling Cape Breton as a desirable location for some specifically targeted machine tool and precision machinery companies. Similar niches could be developed around the electronics and navigation capacity of Micronav, and fibreglass boats, etc. The basis of these groupings is not just similarities in hardware and physical facilities but also common technical skills and knowledge. There are opportunities for technical specialties which would make the Island attractive for industrial development. However, the capability to develop, design and sell products or services whose market position is dependent on a superior technical environment is crucial. (Savoie, 1990, p. 58)

Doing Well by Doing Good: New Dawn

New Dawn Enterprises Ltd. of Sydney is a unique organization that manages to make an overall profit by providing public services through private enterprise. It was started in 1975 by two members of the University College of Cape Breton faculty, who received small federal government grants to carry out projects during the summer months. Their main undertaking during that first summer was to renovate uninhabitable buildings through make-work projects, and rent them at low rents. Their experience taught them they would need to explain to the construction industry that they were not competing against them for the same dollars. In fact, they persuaded representatives of some of the best construction companies to become members of their board, and convinced lawyers and other professionals to give their time free of charge as a service to the community. In 1992 there were eleven members of the board, four from UCCB, four from the public service, and three from the private sector. They engaged a staff of sixteen, all drawn from the private sector. Housing is still one of New Dawn Enterprises' main activities, and is handled by a subsidiary, the Cape Breton Association for Housing Development. Other subsidiaries are: Cape Care Services Ltd.; Highland Resources Ltd.; New Day Ventures Ltd.; and Volunteer Resources Ltd. New Dawn also operates a guest home for older people and the Sydney Senior Care - Home Living Ltd.

In his annual report for 1992, the chairman of the board stated:

> When New Dawn was first introduced to the Cape Breton community in the mid-seventies as an example of how to organize a business venture other than in the traditional private-sector way there was a fair amount of interest and excitement but also doubt and scepticism that volunteers could stand the gaff. It took patience and courage and vision on the part of many committed volunteers to prove that a community development corporation could work in Cape Breton and by the mid-eighties New Dawn was established as a viable public business with potential for growth.

He also said:

> For the year 1992, New Dawn had as its primary objective to consolidate the several business initiatives it had undertaken over the past few years. Pine Tree Park, Cape Care and Home Living each required a great deal of attention to bring them through the early stages of their growth and development. By focusing the energies of the New Dawn staff on these new and rapidly developing companies considerable success was achieved in that each of these companies more than met their financial objectives for 1992.

New Dawn is performing an entrepreneurial function. As the executive director put it in his 1992 report: ". . . Every business and social activity operated by New Dawn was not acquired but rather was created." Moreover, even though New Dawn was established to assist underprivileged groups, and depends mainly on volunteers, in 1992 it made an overall profit of just under $211,000 on a total revenue of $3.6 million. This profit was greater than expected. Housing is both its major and most profitable enterprise. Its Pine Tree Park made an operating profit of $67,000, the Cape Breton Association for Housing Development a profit of $37,438 and its guest house a profit on operations of $23,974, from which it made a mortgage payment of $17,974. By the end of 1993, the Housing Association expected to be operating nearly 300 units, providing low rental accommodation for the elderly. New Day Venture is relatively new, and is primarily concerned with repair, maintenance, and upgrading of housing units. In 1992, it spent more than $900,000 for such purposes. In 1992, New Dawn also began work on a new guest home, the old one having become irreparable. This project will cost $1.38 million.

The Voluntary Resource Center coordinates such project as Meals on Wheels for Senior Citizens, Each-One-Teach-One (an adult literacy program), and child day-care. It is managed by UCCB faculty members and employs more than 200 volunteers. Cape Care Services provides such services as health, personal care and housekeeping. During 1992, it surpassed its projected growth and now serves 200 clients. Senior Care-Home Living employs 10 care-givers and houses 30 seniors. This project actually makes a small profit.

But New Dawn is doing more than making profits out of low-rental housing. It is trying, at least, to build communities. They involve their tenants in the management and maintenance of their homes, and in planning care and activities suitable for senior citizens. For example, they took over from the armed forces a radar base that was being abandoned, with a swimming pool and gymnasium as well as housing. They remodelled it, provided services, organized activities, and created a new community of senior citizens. In another case there was a low-income community that was badly in need of a dentist. It was not an area that would be attractive to an established dentist, and a young person, fresh out of dental school, probably would not have the capital to obtain and equip a dentist's office. So New Dawn built and equipped a dentist's office, offered it at a modest rent, and thus encouraged a dentist to move into the area. It should also be said that New Dawn is a non-profit organization, in the sense that any profits they make are ploughed back into the activities of the company.

New Dawn Enterprises illustrates the strong sense of community that prevails in Cape Breton. It also demonstrates the latent entrepreneurship with which Cape Breton is blessed. It is, of course, very small in comparison to such dinosaurs as DEVCO and SYSCO. But if enough small projects emerge to harness the energies and talents of the people of Cape Breton - and if the people of Cape Breton understand fully that the future of the Island lies in its human resources rather than its natural resources - the Cape Breton economy, and the Cape Breton society, may finally have reached a turning point.

The University College of Cape Breton

Cape Breton's University College is undoubtedly the most valuable asset it has for future economic and social development. Born barely two decades ago, as a result of the union of the Sydney branch of St. Francis Xavier University and the Nova Scotia Eastern Institute of Technology, it is already playing a major role. It is not only training managers, scientists, engineers, technicians and other professionals needed for development but is also performing an entrepreneurial function by establishing high-tech enterprises. It also provides a centre of culture that helps make Sydney an attractive place for entrepreneurs to settle.

As I have said elsewhere, no doubt this very youthfulness accounts for some of the vitality, verve, dynamism, flexibility and inventiveness that characterize the UCCB story to date. The marriage of a liberal arts college with a community college focused on technology might have been expected to be barren and to end in early divorce. Instead, it has been extraordinarily durable and fruitful. One might distill the essence of UCCB by saying that it has its head in the clouds, where it belongs; but its feet are firmly planted on the ground where they belong. In short, UCCB provides a unique blend of pragmatism and vision. (Higgins, 1993, p. 151)

Its calendar states its specific objectives:

1.   To educate men and women by developing the ability to think clearly and the readiness to challenge and to criticize, and by encouraging initiative and responsibility, regular and systematic application to work, and orderly habits of mind and conduct;

2.   To relate its programs to the particular needs of the community and to relate Cape Breton's particular needs and attributes to the wider national and international community;

3.   To enhance the quality of life for its students and the wider community through art, literature, music, theatre, etc.;

4.   To preserve, enhance and represent what is best in the cultural heritage of Cape Breton;

5.   In all that it does, to provide perceptive, creative and responsible leadership to the community.

Many academic institutions make lofty statements about their ideals. A lofty few don't even need to do so. The remarkable thing about UCCB - raw young institution that it is - is that this statement of objectives accurately describes what it actually does.

Education and Training

Let us look first at what the University College is doing in the field which people most generally associate with universities and colleges: higher-level education and training. Its program includes the following degrees and diplomas:

> A general B.A. in three years; a four-year B.A. (Major) with concentration in one or more fields; a B.A. in Community Studies; a Bachelor of Business Administration. (an interesting feature of this program is that it provides an option for internships, permitting the degree to be completed while gaining on-the-job experience); a joint B.A. in Community Studies and a Bachelor of Business Administration; a four-year Bachelor of Science (specializations are available in Biology, Mathematics and Psychology); a Bachelor of Technology (Environmental Studies), the first of its kind in the Atlantic provinces.

In addition to these university degrees, UCCB offers a diploma in Engineering with two years of study, leading to a Bachelor of Engineering at the Technical University of Nova Scotia after three more years study. A similar transfer program is available in Computer Science. In addition to these, diplomas in Applied Arts and Technologies are available in a wide range of Business and Engineering subjects, from fields like accounting, marketing, management and data processing to chemical, power, communications, environmental, mechanical, mineral and construction engineering. Finally, within the Cooperative Education Program, there are nine technology fields which alternate three four-month work placements with four-month periods of study.

Apart from these degree and diploma programs, UCCB provides a wide variety of non-credit courses through its Extension and Community Affairs division, some of them broadcast by satellite. The aim of the division is quite explicitly economic and social development. The University College has also been engaged in international cooperation projects, such as training Indonesians for the coal industry, technical training for Nigerian and Libyan students, and sending instructors to countries in Africa, the Caribbean, and South America.

There are many illustrations of the University's capacity to combine respect for solid academic tradition with innovation. For example, in the Arts program there are standard courses in drawing, painting, and history of art. But there are also courses in Gaelic; Celtic language, literature, history, and music; folklore and vernacular architecture. The history department offers courses in American and European history, but also in Mi'Kmaq history, Atlantic colonial history, and - rare enough in Canadian universities - in Latin American history. The Philosophy department gives courses in Business Ethics and Moral Dilemmas in Business. The Division of Development Studies and Applied Arts has a course in Applied Research involving group projects in "research (which) is expected to have relevance to particular problems and issues of the local community or region;" and another on Community Volunteer Work which requires students to spend 160 hours in actual social work during the year, as well as "general background research and reading."

Nor is recreation and entertainment neglected, either for the faculty and students or for the community at large. In the field of sport, one of UCCB's most notable achievements was to sponsor and to serve as host for the Sixth Canada Winter Games in 1987. UCCB housed almost 3,000 athletes for the games, and the Canada Games complex which resulted from these efforts have made the University a leading force in sport for the entire region. The UCCB Art Gallery was the first on the Island, and remains the only full-time gallery. Its permanent collection is one of the finest in Nova Scotia, and in its fourteen year life it has displayed over two dozen special exhibitions. Since the mid-1960s the UCCB Dramagroup has presented a Festival of Plays each year, from February to May. Plays by leading playwrights are staged by UCCB students, members of the Play Production Course, and community organizations.

Continuing Education

Finally, under the heading of training and education, mention must be made of UCCB's program of continuing education. Most departments of extension or continuing education endeavour to do two things: provide courses outside of working hours for people who wish to pursue degrees while keeping their jobs; and provide non-credit courses for people who enjoy learning and wish to keep up with the advance of knowledge. UCCB's Department of Continuing Education does both of these things, but it does more. It also provides directly applicable training for people actively engaged in industry, commerce, finance, and the professions.

Over 3,500 students enroll in non-degree continuing education programs. It is interesting to note that the program attracting much the largest number of students was the concert series, with nearly 1,000 persons enrolled.

Research

Recognizing that research is a major function of any university, and conscious of the fact that even instruction can be seriously damaged if the faculty is not actively engaged in research, UCCB has compensated for the absence (thus far) of programs of postgraduate training by establishing a range of very active research institutes and centres which is remarkable for so small an institution. Moreover, all of them have an impact, direct or indirect, on the economic and social development of the region.

The Bras d'Or Institute

Most directly involved in development activities is the Bras d'Or Institute, which now has 22 years of experience in that field, pursuing its "goal of stimulating research, development, and enquiry relevant to Cape Breton Island." The Institute has interpreted its mandate in highly pragmatic terms. A mere list of the development projects undertaken by the Institute covers ten pages. Here, a few examples must suffice to give some sense of the Institute's highly varied but carefully managed activities.

- The "Growing for the 80s program" which covers such topics as greenhouse management and growing fruit trees, is presently in it's tenth year. Organizations such as the "Cape Breton Fruit Tree Association" and the "Cape Breton Part-Time Farmers Association" were formed as a direct result of this successful program. The "Cape Breton Fruit Tree Association" has established an expanding fruit-growing industry for Cape Breton.

- The "Mira Community Pasture Cooperative" was developed in response to recommendations by the Institute. The group is involved in such activities as barn construction and the hosting of young people under the Katimavik program.

- Agra-Tel: an agricultural information system opened in March of 1984 to provide a telephone-accessed library for Cape Breton.

- The Institute became involved in the building of an inshore fishing boat in 1978-79, to be used to carry out exploration of naval equipment and techniques. The vessel was launched in early autumn 1980.

- The Institute entered into a joint research project with the Cape Breton District Office of Lands and Forests and Acadia University in 1980-81 to evaluate the effects of woodlot management techniques on songbird and small animal populations.

- Professional assistance was provided in 1980-81 to the Mira Community Pasture Cooperative to raise the level of organic matter in their pasture soil, and to New Dawn Enterprises Ltd. for implementing their farm-woodlot project.

- A 1983-84 saw the inauguration of an education program for the fire service. A ten-week course in *basic firefighting* was offered.

The Tompkins Institute for Human Values and Technology

The aim of the Tompkins Institute might be described as "development with a human face." Established in 1974, "the Institute's general objective is to investigate the socio-ethical context of technological change." In slightly more detail, the Institute describes its activities in these terms:

> Within the University College of Cape Breton, the Tompkins Institute sponsors efforts towards programme innovation and is involved with studies on how institutions of higher learning can best respond to technological and societal change. In addition, the Institute acts as an intellectual animator for both the University College and the local community at large.

Once again, a list of the Institute's activities since 1977 covers several pages, which cannot be reproduced here.

The Centre for International Studies

The deep concern of UCCB for Cape Breton does not mean that the rest of the world is overlooked. The Centre for International Studies, founded in May 1978, has as its mandate "to develop greater general awareness of the relevance and importance of international affairs to Canadians, to encourage research and publications, to sponsor guest speakers and seminars on specific topics, and to establish relationships with universities and institutes both within Canada and in other countries." A description of its activities during the last decade also takes ten pages.

The Beaton Institute

The Beaton Institute is somewhat different in character from the other institutes and centres. It is primarily a repository and archives for Cape Breton history, and for the UCCB. However, it also fosters research and performs research on its own. By helping to keep alive an interest in the history of the Island and in its cultural heritage, it contributes to the sense of unity among the people of Cape Breton, a fundamental factor in the economic and social development of any region.

From its beginnings on September 11, 1951 as St. Francis Xavier Junior College, UCCB has grown exponentially. In its first year, there were sixty-five full-time students and eighty-five part-time students. Today, there are more than three thousand students. More impressive than its growth, however, is that throughout its more than four decades of expansion, it has retained its fundamental and unique character. The College has demonstrated its determination to combine solid scholarship with service to the community at large, and with what we would now call a significant contribution to the economic and social development of Cape Breton.

Conclusions

To a development economist viewing Sydney and Cape Breton from the outside, the path to development of Metro Sydney seems clear: Cape Breton must turn away from "natural resources and know-how," and towards "human resources and knowledge." However, this path may not yet be visible to many residents of Cape Breton, who still yearn for the past glories of the "industrial heartland" that Sydney once was. Certainly, some Cape Bretoners may still catch fish, saw lumber, mine coal, make steel, and sell scenery to tourists, within the limits imposed by the Island's dwindling stock of natural resources and the markets open to sales of final products. But there is little to suggest that these traditional industries can absorb a growing labour force into productive employment. There seem to be no limits to the number of jobs created by the other route, except the supply of innovative entrepreneurship, willingness to take risks, scientific and technical skills, and the provision of the right kind of education and training. The University College of Cape Breton can be of enormous assistance in removing any deficiencies in availability of all of these elements of the development process.

Because it is less advanced and less diversified than the economies of some other cities in the Maritimes urban structure, the Sydney economy is probably less affected by the three shocks than, say, Halifax, Saint John, and Moncton. Sydney's fate will be primarily the outcome of its own internal dynamics - or statics - rather than the product of outside shocks. The static force is the continued decline of her fishing and fish-processing, coal and steel industries. The dynamic force is the surge of entrepreneurship, creating new small industries, using advanced technology to produce manufactured goods or services. The struggle between the static and dynamic forces has been going on for a very long time. Which will win? It is impossible to predict the outcome with any precision; but given the number and nature of the new entrepreneurs, I would bet on the dynamic forces. Even the reductions in government spending may turn out to be a blessing in disguise. Most of the government spending in the past has been directed to a vain effort to keep the traditional large-scale industries going, keeping alive vain hopes that past glories can be reborn, and delaying the search for something new. Once the people of Cape Breton accept the fact that the fishing and fish-processing, coal and steel industries can never be quite what they once were, their energies, talents, training and education can be directed towards more hopeful ventures.

REFERENCES

Benjamin Higgins, "Entrepreneurship and Economic Development: the Case of Cape Breton," in Donald J. Savoie and Ralph Winter (eds.), *Les provinces Maritimes: Un regard vers l'avenir/The Maritime Provinces: Looking to the Future* (Moncton: Canadian Institute for Research on Regional Development, 1993), pp. 125-56. See also Benjamin Higgins, *Cape Breton and its University: Symbiotic Development* (Sydney: University College of Cape Breton Press, 1994).

Benjamin Higgins and Donald J. Savoie, *Regional Development Theory and its Applications* (New Brunswick, N.J.: Transactions Publishers of Rutgers University, 1994).

Donald J. Savoie, *Building a Competitive Cape Breton: Towards an Economic Development Plan for Enterprise Cape Breton Corporation and for Cape Bretoners* (Sydney: Enterprise Cape Breton Corporation, 1990).

Employment and Immigration Canada, Metropolitan Halifax Canada Employment Centre, *Area Profile*, March 1994; and *Industry Profile: Manufacturing*, April 1994.

Gordon DeWolf, "The Effects of Government Incentives and Other Initiatives on a Marginal Region: The Case of Cape Breton, Nova Scotia," in Reginald Byron (ed.), *Public Policy and the Periphery: Problems and Prospects in Marginal Regions*, printed in Canada by the Queen's Printer, Halifax, for the International Society for the Study of Marginal Regions, 1988, p. 254.

John Mellor, *The Company Store: J.B. McLachlan and the Cape Breton Coal Miners 1908-1925* (Halifax: Goodread Biographies, 1983), p. 289.

Statistics Canada, *Special Data, Custom Products Services, Advisory Services*, December 1993.

Tom Kent, "The Cape Breton Development Corporation: One Canadian Case of Planning on the Spot," in Benjamin Higgins and Donald J. Savoie (eds.), *Canadians and Regional Development at Home and in the Third World* (Moncton: Canadian Institute for Research on Regional Development, 1988), p. 87.

9

SAINT JOHN:
ARE ITS STRENGTHS ITS WEAKNESSES?

George J. De Benedetti

> Traditionally the central problem in the study of the economy of Saint
> John has been to explain the failure of the city to make the necessary
> adjustments to compensate for the dislocations occasioned by the
> stagnation of the wood trade following Confederation . . . Businessmen
> failed to make the transition to metal ships . . . [1]

Historically, manufacturing has been the principal activity in Saint John. Even
in the great era of the merchant in the nineteenth century, "many important
shippers and wholesalers owned, in whole or in part, the means to process the
basic commodities of their region."[2] Today, Saint John still manufactures heavy
industrial products and is considered the manufacturing heart of the Maritimes.
The Irving refinery and the Saint John Shipbuilding yard are but two examples.
Can such dependence on manufacturing sustain Saint John in an economy that is
more geared to services, international competition, and reduced public spending?
Manufacturing, the very strength of the Saint John economy, could turn out to
be the source of Saint John's vulnerability in the new economy.

Some Facts

The Saint John metropolitan area is the second largest centre in the Maritime
provinces, and the largest centre in New Brunswick. The population of the Saint
John metropolitan area is 124,981. The population in the city of Saint John itself
is 74,969.[3] Since 1981, the population of the Saint John metropolitan area has
grown by 9.6 percent, while the population of the city itself has declined by 7.4
percent.[4] The Saint John metropolitan area has a labour force of approximately
62,000 people, 8,000 of whom are bilingual.[5] The participation rate for the Saint
John metropolitan area is 63.9 percent and the unemployment rate is 11.4
percent. The female participation rate of 54.9 percent is among the lowest in the
urban communities in Canada.[6]

   The major employers by sectors in the city of Saint John are as follows:
Health care - Saint John Regional Hospital, Saint Joseph's, and Centracare
employ 3,800 persons; Shipbuilding - Saint John shipyard, which was awarded
the $6-billion federal government frigate contract, presently employs 3,500

people; pulp, paper and forestry products - Irving Paper (newsprint), Irving Pulp and Paper (softwood kraft), and Irving Tissue, which produce over 2,000 tonnes of paper products daily, representing 37 percent of the province's total production, employ 2,500 persons; Transportation - three airlines, the port, forty trucking firms, many brokers and the airport employ 2,200 persons; Telecommunications - NBTel and various telemarketing operations employ 2,000 persons; Food and beverages - Moosehead Brewery, Baxter Dairies, the Lantic Sugar refinery, Crosby's Molasses, Atlantic Wholesalers, and Mother Nature's employ 1,200 persons; Financial services - financial institutions employ 1,500 persons; Oil refining and petroleum processing - the Irving refinery, the largest in Eastern North America, with a production capacity of 250,000 barrels per day, employs 1,000 persons; Power generation - the Colson Cove station, the Courtney Bay station and the nearby Point Lepreau Nuclear Power generating station, employ 1,000 persons; Education - the University of New Brunswick, Saint John, and the New Brunswick Community College, the largest community college in New Brunswick, employ 550 full-time persons.[7]

Evolution of the Industrial Structure and the Distribution of Earned Income

The Saint John metropolitan area increased its dependence on the manufacturing sector and failed to diversify more towards a service economy between 1981 and 1991. In the goods-related industries, there has been disproportionate growth in employment and an increase in the share of earned income in the primary and the manufacturing sectors, and a disproportionate decline in employment and the share of income in the construction and the transportation sectors. In services, employment fell in the business and other services sector, and the finance, insurance, and real estate sector. The share of earned income for these two sectors has also fallen (see table 1).

To further illustrate Saint John's dependence on manufacturing, consider the main differences in the distribution of the labour force by sectors in 1991 between Saint John, and its rivals, Halifax and Moncton. Saint John had twice the concentration of employment in the manufacturing sector. Conversely, Halifax and Moncton each had almost twice the concentration of employment in business and other services. In other service sectors, Saint John had a larger share of its labour force in the hotels and restaurants sector, but in public administration, Saint John's share was below the other two metropolitan areas (see table 2).

The employment growth pattern in Saint John, like its industrial structure, has been skewed toward primary and secondary activities. In Saint John, manufacturing employment grew at twice the rate of that of Halifax between 1981 and 1991. Conversely, in the construction sector, employment fell in Saint John, and rose in Halifax and Moncton. Part of the shift in employment from the

Table 1

Evolution of the Industrial Structure and Earned Income
Saint John Metropolitan Area

	Distribution of Employment				Distribution of Employment %		Distribution of Earned Income %	
	1981	1991	Change	% Change	1981	1991	1981	1991
Total	57,340	65,940	8,595	15.0	100.0	100.0	100.0	100.0
Primary	675	1,110	435	64.4	1.2	1.7	1.0	1.8
Manufacturing	8,775	9,810	1,035	11.8	15.3	14.9	19.9	21.3
Construction	4,610	4,105	(505)	(11.0)	8.0	6.2	10.2	6.0
Transportation	7,245	6,350	(895)	(12.4)	12.6	9.6	16.3	13.1
Trade	10,850	11,790	940	8.7	18.9	17.9	13.1	12.9
Finance, Insur., Real Estate	3,125	3,070	(55)	(1.8)	5.4	4.7	5.9	5.4
Teaching	3,265	4,030	765	23.4	5.7	6.1	6.6	7.0
Health	5,800	7,530	1,730	29.8	10.1	11.4	9.3	11.6
Hotels & Restaurants	3,650	6,705	3,055	83.7	6.4	10.2	2.1	4.0
Business & Other Services	5,490	4,095	(1,395)	(25.4)	9.6	6.2	7.6	4.6
Public Administration	3,855	4,695	840	21.8	6.7	7.1	7.9	8.7
Not Classified elsewhere	*	*	*	*	*	*	*	*

* not available

Source: Statistics Canada, Special data, Custom Products Service, Advisory Services, December 1993.

Table 2

Experienced Labour Force by Industry Divisions
Saint John, Moncton, Halifax

	Saint John			Moncton			Halifax		
	% Distribution of Employment		% Growth	% Distribution of Employment		% Growth	% Distribution of Employment		% Growth
	1981	1991	1981-91	1981	1991	1981-91	1981	1991	1981-91
Total	100.0	100.0	15.0	100.0	100.0	22.4	100.0	100.0	22.3
Primary	1.2	1.7	64.4	1.4	1.5	30.9	1.4	1.2	1.1
Manufacturing	15.3	14.9	11.8	9.7	7.5	(4.6)	7.7	6.6	5.4
Construction	8.0	6.2	(11.0)	6.0	5.4	10.7	5.2	5.4	26.1
Transportation	12.6	9.6	(12.4)	15.2	10.3	(17.2)	8.6	8.2	17.3
Trade	18.9	17.9	8.7	22.3	21.3	16.9	18.0	17.0	14.9
Fin., Insur., Real Estate	5.4	4.7	(1.8)	5.3	5.1	17.3	6.6	6.3	17.3
Teaching	5.7	6.1	23.4	6.4	6.9	32.9	8.3	7.5	10.3
Health	10.1	11.4	29.8	7.6	10.2	64.4	9.5	10.4	33.4
Hotels & Restaurants	6.4	10.2	83.7	7.0	7.5	31.3	6.3	6.5	25.2
Business & Other Services	9.6	6.2	(25.4)	9.9	11.4	40.3	10.5	11.8	37.0
Public Administration	6.7	7.1	21.8	9.3	9.3	22.3	17.9	15.8	8.0
Not classified elsewhere	*	*	*	*	*	*	*	*	*

* not available

Source: Statistics Canada, Special data, Custom Products Service, Advisory Services, December 1993.

construction sector to the manufacturing sector can be explained by the distortions in the statistics caused by the frigate program. Many trades-persons, such as steam-fitters, welders, etc., who would normally work in the construction industry are now employed building frigates. Despite the nature of the work being the same, when these trades-persons work on a building, their employment is classified as construction, but when they work on producing a ship, their employment is classified as manufacturing.

Employment in the trade sector grew more slowly in Saint John than in the two other metropolitan areas. In other service sectors, employment fell in finance, insurance, and real estate, and in business and other services. By contrast, Moncton and Halifax had substantial positive growth rates in these sectors.

Saint John had a much larger employment growth rate in the hotels and restaurants sector compared to Halifax and Moncton. This was due to the city centre improvements under the urban renewal project which resulted in a deliberate expansion of convention facilities in the city of Saint John in the late 1970s and the 1980s. The three levels of government put substantial monies into the land assembly and the construction of such structures as the Delta Hotel-Brunswick Square complex, Market Square, the Hilton-Trade & Convention Centre complex, and the Aquatic Centre. With the renewal of the urban core, and the creation of new dwellings like condominiums in the downtown area, came many new eating and dining establishments. The frigate construction project attracted visiting civilian and military consultants which created a demand for eating and dining facilities. In other parts of the metropolitan area, there were expansions of hotel-motel and eating establishments, such as the expansion of the room capacity at the Algonquin Hotel in Saint Andrews.[8]

The employment growth rate in the health sector in Saint John was similar to that of Halifax but less than half that of Moncton's employment growth rate. The growth in employment in public administration in Saint John was similar to that of Moncton's but much larger than Halifax's.

The percentage share of earned income in the manufacturing sector grew in Saint John between 1981 and 1991, whereas the distributive share of employment in the manufacturing sector remained approximately the same (see table 1). Although earned income and the distributive share of earned income in the manufacturing sector are high in Saint John, there is vulnerability in employment in the manufacturing sector. Much of the high earnings in manufacturing activity in Saint John is presently centred on the Saint John Shipyard building frigates under the $6 billion defence contract from the federal government. This program began in 1982 and will end in 1996. The completion of this program could cause a loss of 1,500 to 3,500 jobs, many of them high-paying, if no substitute activity is found. (For a phase-down schedule of employment, see table 3.) This will not only greatly affect manufacturing earnings, but will of course have ripple effects in the service sectors, on retail sales, and the value of real estate.

Table 3

Phase-down Schedule of Employment
Frigate Contract - Saint John Shipyard

Year	Schedule 1	Schedule 2
1992	3,550	3,550
1993	3,400	3,400
1994	3,100	3,100
1995	2,700	2,700
1996	1,800	2,400
1997	900	2,100
1998	0	2,000

In Schedule 1, the assumption is that Saint John Shipbuilding Limited does not attract new business.

In Schedule 2, the assumption is that Saint John Shipbuilding Limited pursues new options for the shipyard and/or resumes previous activities.

Source: Department of Economic Development, City of Saint John, March 25, 1994.

Saint John, unlike Moncton and Halifax, is still dependent on the production of goods and is failing to transform its economy more toward the service sectors. Any unusual growth in the service sectors has been in the hotels and restaurants sector, where wages tend to be lower than in other service sectors. In service sectors such as health, teaching, business & personal services, Saint John did not fare as well as Moncton in its employment growth.

The Port

For centuries, the port of Saint John, at the mouth of the St. John River, has been an important gateway to the world. Historically, many activities in Saint John centred on shipping, ship-building, manufacturing and commerce related to the port. The Saint John port is not as well situated geographically as the port of Halifax to capture the passing traffic between Europe and North America on the North Atlantic. The Halifax port is also more specialized in container traffic. Saint John by contrast is much more suited to bulk shipments, such as petroleum, pulp and paper products, lumber, and potash both because of the special facilities there, and that time is not as critical a factor for bulk shipments as it is for container traffic. Large shipments of salt, raw sugar, chemicals, and molasses pass through the port facilities. The Port Corporation has also built a specialized dry-bulk terminal for shipping New Brunswick-mined potash.[9] Both major Canadian rail lines, Canadian National, and a subsidiary of Canadian Pacific, the Canadian Atlantic railway, serve the port. Overnight trucking services from Saint John can reach the Northeastern United States, Quebec, and Ontario within twenty-four hours. Canadian exporters have access to shipping lines that travel regularly to more specialized markets such as the Caribbean, central America, South America, Asia, Africa, the Mediterranean, the Red Sea and the Arabian Gulf, with connections to the Far East and Southeast Asia. That said, the United Kingdom and Northern Europe remain its traditional markets.[10]

Historically the port of Saint John has served as a "winter port" for Ontario and Quebec. Although its role has diminished since the 1970s, when the federal government extended ice-breaking services to Montreal, Saint John still serves as an alternate port when extreme ice conditions prevail in the Great Lakes in the St. Lawrence River system.[11] For example, when the ports of Montreal, Trois-Rivières, and other river ports were closed for almost four weeks in February 1993 because of ice conditions, several shipping lines used the container facilities at the port of Saint John for the movement of containerized cargoes to and from central Canada and the American midwest markets.[12]

The annual volume of traffic in the period 1988-1993 has fluctuated between fifteen million and nineteen million tonnes per year. Although the total traffic volume compares favourably with the port of Halifax, the distribution of cargo in Saint John is skewed towards the movement of the products of the Irving refinery. Approximately three million tonnes per year move through the facilities owned by the Saint John Port Corporation. The balance of the cargo is almost exclusively petro-chemical products, both crude and refined, which move through the privately-owned Irving Oil facilities at Saint John (table 4).

A strength of the port is in the movement of forest products. The Saint John Forests Products Terminal at Navy Island is a major load centre for forest products in Eastern Canada and the Eastern seaboard. Indeed, it is the largest such terminal north of Mobile, Alabama, with exporters from New Brunswick,

Table 4

Port Traffic Volumes by Commodity, 1989-1993
('000 metric tonnes)

Port of Saint John

Commodity	1989	1990	1991	1992	1993
Petroleum[a]	11,649	11,793	14,112	12,879	16,581
Potash	1,335	1,524	1,563	1,511	1,316
Forest Products	888	795	789	858	763
Sugar[b]	246	266	215	264	263
Containers	132	118	110	109	231
Salt	140	171	171	187	233
Other Cargo	310	323	134	123	183
TOTAL	14,700	14,990	17,094	15,931	19,570

[a] Petro-chemical products move through the privately-owned Irving Oil facilities
[b] Sugar moves through the privately-owned facilities of Lantic Sugar refinery

Port of Halifax

Commodity	1989	1990	1991	1992	1993
Petroleum	8,606	9,063	8,730	8,275	8,241
Gypsum	3,204	3,221	2,092	2,474	2,568
Grain	499	455	469	288	356
Containers	3,889	3,909	3,066	2,463	2,519
Other	586	639	536	464	428
TOTAL	16,784	17,287	14,893	13,964	14,112

Source: Supplied by Saint John Port Corporation and Halifax Port Corporation.

Nova Scotia, Quebec, Ontario, Maine and other New England States using the facility.[13] A new floating 'roll-on-roll-off' ramp, which enables cargo to be loaded and unloaded on ships at various tide-levels, enhances the strength of the port in the movement of forest products.

Proposed Abandonment of the Canadian Atlantic Railway Line

The Canadian Atlantic Railway, a subsidiary of CP Rail, is the vehicle by which many forest products shipments are moved from Ontario, Quebec, through Maine to the port of Saint John.[14] In 1993, Canadian Pacific Limited applied to the National Transportation Agency to abandon the operation of the Canadian Atlantic Railway. This line provides access to the port of Saint John through Southern New Brunswick, Maine, and into Quebec *via* Sherbrooke to Montreal. A complete abandonment of the line would have serious consequences for traffic passing through the port of Saint John because there are important producers located along the railway line, including Georgia Pacific, which has a significant operation at Woodland, Maine, and whose traffic is routed through St. Stephen and McAdam.[15]

What would be the effect of abandonment on port volume? The Saint John Port Corporation has produced forecasts of general cargo volumes based on three scenarios (see table 5). All scenarios assume no recurrence of the icing conditions in the St. Lawrence River that resulted in increased volume in 1993. Scenario "A" is a traffic forecast prepared by the Port Corporation before CP Rail's application to abandon its main line from Sherbrooke to Saint John, New Brunswick. Scenario "B" assumes the abandonment application is granted, i.e., there is no rail service along the CP alignment from West Saint John to Montreal but that there would be a rail connection from the port terminal facilities in West Saint John by either a short-line operator or CN Rail to the CN railyard in East Saint John. Scenario "C" assumes the abandonment application is granted and that there is no subsequent connection by a short-line operator to the port terminal facilities in West Saint John.[16]

If a short-line operator was found to operate part of the line, there would be reductions in traffic volumes from 23 percent in 1994 to 44.2 percent in 1997. If the line were abandoned completely, the reductions in traffic would be 27.7 percent in 1994 to 45 percent in 1997 (see table 6).

Under Scenario "B," the Port Corporation is arguing that there would be a reduction in the growth opportunities of handling forest products, due to the loss of efficiency in moving cargoes directly to the facilities at the port of Saint John *via* CP Rail. An interline operation, connecting with CN Rail, would increase the mileage to or from central Canada. The volume of forest products would be reduced to the traffic that is available directly on CN Rail facilities.

Table 5

Volume Forecasts, Three Scenarios[*]
Port of Saint John

(General Cargo, 000's metric tonnes)

	1994			1995			1996			1997		
	A	B	C	A	B	C	A	B	C	A	B	C
Forest products	1,005	805	780	1,040	780	780	1,105	780	780	1,165	780	780
Containers	160	100	80	190	100	75	190	90	70	190	80	70
Other cargoes	10	0	0	20	0	0	20	0	0	20	0	0
Total	1,175	905	860	1,250	880	855	1,315	870	850	1,375	860	850

[*] Scenario "A" is a traffic forecast prepared by the Port Corporation before CP Rail's application to abandon its main line from Sherbrooke to Saint John, New Brunswick.

Scenario "B" assumes the abandonment application is granted, i.e., there is no rail service along the CP alignment from West Saint John to Montreal but that there would be a rail connection from the port terminal facilities in West Saint John by either a short-line operator or CN Rail to the CN railyard in East Saint John.

Scenario "C" assumes the abandonment application is granted and that there is no subsequent connection by a short-line operator to the port terminal facilities in West Saint John.[17]

Source: Submission of the Saint John Port Corporation to the National Transportation Agency in opposition to the application of Canadian Pacific Railway to abandon the operation of the "Canadian Atlantic Railway," NTA File Nos. T6120-2 and T6120-3, undated, pp. 13-18.

Table 6

Volume Forecasts - Port of Saint John
Reduction in Volume Relative to Scenario A *
General Cargo, 000's metric tonnes

| | 1994 | | 1995 | | 1996 | | 1997 | |
	B	C	B	C	B	C	B	C
Forest products	200	225	260	260	325	325	385	385
Containers	60	80	90	115	100	120	110	120
Other cargoes	10	10	20	20	20	20	20	20
Total	270	325	370	395	445	465	515	525
% Change	- 23.0	- 27.7	- 35.6	- 38.0	- 40.3	- 42.1	- 44.2	- 45.0

* Scenario "A" is a traffic forecast prepared by the Port Corporation before CP Rail's application to abandon its main line from Sherbrooke to Saint John, New Brunswick.

Scenario "B" assumes the abandonment application is granted, i.e., there is no rail service along the CP alignment from West Saint John to Montreal but that there would be a rail connection from the port terminal facilities in West Saint John by either a short-line operator or CN Rail to the CN railyard in East Saint John.

Scenario "C" assumes the abandonment application is granted and that there is no subsequent connection by a short-line operator to the port terminal facilities in West Saint John.[18]

Source: Submission of the Saint John Port Corporation to the National Transportation Agency in opposition to the application of Canadian Pacific Railway to abandon the operation of the "Canadian Atlantic Railway," NTA File Nos. T6120-2 and T6120-3, undated, pp. 13-18.

This represents approximately 780,000 tonnes over a two to three-year period.[19] Container traffic would also decline because of the increased amount of time it would take due to these interline inefficiencies. Under Scenario "C," the volume in forest products would decline immediately to the stable level of approximately 780,000 tonnes. There would also be the added drayage charges in moving the cargo from the CN Rail yard to the terminal facility on the opposite side of the harbour.[20] There would be a large reduction in container volumes from levels of 200,000 tonnes in 1993 to an annual volume of approximately 70,000 tonnes.

The Port Corporation estimates that the decline in its revenues in 1994 would be $980,000 and there would be 600 jobs lost due to a reduced port and rail activity in 1994. By 1997, the loss in port revenue would be $1,635,000.[21]

Guilford Transportation Industries, Inc. (GTI) of North Billerica, Massachusetts is very much interested in operating part of the line served by the Canadian Atlantic Railway.[22] If Guilford purchased the running rights over the line, it would operate a service from Saint John to Mattawamkeag, Maine. Guilford, which owns the Maine Central Railway, would then make use of the Maine Central lines to Albany. At Albany, New York, there would be a connection to points south, and to Montreal by way of the Delaware and Hudson Railway. This more circuitous route would make the line unattractive for those shipping from Montreal. However, a short-line operation, such as Guilford, would probably change the trade patterns to and from the Saint John Port. The Guilford line would give more direct access to markets and producers in New England and the rest of the United States. There would also be the added potential to ship to Western Canada over American railway lines, whose rates are lower than Canadian railways'.

Besides the threat of the proposed abandonment of the Canadian Atlantic Railway, there is the threat that the proposed merger of CN and CP operations in Atlantic Canada poses for Saint John. In the short term, the predicted effects would be similar to those outlined in Scenarios "B" and "C." In the longer term, with CN's financial interests in the container facilities at the port of Halifax, rail traffic to the port of Saint John could be further reduced.

Saint John as a Telecommunication Centre

NBTel is one of the most progressive telephone companies in the world. It is, for example, the first telephone company in Canada to have 100 percent digital switching capability, which enables the integration of voice with computers. NBTel is a leader in the deployment of CSS7 network capacity, of which one feature is Calling Line Identification. With the appropriate hardware and software, Calling Line Identification permits a telemarketing operation to correlate incoming calls with existing client records, even before the customer service agent says "Hello."[23] There are other innovations, such as, the development of interfaces between computer hardware and Northern Telecom switches, which make NBTel an industry leader. NBTel in Saint John is the centre of expertise for Centrex and does all the planning for the system in Canada.

> The mandate of the National Centrex Business Development Centre in Saint John is to develop, on behalf of the nine major Canadian telecommunications companies, a continued evolution of advanced communications systems. These services form an integrated international network, all captured under the market name "Centrex." . . . Using the power of Centrex, a customer with multi locations in Canada can appear as a single entity, thereby increasing productivity and competitiveness in a global marketplace. A telemarketing operation in New Brunswick can answer inbound calls from all across the country, taking advantage of the lower business costs in the region, without compromising business expectations or customer service. . . "Centrex is a way to provide reliable communication services at a reasonable cost without the [customer incurring the] expense of equipment and the people to manage it" (Lowell Kessler, President of the National Centrex Users Group).[24]

Northern Telecom is also located in Saint John, with approximately sixty employees involved in writing technical manuals for Centrex operations.

The advanced technology used by NBTel, and the remission of the provincial sales tax on 800 numbers in New Brunswick,[25] has done much to attract companies to locate their "back offices" or call centres in New Brunswick. Some of the companies that have established their call centres in New Brunswick are Purolator Courier, Federal Express, Canada Post, Camco, Phone Works, McCain Foods, Connect North America Corporation, Livingston International, Unisys, Baxter Foods, and CP Express & Transport. The phone centres associated with Livingston International and Baxter Foods are located in the city of Saint John. Recently Canada Trust has set up their Easy-Line-Banking operations in Saint John, which allows customers all over Canada to conduct their banking transactions with Canada Trust at any time of the day. Medi-Trust Pharmacy Services Inc., a mail-order supplier of pharmaceutical drugs, has also established in Saint John. Such call centres strengthen the notion that New Brunswick is a good place to do business if you need access to modern telecommunication technology.

Complementing the presence of NBTel and Northern Telecom in Saint John is Digital Products Limited. The company manufactures switching equipment, test equipment, and software for NBTel and Northern Telecom. Beyond this local base, Digital Products Limited also exports products to telephone companies throughout North America.[26] They also supply electrical engineering services, systems-integration and control panels, sets, and software for the telecommunications and the aerospace industries. This firm has developed a computer interface module for office telephone systems that can control in-coming and out-going telephone calls. For example, an office telephone system can be programmed so that employees can call home only during official coffee breaks or after regular business hours. The system can screen incoming calls, and direct calls from certain telephone numbers to reach only designated employees. Digital Products Limited also refurbishes telephones for NBTel, and acts as a paint division for all telephone plastics in the Maritimes. The company has 82 employees: their success is based on forming partnerships with NBTel, Nova Scotia Power Commission, and the Irving companies. By working in partnership with such companies, they become familiar with the technology and the needs of the industry, and therefore can solve problems by providing appropriate solutions. They also service cable companies such as Fundy Cable, and provide security systems for them.

Although there is potential for companies like Digital Products Limited to establish themselves in Saint John to serve the telecommunications industry, there are few such firms in the Saint John area. Firms that specialize in software development in New Brunswick generally locate in the Fredericton area where, among other factors, they have access to faculty members with expertise in computer science and engineering in the Graduate School at the University of New Brunswick. Without the potential to form partnerships with NBTel and companies in the Irving Group, companies would find it less attractive and more difficult to establish in the Saint John metropolitan area than they would find it in Fredericton, Moncton, or Halifax.

Prospects for Growth

Growth prospects for the Saint John metropolitan area are mixed. The area will encounter some adjustment problems in the short term. The city is very dependent on manufacturing, and its hinterland on primary production. Many manufacturing jobs are dependent on public sector spending. It will be difficult to find a replacement activity for the $6-billion frigate program from which the city has benefited for fourteen years, given that the federal government is cutting back on defence expenditures. The construction of the fixed link from New Brunswick to Prince Edward Island will create additional manufacturing activity in Saint John, especially for Irving companies that can supply materials and services. For example, Ocean Steel can supply the structural steel for the bridge complex, and Strescon can contribute to the building of the concrete bridge spans. However, the activity associated with the fixed link will not create enough jobs to replace the jobs lost at the completion of the frigate project. Premier McKenna and city officials have talked about starting construction on a second nuclear power plant at Lepreau. However, it is unlikely that the federal government and the provincial government are in a position, with deficit reduction targets, to initiate construction of a second nuclear power plant. Also, the slow recovery of the North American economy from the recent recession is limiting the potential demand for power.

The Saint John metropolitan area does not have as well a developed service sector as does the Moncton area. On the other hand, Saint John has a manufacturing sector that Moncton would envy. There is as well some potential for increasing activities in the tourist industry. With its rich heritage and the revitalization of the downtown area, with the newly-renovated Imperial Theatre, and the increase in hotel, convention, and eating facilities, the city has become more attractive to tourists, including those from visiting cruise ships that now make Saint John a port of call in the summer.

In building his empire, the late K.C. Irving built Saint John into a manufacturing pearl, and caused the city of Saint John to grow, especially since the 1950s.

> . . . [He] built the oil refinery. . ., used it as a springboard into allied fields, bought a shipyard and went into shipbuilding, expanded his pulp production into a new line, planned a newsprint mill, [and] bought into New Brunswick's last English-language newspaper that he didn't already own. . . By 1960 Irving was responsible for well over half of the $144 million that was being, or just had been, spent on new projects. He had done much to make Saint John the twelfth or thirteenth industrial city in Canada. On a per capita basis, Saint John ranked very near the top: Toronto and Montreal did not exceed it and Vancouver stood well behind.[27]

Today, the Irving companies' dominance in the city is formidable (see appendix A). Such dominance could stifle the initiative of small entrepreneurs. It is commonly held that in order to get established in Saint John, a small entrepreneur requires the cooperation or the tolerance of the Irving companies. If the Irving Group saw an opportunity to establish its own operation to supply not only its own companies but also others in the city, it would be tempted to do so, and it has the power to drive out small competitors. Also, a small firm that wishes to do business in Saint John might feel expected to patronize Irving companies. For example, a new business owner might worry about being able to place a food item in Irving convenience store unless the new business makes a commitment to purchase oil and gasoline, stationary supplies and other materials from Irving companies. Even if Irving companies did not actively encourage new firms to buy Irving products, or actively drive out the competition, many fear the power of the Irvings. In a recent biography of K.C. Irving, the late Premier Richard Hatfield is quoted as saying:

> Some people are never going to believe that he [K.C. Irving] doesn't order provincial governments around. I have no evidence but my guess is that from the thirties to the sixties his political influence was far

> more indirect than real. I don't believe he ever snapped his fingers and had premiers jump. *I do believe that people were afraid of him. They believed that whatever he wanted he got.*[28]

That belief continues. It may generate an entrepreneurial chill for small companies that might otherwise establish themselves in Saint John. They prefer a more open market environment, and are likely to seek it by establishing in Moncton or Fredericton or outside the province entirely.

The possible loss of the Canadian Atlantic Railway connection to Montreal will reduce port activity and the overall level of economic growth. The success of Guilford, or some other line, to operate as a short-line operator may be contingent on the company striking a deal with the Irvings who own the New Brunswick Railway Company, which owns the entire right of way, and virtually all the track on the New Brunswick portion of the line. They currently lease these rights to CP Rail.

Saint John's strengths will create potential for growth in the longer run. Although dependent on manufacturing, the manufacturing activity of the latter decades has been more of the high-technology variety. Much of the expertise developed in the building of the frigates, for example, is transferable to other activities. As the world becomes more environmentally-conscious, there will be an increased demand for double-hulled tankers that can minimize potential oil spills. The Saint John Shipyard has gained the needed expertise in its manufacture of frigates. The yard has been actively marketing its capabilities to Saudi Arabia and other countries. There has also been some positive spillover effects in the telecommunications industry in Saint John related to the deployment of CSS7 network capacity by NBTel, mentioned earlier. Some positive externalities or spillover effects from the construction of the frigates have been transmitted outside the Saint John metropolitan area. Lexi-tech, an Irving company in Moncton, which supplies computerized language translation services was a spin-off activity of the frigate construction program, where technical manuals had to be prepared in both official languages. Leaders in the metropolitan area should ensure that more dynamic service activities are introduced to balance the employment in the goods-producing sectors.

Globalization

Saint John is well situated geographically to capitalize on the North American Free Trade Agreement. It is 110 kilometres from the United States border, 678 kilometres from Boston, and 1,032 kilometres from New York.[29] Ironically, the closure of the Canadian Atlantic Railway and the operation of a Guilford Line could actually work to Saint John's benefit, in providing a more direct link to the United States and to Mexico. However, proximity and access are only advantageous if the products manufactured locally are competitive internationally, or if firms in New England and Eastern Canada wish to take advantage of the port of Saint John. Moreover, the rules under the new GATT arrangements and NAFTA work against areas like Sussex, the dairy capital of New Brunswick and Saint John's most important satellite town. With the gradual elimination of quotas and marketing boards, and the tariff reduction sought by the United States over the next decade, Sussex dairy producers will become less competitive with their American counterparts. More dairy products would likely be imported from the United States, and the reduction in the production of dairy products in Sussex would diminish the level of economic activity in the Saint John hinterland, and thus would reduce the rate of growth for the Saint John metropolitan area. More non-traditional exports will have to be found. For example, there is a growing demand for modular home kits in Japan, Germany, and China. More of these kits could be built in Sussex and Buctouche, which could strengthen the wood products industries and increase the shipping activities of Kent Lines, which uses the port of Saint John.[30]

With NBTel being a leader in the telecommunications industry, there is potential for developing more non-traditional service exports. The growth and development of NBTel will provide some dynamic growth in labour-force skills and will stimulate growth of the metropolitan area. There is also potential for non-traditional exports from companies such as Maritime Information Technology (MIT) Inc. This Irving company, with 125 employees, can undertake facilities management, software development, support and training, and information technology procurement for a broad range of business and government departments.[31] Although MIT mainly serves Irving-owned companies, the possibility exists of supplying management information to other companies and governments inside and outside New Brunswick. This would contribute to the diversification of the present export base.

Conclusion

We have seen in this chapter that while the relative share of employment in the primary and manufacturing sectors in the other centres shrank, Saint John maintained its dependence on these sectors for employment and increased its dependence on manufacturing for income. While Saint John remains the manufacturing heartland of the Maritimes, with potential for additional manufacturing of a high-technology nature, Saint John is failing to transform its economy away from primary and manufacturing activities toward services. In the quotation at the start of this chapter, Acheson commented on the failure of entrepreneurs to adjust to conditions and changing times in the last century. It appears that Saint John is still lagging in its transformation to a more modern economy based on a strong tertiary sector and the information economy. In a study of population growth and the industrial structure of small towns in the Maritime provinces, the authors discovered that towns that were largely dependent on "smokestack industries" and that did not have a favourable mix of goods-producing and service-producing sectors were destined to experience negative population growth.[32] A metropolitan area like Saint John, which is more dependent on the goods-producing sectors than other metropolitan areas in the Maritimes, could face a declining growth trend, if not the negative growth already faced by many small towns in the Maritimes in similar circumstances. As noted earlier, Saint John's employment growth rate was below that of Moncton and Halifax (see table 2).

Like manufacturing, the presence of large companies, such as Irving and NBTel, has also been a strength for Saint John, but their dominance may discourage small emerging firms of the type found in the growing service sector in other centres. This may make it difficult for Saint John to undergo the structural transformation and the expansion of its entrepreneurial pool, elements necessary to withstand the shocks of globalization, reduction in public spending, and the information economy. Are Saint John's strengths, its weaknesses?

APPENDIX A

Sample of Irving Companies
Based in Saint John

Atlantic Land Dealers Limited
Atlantic Towing Ltd.
Barrington Industrial Services
Canaport Limited
CFM Rubber
Chandler Sales Ltd.
Commercial Communications
Commercial Equipment
Commercial Properties Limited
Custom Fabricators and Machinist (CFM)
Gulf Operators Ltd.
Industrial Security
Irving Equipment
Irving Forest Services Limited
Irving Oil Limited
Irving Oil Limited - Lubricants Plant
Irving Oil Limited - Refinery
Irving Oil Terminal Limited
Irving Oil Transportation Limited
Irving Paper Limited
Irving Pulp and Paper Limited
Irving Tissue Company
J.D. Irving Ltd.
Kent Building Supplies Ltd.
Kent Line International Limited
Kent Line Ltd.
Maritime Information Technology Inc.
Maritime Tire
Marque Construction Limited
New Brunswick Broadcasting Limited
New Brunswick Publishing Limited
New Brunswick Railway
Ocean Steel & Construction Ltd.
Plasticraft Limited

RST Industries - Transportation
Saint John Shipbuilding Limited
SMT Eastern - Bus Line
Speedy Propane Ltd.
Strescon Limited
Thorcom Inc.
Thornes
Universal Sales
Work Ready Professional Corp.

Other Major Employers
Saint John

Atlantic Wholesalers
Bank of Canada (N.B.)
Bank of Montreal (N.B.)
Bank of Nova Scotia (N.B.)
Baxter Foods Ltd.
Brookville Manufacturing Limited
Brookville Transport Limited
Bruncor Inc.
Brunswick Data Inc.
Canada Employment & Immigration (SJ)
Canada Games Aquatic Centre
Canada Post
Canada Trust - Easy-Line
    Customer Service Centre
Canadian Atlantic Railway
Centracare Inc.
City of Saint John
Clow Canada
Coates Distributors Limited
Connors Bros. Ltd.
Crosby's Molasses Co. Ltd.
Customs Canada (SJ)
Delta Brunswick Hotel
Digital Products Limited
Downey's Ltd.
E.P.C. Industries Limited
Fundy Cable Limited
Fundy Linen Limited
Gardner Electric Ltd.
Hilton International Hotel
Investor Group
Ipex
K-Mart Canada
Keddy's Fort Howe Hotel
Lantic Sugar Limited
Marine Atlantic Inc.

Maritime Paper Products Limited
MediTrust Pharmacy Services
Meridian Construction Ltd.
Moosehead Breweries Ltd.
Mother Natures Restaurant and
    Pita Bakery (and Dusenbagels)
NBTel Interactive Ltd.
NCH Promotional Services Ltd.
New Brunswick Community College
New Brunswick Red Cross Society
N.B. Telephone Company Ltd (NBTel)
Newdick Enterprise (McDonald's)
Northern Telecom
PCL & Eastern Packaging Ltd.
Power Comm. of the City of Saint John
Province of New Brunswick
Revenue Canada - GST (N.B.)
Revenue Canada - Taxation (N.B.)
Rocmaura Nursing Home
Ronald's (Quebecor) Printing Ltd.
Royal Bank of Canada (N.B.)
Saint John Port Corporation
Saint John Regional Hospital
School District 6; School District 8
Sears Canada Inc.
Sobey's
St. Joseph's Hospital
Stentor Resource Centre Inc.
T.S. Simms & Co. Limited
T.W. Graham
Transport Canada
Univ. of New Brunswick - Saint John
Wal-Mart Canada
Wayside Industries (Bob Snodgrass)
Worker's Compensation Board
Zeller's

Source: Department of Economic Development, City of Saint John, Saint John, New Brunswick, March 1994.

NOTES TO CHAPTER NINE

1. T.W. Acheson, "The Great Merchant and Economic Development of St. John 1820-1850," *Acadiensis*, vol. VIII, no. 2, pp. 4-5.

2. Ibid. p. 3.

3. Statistics Canada, Census of Canada, "Population and Dwelling Counts," Statistics Canada, Catalogue no. 93-303, p. 25.

4. Statistics Canada, Census of Canada, New Brunswick Part I, Census Divisions and Subdivisions, Catalogue no. 94-107. Profiles of Census Tracts in Moncton and Saint John, Part A, Catalogue no. 5-321. Profiles of Census Divisions and Subdivisions in New Brunswick, Part A, Catalogue no. 95-369.

5. Statistics Canada, Census of Canada "Population and Dwelling Counts," Statistics Canada, Catalogue no. 93-303, p. 25.

6. Statistics Canada, Census Divisions and Subdivisions, Ottawa, 1993, Catalogue no. C2275.

7. City of Saint John, Department of Economic Development, "Report on the Cost and Availability of Labour in Saint John, N.B.," 5 May, 1993, p. 2, and in a telephone conversation with Mr. Dan Leblanc, Department of Economic Development, city of Saint John, 25 March, 1994.

8. Telephone interviews with Mr. Guy Levesque at ACOA, Moncton, N.B., 25 March, 1994, and Mr. John Shackleton, Manager of Market Square, Saint John, 28 March, 1994.

9. Saint John Port Corporation, Saint John, N.B., pamphlet entitled, "Port of Saint John," undated, p. 3.

10. Based on an interview with Mr. K.R. Krauter, General Manager & Chief Executive Officer, Saint John Port Corporation, Saint John, N.B., 19 January, 1994.

11. Ibid.

12. Submission of the Saint John Port Corporation to the National Transportation Agency in opposition to the application of Canadian Pacific Railway to abandon the operation of the "Canadian Atlantic Railway," NTA File nos. T6120-2 and T6120-3, undated, p. 7.

13. Ibid., p. 12.

14. Based on an interview with Mr. Ralph Murray, Transportation Policy Manager, city of Saint John, Saint John, N.B., 19 January, 1994.

15. Ibid.

16. Submission of the Saint John Port Corporation to the National Transportation Agency in opposition to the application of Canadian Pacific Railway to abandon the operation of the "Canadian Atlantic Railway," NTA File nos. T6120-2 and T6120-3, undated, pp. 13-8.

17. Ibid.

18. Ibid.

19. Ibid.

20. Ibid., p. 14.

21. Ibid.

22. Based on an interview with Mr. Ralph Murray, Transportation Policy Manager, City of Saint John, Saint John, N.B., 19 January, 1994. On April 20, 1994, CP Rail announced it will decide at the end of May with which of two parties, Guilford Transportation Industries (GTI) and CANTRAK, a group of American and Canadian investors based in Bear, Delaware, it will continue to negotiate.

23. City of Saint John, Department of Economic Development, "Location Proposal for Canada Trust," Saint John, 8 September, 1993, p. 6.

24. Information supplied in a facsimile by Ms. Sue Clack, Manager, Corporate Communications, NBTel, 24 March, 1994.

25. New Brunswick had an initial advantage in remitting the provincial sales tax on 800 numbers. Nova Scotia and Manitoba followed suit and other provinces are expected to do the same.

26. Information on Digital Products Limited is based on an interview with Mr. W. Kelly, President of the Company, in Saint John, N.B., 14 January, 1994.

27. Douglas How and Ralph Costello, *K.C.: The Biography of K.C. Irving* (Toronto: Key Porter, 1993), p. 137.

28. Ibid., p. 256. *Emphasis mine.*

29. City of Saint John, Department of Economic Development, *Saint John, New Brunswick: Community Profile,* undated, *circa* December, 1993, pp. 1-2.

30. Based on an interview with Mr. James Balcomb, General Manager, Fundy Region Development Commission Inc., Saint John, N.B., 10 November, 1993.

31. *In Business* Section, Saint John *Telegraph Journal*, 20 July, 1993.

32. George J. De Benedetti and Richard J. Price, "Population Growth and the Industrial Structure of Small Towns, 1971-1981," in McCann, Larry, (ed.), *People and Place: Studies of Small Town Life in the Maritimes* (Fredericton, 1987), pp. 191-208.

10

MONCTON, MAKING THE TRANSITION:
MYTH OR REALITY

Donald J. Savoie
Yves Bourgeois

As the editors have already pointed out, the central purpose of this collection of essays is to analyze the capacity of Maritime urban centres to cope with the restructuring of the national and global economies. Monctonians will be quick to point out that their city, perhaps more than any other in the region, has felt the sting of this restructuring process, but that their community nonetheless has succeeded in putting in place a solid footing for future economic growth. They will talk about the closure of the CN repair shops in 1988 which resulted in the loss of over 1,000 jobs, cutbacks in the VIA Rail operations and the planned closure of the Department of National Defence's Supply Depot.[1] Monctonians, however, will also be quick to argue that they have been particularly adroit at managing the adjustment process. They are not alone in making this argument. Outside observers, including the national media, have reported time and again on Moncton's ability to bounce back. Government representatives from elsewhere, including cities in the United States, have come to study how Moncton promotes economic development, with the hope of improving the planning of their own economic adjustments.[2]

The purpose of this chapter is to review the challenges Moncton has had to face in recent years, and the measures it has taken to deal with these challenges. It compares the structure of the Moncton economy of today with that which existed when the challenges surfaced. The chapter also attempts to determine to what extent Moncton has made the transition to a modern self-sufficient economy capable of competing in the regional, national and global economies.

The Challenges

Moncton has witnessed many economic storms over the past twenty years and not all of them were driven by the public sector. Two leading private firms, for example, closed down important economic activities in Moncton in the 1970s. Marven's biscuits, started by a local entrepreneur Joe Marven at the turn of the century, went on to sell a variety of products throughout Canada. After several years of solid growth, Marven's moved his factory in 1917 to the site of a former cotton mill built in 1882-83. A year later, the firm had become Canada's third largest biscuit manufacturer. However, in 1958 the company was bought out by George Weston Company, a large national firm. It closed down the Moncton operations in 1978 with a job loss of 65 employees. At its peak Marven's had employed about 200 people.[3]

Eaton's had in 1920 established a mail order house in Moncton to serve the Maritime provinces. It decided on the Moncton location because the city was already an important railway centre, a key asset at the time for catalogue sales. But in 1976, Eaton's decided to close the mail order house as part of a restructuring plan, throwing 1,300 people out of work.[4]

But, more than any other event, it was the closure of the CN shops that "shocked" the city.[5] In some ways, the closure of the shops went to the heart of Moncton's *raison d'être* - the transportation and distribution centre of the Maritimes. Moncton had, with a great deal of pride, long claimed to be a *railway* town and boasted of being the *Hub City* of the region. CN had been to Moncton what the auto industry is to Windsor, Ontario. Indeed, no one doubted that Moncton was a company town and that CN was the company. Somehow, Monctonians also assumed that the shops would continue to operate come what may. To be sure, most Monctonians had heard stories for some time that the shops were overstaffed and its workers were underemployed. Still, CN was a crown corporation and it was expected that powerful federal politicians from the region would stand up for Moncton at the first hint that the shops might close. And, over the years, Moncton had some powerful friends at court in Ottawa, notably Honourable Roméo LeBlanc, a high-profile minister in the Trudeau cabinet, and representing the neighbouring riding of Beauséjour from 1974 to 1984. With the Mulroney government coming to office in the fall of 1984, however, Moncton lost most of the clout it had in Ottawa. New Brunswick had, at least for the first few years of the Mulroney administration, a junior minister in cabinet - Gerald Merrithew from Saint John. Not only was he a junior minister, he also had a reputation of being preoccupied with the interests of Saint John, a city he felt had been neglected during the Trudeau years in favour of Moncton and surrounding areas.

With weakened representation in Ottawa, rumours soon surfaced that the future of the repair shops was in doubt. Still, the news of the closure came as a shock to "virtually all Monctonians" when CN made the announcement in the fall of 1985.[6] A good number of Monctonians felt that Ottawa had delivered a death blow to the city. Local historian Alex Pincombe had warned earlier that: "My knowledge of the history of the region easily reveals the importance of the railway. I shudder to think what would happen. They (the feds) would be removing the cornerstone from our economy."[7] The local newspaper, *The Times and Transcript*, observed that "Moncton did not create the CN shops. The CN shops created Moncton."[8] One also increasingly heard references to Moncton becoming a "ghost town."[9] Spontaneous demonstrations took place, with some demonstrators carrying posters saying: "The City will die without the shops."[10] Even out-of-province newspapers ran stories reporting that Moncton was about "to suffer a serious blow to its economy and to its identity as a once-bustling railway city."[11]

On the face of it, at least, the media and Monctonians had every reason to ring the alarm bell. The CN shops were Moncton and New Brunswick's largest single industrial employer. At the time the closure was announced, some 1,150 workers were still employed at the shops, down from a peak of 3,000 workers in the 1960s. Local businesses and economic development groups were quick to add up the cost - $13.5 million loss in disposable income over two years, $9.4 million in increased costs in social services benefits, $7 million loss in purchasing power in the region, an estimated loss of 590 to 680 indirect jobs, $16 million in retail sales in the city and a 5 percent reduction in housing prices in the Greater Moncton area.[12] The immediate job loss of over 1,000 accounted for 2.5 percent of the area work force, with the average income of shops workers amounting to $27,900 compared to the overall average of $17,300.

A Save Our Shops (S.O.S.) committee was established and quickly began to apply pressure on Ottawa to direct CN to reverse its decision. To be sure, strong pressure was applied and a few unfortunate incidents occurred, including a widely-reported incident when the prime minister visited Moncton.[13] But CN stuck to its decision and the shops were finally shut down in January 1988, after eighty-one years of operation at that site.

A few years later Ottawa announced its plan to close the Canadian Forces Base No.5 Supply Depot located in Moncton. The base was established in 1940, and it became the largest equipment depot of World War II, with over 1,500 personnel at its peak. In time, it became one of four such depots in the country and responsible for receipt, warehousing and shipping of supplies used by the Canadian Armed Forces in the Atlantic region, other parts of Canada, and by Canadian NATO and UN forces abroad. It was rumoured that Ottawa was thinking of closing the base in the late 1970s, but that Roméo LeBlanc used his influence to kill that suggestion. The 1992 federal budget, however, finally did unveil plans to consolidate DND's four regional supply depots into two central depots, in Edmonton and Montreal.[14]

Again, a Save Our Base committee was struck. It, in turn, pointed to serious consequences for the city should the base close. It pointed to a loss of 445 direct jobs (102 military and 343 civilians) and a likely indirect loss of about 250 more. Some fifty university students would no longer have access to summer jobs. Direct payroll loss was estimated at about $15 million, with nearly 300 local and regional businesses expected to feel an impact through loss of sales and service contracts. The committee ranked the base as Moncton's 11th largest employer, and argued that its closing would entail a population loss of nearly 700 people over a six-year period.[15] The committee has argued repeatedly that Ottawa has targeted Moncton unfairly for cutbacks, in light of the closure of the

CN shops and several cuts to CN and VIA Rail operations. Still the plan to close the base was proceeding on schedule.

The Response

There is no doubt that Moncton fought hard to keep its CN repair facilities open and that it has applied strong pressure on Ottawa to reverse the decision to close the CFB supply base. In this sense, it is no different from any other city or region in Canada. The federal government is fair game for anyone to apply pressure to secure new spending or to keep doing what it is doing in a given region. The call for Ottawa to cut back its spending is always applauded provided, of course, that the cuts are made somewhere else.[16]

But Moncton has done a great deal more than simply apply pressure on Ottawa. Moncton Industrial Development Ltd. (MID), an office supported by the municipal government, launched an ambitious promotional campaign in 1985. It ran a series of full-page ads in a number of national business magazines, including special business supplements and a series of full colour ads which were introduced in 1987. MID subsequently passed on its promotional mandate to the Greater Moncton Economic Commission (GMEC) in 1991, and that new agency continued the promotional campaigns.[17]

The central purpose of the campaign was to promote Moncton as a place to invest in or to launch new economic activities. Through the ads and various information sessions of one kind or another, MID and GMEC have pointed to Greater Moncton as the geographic centre of the three Maritime provinces, with all land traffic going east and south having to pass through the city. They add that, because of its central location, Moncton has the largest retail market in Atlantic Canada with some 1.2 million people, having a combined purchasing power of about $8 billion, living within a three-hour drive of the city.

The campaign also pointed to the city's labour force as an important asset. Greater Moncton's population is now over 100,000. The city has seen a remarkable growth in population throughout this century (537.5 percent compared with 114.3 percent for the province as a whole). More importantly, the city can boast about a stable and skilled labour force, available at competitive wage rates, compared to the province and even to the country as a whole. The proportion of Greater Moncton's population of working age was 2.3 percent higher than the provincial average in 1986. Though in more recent years the city has seen shortages of highly skilled labour in some of the new technological industries such as telecommunication, there are usually many candidates who can be recruited for almost any position. However, the most important competitive advantage of Moncton's work force is its bilingualism. Most observers and government officials at all three levels promoting Moncton as a place to invest invariably will point to bilingualism as one of the city's leading selling points. According to Statistics Canada (1986 Census), over 30 percent of the population of the Greater Moncton area is bilingual. Little time or money is needed for second-language training. Another important advantage of Moncton's labour force is its education level. A higher proportion of Greater Moncton's population had either a high school certificate or diploma, (+0.1 percent), a technical diploma or certificate (+6.0 percent) or university degree (+1.8 percent) in 1986 than any other community in the province.[18] Table 1 shows the level of academic achievement, and that 10 percent of Moncton's population has a university education, the same figure as for Canada.

Table 1

Level of Academic Achievement

Highest Level of Schooling Achieved	City of Moncton (%)	Census Area (%)	Canada (%)
Less than grade 9	17	17	17
Grade 9-13	26	27	27
High school certificate or diploma	12	12	13
Trade certificate or diploma	2	3	3
Other non-university:			
without certificate	6	5	7
with certificate	16	17	14
University:			
without degree	11	10	9
with degree	10	9	10
	—	—	—
	100	100	100

Source: Statistics Canada, 1986 Census.

Based on Statistics Canada (1986 Census) figures, the Moncton region's labour force is distributed as follows: 45.2 percent in service industries, 22 percent in trade, 13.4 percent in transportation, communications and other utilities, 7.9 percent in manufacturing, 5.6 percent in finance, insurance, and real estate, 5.1 percent in construction, and 0.8 percent in primary industry. Greater Moncton had a higher proportion than the provincial average of its labour force in the following sectors: transportation, communications and utilities (+5.5 percent), trade (+5.0 percent), service industries (+1.3 percent), and financial insurance, and real estate (+2.0 percent). The region had a lower proportion of its labour force in the primary (-6.5 percent), manufacturing (-6.1 percent) and construction (-.12 percent) sectors. In terms of economic growth between 1981 and 1986, the Greater Moncton area's labour force expanded by 12 percent in the trade sector, 16 percent in construction industry, 0 percent in the transportation, communications and utilities sector, 12 percent in the trade sector, 16 percent in finance, insurance, and real estate sector, 19.6 percent in the community business and personal service sector and 11 percent in the public administration sector. The provincial averages were 47, 0.1, 2.2, 9.5, 8.8, 18.3 and 11 percent, respectively.[19]

Compared to the rest of Canada, Moncton's wage rates are also very competitive. The city's average wage rate is even lower than the provincial average. Moncton's strength in the retail and financial sectors is perhaps a major reason for this lower average rate. According to Statistics Canada 1986 Census figures, Greater Moncton's manufacturing (-$2.25), construction (-$1.80), transportation, communications and utilities (-$1.83), services (-$0.81), and public administration (-$0.04) sectors have lower average hourly earnings than the province as a whole. The city's insurance and real estate sectors were the only groups with average hourly wage rates higher than the provincial industry averages (+$1.80). The Greater Moncton area's average household income ($21,801 for males and $11,314 for females), however, exceeded the provincial average ($18,882 for males and $10,293 for females) in 1986.[20]

The local development agencies can also point to a number of other important advantages: real estate, including serviced industrial lots available at reasonable prices; an all-weather airport; and the development of sophisticated communications networks. Recreational facilities, including the Atlantic ocean - notably Parlee Beach and Kouchibougouac National Park - are also easy to reach. In addition, they point to two universities - Université de Moncton and Mount Allison University - both of which are able to provide important information and support for business and economic development.

Both the provincial and federal governments also have sought to play a role in promoting economic development in Moncton. At the provincial level, a new government led by an energetic young premier, Frank McKenna, came to office in 1987 pledged to do things differently. McKenna himself wanted above all to lead the province out of its dependency on federal transfer payments and sought to "energize" the provincial economy and, in particular, the business community. He won every seat in his first general election campaign. Though he had plenty of candidates vying for cabinet posts, he appointed four Moncton area members of the legislative assembly to his cabinet.

Moncton had no or weak representation in the provincial cabinet since the late 1970s, after Paul Creaghan left the cabinet. With new clout in Fredericton, Moncton would now be able to speak up at the cabinet table whenever new initiatives were being proposed. If nothing else, the city of Moncton would have three members in cabinet able to press for their community's fair share.

It soon became clear that the McKenna government would turn to entrepreneurship and to the aggressive pursuit of outside investors to achieve economic development in the province. Perhaps more through good luck than good management, that approach appears to have been particularly well suited for Moncton's emerging economic circumstances and advantages.

Provincial government figures show that Moncton has done particularly well, compared with other regions in the province, in taking advantage of provincial government programs. More Moncton entrepreneurs applied for such provincial government programs as the "New Brunswick Entrepreneur Program" and the "Self-Start Program" than entrepreneurs from other communities. Moncton was also able to attract a number of high-profile out-of-province investors to locate new economic activities to the community. More is said about this below.

The federal government has also been active in promoting economic development in Moncton in recent years. Ottawa moved in 1987 to establish the Atlantic Canada Opportunities Agency (ACOA). Unveiled in a blaze of publicity by former Prime Minister Brian Mulroney, ACOA represented a new beginning in regional development.[21] The prime minister declared: "We begin with new money, a new mission and a new opportunity. The agency will succeed where others have failed."[22] The agency broke from past efforts in several ways. For the first time in Canadian history, the head office of a federal government department would be located outside of Ottawa. A deputy minister would be appointed to direct the work of the agency, and he or she would also be located outside of Ottawa in the department's head office. ACOA was given a substantial amount of "new" money, over $1 billion over five years. Other federal government economic programs and their resources were also transferred to the new agency. The work of the agency would also be directed by an advisory body consisting of local business and community representatives. In unveiling the agency, the prime minister made it clear that it was designed for Atlantic Canada and that Atlantic Canadians themselves would have to provide the knowledge, the skills, the creativity and the energy to conceive and pursue new economic activities. In brief, the prime minister issued a challenge to Atlantic Canadians - future growth would have to be generated largely by the region itself. It soon became clear that entrepreneurship would become key to future federal development efforts in Atlantic Canada.

As could be expected, intense behind-the-scenes jockeying for the agency's head office surfaced the moment it became clear that it would be located outside of Ottawa. Halifax-area politicians, with the support of politicians from

Newfoundland and Labrador, once it became clear that the latter province would not be able to secure the office, pushed hard for ACOA's head office to be located in the Halifax area.

In the end, however, Mulroney took his own counsel on this issue, and picked Moncton. There is no doubt that this boosted business confidence in the city. Not only did it mean new jobs (over 100, and highly-paid), it also meant Moncton would become more visible to the business community throughout Atlantic Canada since business would have to turn to the agency's head office whenever it had business plans of a large or significant nature to promote. In time ACOA closely identified itself - even more than initially envisaged - with entrepreneurship. It promoted entrepreneurship as the way ahead for the region time and again through special programs, high profile advertising campaigns and in its own publications. Moncton, in turn, became closely identified with ACOA and its campaign. As is well known, success breeds success in regional development and, conversely, failure breeds failure. Many of the cases ACOA pointed to as "role models" for current and aspiring entrepreneurs were from the Moncton area. Local business leaders and government officials report that Moncton entrepreneurs took the campaign to heart, and before long they began to believe their community indeed was the region's entrepreneurship capital. They also took great pride in their city's ability to bounce back from the closure of the CN shops, and began to assume that all or most of the rebound was due to entrepreneurship. As we will suggest, the truth is that this view is part fact, and part myth. Still, it served to give the local business community a sense of confidence, a key ingredient in any successful attempt to promote local economic development.

ACOA put together two programs - the Action Program and the Cooperation Program.[23] The Action Program provides business guidance and financial support in the form of cash grants and loan guarantees to entrepreneurs from eligible sectors (aquaculture, business service, commercial R & D, manufacturing & processing, mining, and tourism) who are interested in starting a new business, or in expanding or diversifying an existing one. The Cooperation Program is a regional development program shared between the federal government and the provincial governments of the Atlantic provinces. The main goal of that program is to target and develop areas and industries within Atlantic Canada in order to improve the overall economic prosperity of the region. This goal is achieved through Cooperation Agreements which establish development and funding priorities. New businesses and existing ones can both benefit from the Cooperation Program.

The Cooperation Program is in reality a continuation of an established pattern of federal government programs, originating with the General Development Agreements (GDAs), in place between 1973 and 1983 under the Department of Regional Economic Expansion (DREE); and the Economic and Regional Development Agreements (ERDAs) under the Department of Regional Industrial

Expansion (DRIE) which, in turn, were in place between 1983 and the time when ACOA turned them into Cooperation Agreements. All these agreements have several things in common: they are broad enabling documents that clear the way for both levels of government to support economic development measures; they support a wide range of initiatives in such diverse fields as tourism, industrial development, agriculture, mineral development, culture, roads and infrastructure development, research and development, urban development, rural development, and so on; and they provide for joint federal-provincial funding, with Ottawa picking up a larger share of the cost. In the Cooperation Program, ACOA has also sought to extend to federal-provincial agreements its Action Program focus on entrepreneurship. It made some progress on this front, but there is still considerable room for further progress.[24]

ACOA officials report that Moncton has fared very well under both its programs. Nearly 175 projects were approved for Moncton entrepreneurs between 1989-90, with 120 under the Action Program alone. These figures, they report, exceed those for other communities either in New Brunswick or Atlantic Canada generally.

The Facts

It is obvious even to a casual observer that Moncton has changed for the better in recent years. Nowhere is this more evident than in the city's downtown which has been transformed from a dying retail area to a dynamic financial and administrative centre, with additional facilities such as the restored Capitol Theatre. Restoring the theatre to its original role as a home for live performance at a cost of $3.8 million, speaks to the new-found dynamism of the city. To be sure, the federal and provincial governments contributed to the project to the amount of $2.5 million. But the local business community has also contributed by buying seats and opera boxes, at prices ranging from $250 to $15,000.[25]

But the downtown area tells only part of the story. Two studies carried out at the Canadian Institute for Research on Regional Development, one involving a survey of the yellow pages of the NBTel directories for 1972, 1980 and 1991, and the other a survey of four series of reports are quite revealing.[26] The studies reveal that Moncton has witnessed strong growth in the provision of "sophisticated" services. The number of lawyers, architectural firms, consulting engineers, and other consultants, as well as firms involved in both computer and cellular telephone sales and service, has increased considerably more than the population as a whole. This suggests that these firms are expending their effort on satisfying people who have come to Moncton from outside the region.

Table 2 also shows a healthy development in the manufacturing sector, at a time when other regions saw their manufacturing sector hard hit. Solid growth is evident in printing and publishing, as well as in chemicals and plastics.

Table 2

Number of Manufacturing Firms by Sector

Sectors	1972	1983	1990
Food and beverage	14	17	18
Metal products	26	32	32
Wood products, furniture and fixture	23	27	25
Non-metallic mineral products	7	8	8
Electrical products	11	14	15
Textile and knitting mills	7	9	4
Printing and publishing	7	9	17
Petroleum and petroleum products	3	4	9
Chemicals, rubber and plastics	8	9	16
Paper and allied industries	3	4	4

Source: Donald J. Savoie and Ralph Winter, (eds.), *The Maritime Provinces: Looking to The Future* (Canadian Institute for Research on Regional Development, Moncton, 1993), p. 168.

The studies also report remarkable development in the three industrial parks in the Moncton area. One is filled virtually to capacity, another has had to expand substantially its number of serviced lots to accommodate new demands, and the third (Dieppe) has seen several new high profile businesses locate there. The Dieppe park is also expanding to accommodate new tenants.

Moncton has seen important major developments in the telecommunications industry. CAMCO, a subsidiary of General Electric, decided to centralize all its Canadian customer service operations in Moncton. It pointed to the city's bilingual work force as a key factor in its decision. CP Express and Transport picked Moncton over Winnipeg, North Bay and Ottawa to locate its customer service and billing centre. Again, Moncton's bilingual work force was a key factor. Lexi-tech, which provides computerized translation services to both Canadian and international markets, has most of its operations in Moncton. Datacor/ISM offers data management services to customers all over North America and has its operations in downtown Moncton.[27] Purolator Courier recently decided to open its national customer service centre in Moncton, creating

400 new jobs with an annual payroll of $8 million. Again, Moncton's bilingual work force was singled out as an important determining factor in site selection. COM DEV Atlantic, a manufacturer of sophisticated electronics for the aeronautic and satellite communications market, decided to open a plant in Moncton, employing 15 people in its first year of operation. The company maintains there is a potential for as many as 500 new jobs at the plant by the end of the decade.[28]

All in all, Moncton has seen over $100 million in investment from outside investors during the early 1990s. This is no small achievement, given Canada's deep recession during the same period.

But this, too, only tells part of the story. Entrepreneurship has flourished in the city as perhaps nowhere else. Table 3 reveals that almost half of the new jobs in the area were created by firms with 25 employees or less, and over ninety percent of all new jobs were created by firms with 100 employees or less. Furthermore, overall, the small firms increased employment by nearly fifty percent in five years, while the large firms barely changed (a 4 percent increase in five years). Although the large firms are very important to Moncton's economic base and do provide economic stability, recent history clearly suggests they will create only a limited number of new jobs in the area.

Table 3

Manufacturing Employment by Company Size

Size of Company (Employees)	1985 Employment	1990 Employment	Change	% Change
1-25	677	1,005	328	48
26-100	1,165	1,446	281	24
100 + (excluding CN)	1,555	1,620	65	4
TOTAL	3,397	4,071	674	20

Source: Statistics Canada, Catalogue No. 31-203, 1991.

Conclusion

Has Moncton made a transition to a more self-sufficient economy, one capable even of absorbing further cutbacks in federal government spending, and capable of competing in the regional, national and global economies? The short answer is: not yet. There is much more to be done. Still, Moncton has made strong progress, probably more than any other community in the region, towards both shock-hardiness and growth-readiness. To be sure, Moncton has been able to diversify and develop its economic base and has brought a degree of stability to its economy. Accordingly, Moncton is much better positioned today than it was, say, ten years ago to absorb an economic downturn in any of its sectors.

Table 4 presents information on earned income for four Maritime cities - Charlottetown, Halifax, Moncton, and Saint John, by sector. This information reveals that Moncton is showing strength in the manufacturing sector, though not to the same extent as Saint John; in finance, insurance, and real estate, though not to the same extent as Halifax. Moncton, however, enjoys a healthy lead in commerce. Though it still relies on public administration and defence for earned income, Moncton does not do so nearly as much as do Halifax and Charlotte-town.

In brief, Moncton's private sector and its entrepreneurs who have shown a keen sense of dynamism in recent years - together with outside investors which launched new economic activities in areas that hold promise in the global economy - all point in the right direction for the new economy and give cause to be optimistic for the future. The city's bilingual work force, its two universities and varied recreational amenities also suggest a solid base on which to build and to compete successfully in the global economy. Atlantic Canada's continued dependence on federal transfers, however, remains a cause for deep concern.

It is widely believed both in the city itself and in provincial and federal government economic development agencies that Moncton has a strong entrepreneurial spirit. It is clear even to the most casual observer that there is a spirit of confidence among the local business communities. Officials in local development agencies, and in ACOA, insist that this spirit is much stronger in Moncton than elsewhere in Atlantic Canada. It is also clear that during the past several years the various economic development organizations in Greater Moncton have become a cohesive force for growth. Organizations such as MID, DIP, the Greater Moncton Chamber of Commerce, the Moncton Central Business Development Corporation (MCBDC), and Resurgo have successfully pooled resources and supported one another in dealing with various economic issues. Moncton has also seen growth in sectors that hold promise for the future knowledge-based economic activities. Its bilingual work force, its two univer-sities, its high-tech firms, its emphasis on the business service sector and communications certainly point in the right direction to compete in the national and global economies.

Table 4

Comparative Data on Employment Income

	Experienced Labour Force	%	Average Employment Income
Total			
Charlottetown	32,850	-	19,277
Halifax	191,185	-	23,314
Moncton	59,765	-	20,972
Saint John	65,940	-	21,998
Primary			
Charlottetown	1,970	6.0	17,759
Halifax	2,260	1.2	21,075
Moncton	890	1.5	15,920
Saint John	1,110	1.7	23,949
Manufacturing Industries			
Charlottetown	1,805	5.5	19,198
Halifax	12,660	6.6	26,498
Moncton	4,510	7.6	23,352
Saint John	9,810	14.9	31,440
Construction			
Charlottetown	2,150	6.5	18,860
Halifax	10,250	5.4	23,385
Moncton	3,220	5.4	20,512
Saint John	4,105	6.2	21,185

Table 4...

	Experienced Labour Force	%	Average Employment Income
Transportation			
Charlottetown	630	6.0	20738
Halifax	15,680	8.2	28407
Moncton	6,135	10.3	29,769
Saint John	6,350	9.6	29,973
Trade			
Charlottetown	1,500	15.8	14,085
Halifax	32,410	17.0	17,781
Moncton	12,710	21.3	17,482
Saint John	11,790	17.9	15,819
Finance, Insurance, and Real Estate			
Charlottetown	1,085	3.3	24,853
Halifax	12,060	6.3	26,311
Moncton	3,020	5.1	25,027
Saint John	3,070	4.7	25,586
Teaching and Related Services			
Charlottetown	2,605	7.9	26,534
Halifax	14,245	7.5	28,669
Moncton	4,125	6.9	27,243
Saint John	4,030	6.1	25,180

Table 4...

	Experienced Labour Force	%	Average Employment Income
Health			
Charlottetown	3,465	10.6	21,622
Halifax	19,895	10.4	24,143
Moncton	6,115	10.2	22,031
Saint John	7,530	11.4	22,357
Hotels and Restaurants			
Charlottetown	3,100	9.4	8,499
Halifax	12,340	6.5	10,070
Moncton	4,505	7.5	8,659
Saint John	6,705	10.2	8,737
Business and Other			
Charlottetown	3,390	9.4	15,785
Halifax	22,545	11.8	19,761
Moncton	6,810	11.4	15,883
Saint John	4,095	6.2	16,347
Public Administration			
Charlottetown	4,755	14.5	28,290
Halifax	30,135	15.8	31,313
Moncton	5,585	9.3	28,110
Saint John	4,695	7.1	26,869

Source: See Statistical Appendix at the end of the book.

However, more will need to be done on this front, particularly in ensuring closer cooperation between the various university-based research centres and high-tech firms. The new economy places a premium on new knowledge, on a keen sense of entrepreneurship, on a stable well-educated work force, on developing new technologies, on applying the latest developments and processes in the workplace, on computers, on research and development, on aggressive marketing and on highly accessible transportation and communication links with the outside world. These are the ingredients necessary to make a locality or region competitive. Compared to other communities in Atlantic Canada, Moncton can claim more than its share of these ingredients.

All in all, Moncton appears particularly well-positioned to make the transition to the new economy. Indeed, the transition appears to be well-launched. Moncton, as a community, is less vulnerable to cuts in government spending than are Halifax, Fredericton or Charlottetown. Direct government and other public sector activities such as universities and hospitals are far more present in those cities than in Moncton. Moncton has also secured more than its share of developments shaping the new economy - among them high-tech jobs in the development and application of new means of communication. Lastly, officials in government agencies report that Moncton entrepreneurs are particularly aggressive in identifying new markets for their products around the globe. In light of these developments, some Monctonians may even feel smug about their community's recent economic successes and think that they are poised for nothing but solid and sustained growth in the new economy in the years ahead.

They need to be reminded, however, that Moncton cannot divorce itself from the rest of the Maritime provinces. Moncton's economic health is directly tied to what happens in the rest of the region. As it has been well-documented elsewhere, the region as a whole remains overly dependent on the presence of the federal government and on federal transfer payments.[29] Cutbacks in federal spending in Halifax will, of course, have a far greater impact in that community than in Moncton, but Moncton will not be able to escape their effect completely. Similarly, cuts in transfer payments to individuals will hold important implications for Moncton's retail sector, and further reductions in federal transfers to provincial governments will entail cuts in public services which, in turn, will lead to job losses. There are plenty of reasons, not least in Ottawa's difficult fiscal situation, to suggest that the federal government will slowly but surely reduce its level of spending in Atlantic Canada.[30] This suggests that Moncton should look beyond its immediate borders to plan for the new economy. To be sure, it can lead by example, but it can never successfully make a full transition to the new economy without planning its future development efforts in full collaboration with other urban centres in the region.

NOTES TO CHAPTER TEN

1. See, among others, Benjamin Higgins and Andrew Breau, "Entrepreneurship and Economic Development: The Case of Moncton," in Donald J. Savoie and Ralph Winter (eds.), *Les provinces Maritimes: un regard vers l'avenir/The Maritime Provinces: Looking to the Future* (Moncton: Canadian Institute for Research on Regional Development, 1993).

2. See, for example, James Foster, "City Still in Top 5 for Business," *Times and Transcript* (Moncton), 31 July 1993, p. 1.

3. "After 71 years of production, Marven's baked its last biscuit Wednesday," *Times and Transcript* (Moncton), 20 July 1978, p. 1.

4. See John Edward Belliveau, *The Monctonians* (Lancelot: Hantsport, N.S., 1981), p. 301.

5. Higgins and Breau, "Entrepreneurship and Economic Development," p. 170.

6. Ibid.

7. Quoted in an article by Charles Perry in *Times and Transcript* (Moncton), 22 November 1985.

8. See *Times and Transcript* (Moncton), 22 November 1985, p. 1.

9. Ibid.

10. Demonstration in August of 1985; slogan seen on an undated *Times and Transcript* photo clipped from the newspaper and found in its file on the CN shops closure.

11. *The Toronto Star* (Toronto), 21 November 1985, p. 1.

12. Report produced by the *Save Our Shops Committee*, Moncton, undated.

13. The prime minister's wife, Mila Mulroney, was apparently struck in the stomach by a demonstrator.

14. See *Times and Transcript* (Moncton), various dates.

15. "Fact Sheet" produced by concerned citizens, (Moncton), 23 February 1993.

16. See Donald J. Savoie, *The Politics of Public Spending in Canada* (Toronto: University of Toronto Press, 1990).

17. See, among others, Higgins and Breau, "Entrepreneurship and Economic Development."

18. This section borrows heavily from Higgins and Breau, "Entrepreneurship and Economic Development."

19. Ibid.

20. These findings are taken from Ibid., p. 177. See also MID, File Brochure, 1990 and Statistics Canada, 1986 Census.

21. See, for example, Donald J. Savoie, *Regional Economic Development: Canada's Search for Solutions* (Toronto: University of Toronto Press, 2d ed., 1992).

22. "PM Launches New Agency for Atlantic Canada," *Sunday Herald* (Halifax), 7 June 1987, p. 1.

23. See, for example, Savoie, *Regional Economic Development*.

24. Ibid., chapter 12.

25. "Moncton's restored Capitol Theatre catalyst for rejuvenated downtown," *The Brunswick Business Journal*, vol. 10, issue 7, July 1993, p. 1.

26. Copies of the studies are available at the Institute. An excellent summary of them is available in Higgins and Breau, "Entrepreneurship and Economic Development."

27. Rod Allen, "City's Economic Comeback Just Beginning," *Times and Transcript* (Moncton), 6 August 1992, p. 1.

28. Ann Walmsley, "Answering Moncton's Call," *Report on Business Magazine* (Toronto), August 1993, p. 24.

29. See Savoie and Winter (eds.), *The Maritime Provinces*.

30. Ibid.

11

FREDERICTON:
BUILDING ON AN INTELLECTUAL BASE

George J. De Benedetti
Eugen Weiss

Fredericton, the provincial capital of New Brunswick, is situated in the centre of the province along the Saint John River. This growing medium-sized city is the cultural, educational, and administrative centre of New Brunswick. Its Victorian houses and many green spaces make it a desirable place to live and work. Because of the significance of government and higher education in its economic base, many research and knowledge-based industries have developed. Fredericton has the largest concentration of consulting and management firms in the province.[1] Combat Training Centre (CTC) Gagetown, one of Canada's largest and growing military bases, is located in nearby Oromocto.

The city of Fredericton is developing a specific strategy to build on its intellectual base.[2] This should prepare Fredericton well to compete in the global economy, to withstand the reductions in public spending, which are inevitably coming, and to be an important provider of services for the information economy.

Some Facts

The population of the Fredericton Census Agglomeration Area (Fredericton region) is 71,869, 17.7 percent of whom are bilingual. The population of the city of Fredericton itself is 46,466. Since 1981, the population of the region has grown by 9.3 percent, while the population of the city itself has grown by 4.8 percent. The Fredericton region has a labour force of approximately 43,000.[3] The participation rate for the Fredericton region is 71.0 percent, and the unemployment rate is 10.1 percent.[4]

The major employers are: the province of New Brunswick, 4,000 employees; Dr. Everett Chalmers Hospital, 1,750 employees; Government of Canada, 1,500 employees; the University of New Brunswick, 1,450 employees; and the New Brunswick Power Commission, 875 employees. Although outside the Census Area of Fredericton, CTC Gagetown, which is approximately twenty kilometres away, has an important influence on the economy of Fredericton. The military base employs 4,300 persons.[5]

Evolution of the Industrial Structure and the Distribution of Earned Income

The fastest growing sectors in the inter-census years were the service sectors. All the service sectors experienced growth. The health sector was the fastest growing sector, 60.3 percent, followed by finance, insurance, and real estate, 41.1 percent, and the business and other services sector, 37.9 percent (see table 1). There was a decline in the number employed in the goods-producing sectors. Employment in the primary industries declined by 14.9 percent and employment in the manufacturing industries declined by 23.9 percent. Despite an extended search for an explanation for the rapid growth in the health sector, its origin remains a mystery. The rapid expansion of software, consulting, and engineering firms in the Fredericton area accounted for some growth in the business and other services sector. We will explore this at greater length later in this chapter.

If we examine the distribution of employment both in the 1981 and 1991 census years, we see that there was a redistribution toward the service sectors and away from the goods-producing sectors. The proportion of employment in the business and other services sector increased from 11.2 to 12.6 percent in this period. Similarly, the health sector's share of employment increased from 6.7 to 8.7 percent, and the hotels and restaurants sector share increased from 6.5 to 6.8 percent. The declining shares of employment were associated with the production of goods; the primary sector's share decreased from 4.6 to 3.2 percent, and manufacturing, 6.9 to 4.3 percent (see table 1). This pattern in the redistribution of employment paralleled the growth in employment in these same sectors.

When we compare the distribution of employment revenue in the inter-census years, we see that the business and other services sector experienced the biggest increase, 8.9 to 12.0 percent, in the proportion of employment income earned. This shows that this sector not only employed more people, but also that the remuneration, on average, had increased. The average employment earnings were higher in this growing sector of business and other services than that of the declining primary and manufacturing sectors (see Statistical Appendix at the end of the book). This signifies real gains for the economy of the Fredericton region.

How does the industrial structure of Fredericton and its evolution differ from its rival cities? In 1991, Fredericton had twice the concentration of employment in the primary sector than did Moncton and Saint John, and more than twice the concentration than Halifax (see table 2). The Fredericton Valley is fertile ground for farming, and producers have long supplied agricultural products to other parts of the province and for export outside the province.

In the manufacturing sector, Fredericton had much less of a concentration of employment than its rivals: less than a third that of Saint John, a little more than half that of Moncton, and approximately two-thirds that of Halifax. Historically, manufacturing employment has been centred on the woolen mills in Marysville. Today those mills are closed. The concentration in the trade sector

Table 1

Experienced Labour Force by Industry Divisions Saint John, Moncton, Halifax, Fredericton

	Saint John			Moncton			Halifax			Fredericton		
	% Distribution of Employment		% Growth	% Distribution of Employment		% Growth	% Distribution of Employment		% Growth	% Distribution of Employment		% Growth
	1981	1991	1981-91	1981	1991	1981-91	1981	1991	1981-91	1981	1991	1981-91
Total	100.0	100.0	15.0	100.0	100.0	22.4	100.0	100.0	22.3	100.0	100.0	22.2
Primary	1.2	1.7	64.4	1.4	1.5	30.9	1.4	1.2	1.1	4.6	3.2	(14.9)
Manufacturing	15.3	14.9	11.8	9.7	7.5	(4.6)	7.7	6.6	5.4	6.9	4.3	(23.9)
Construction	8.0	6.2	(11.0)	6.0	5.4	10.7	5.2	5.4	26.1	6.8	5.9	6.7
Transportation	12.6	9.6	(12.4)	15.2	10.3	(17.2)	8.6	8.2	17.3	7.4	7.7	6.5
Trade	18.9	17.9	8.7	22.3	21.3	16.9	18.0	17.0	14.9	18.4	17.1	13.6
Fin., Insur., Real Estate	5.4	4.7	(1.8)	5.3	5.1	17.3	6.6	6.3	17.3	3.8	4.4	41.1
Teaching	5.7	6.1	23.4	6.4	6.9	32.9	8.3	7.5	10.3	10.3	9.4	12.0
Health	10.1	11.4	29.8	7.6	10.2	64.4	9.5	10.4	33.4	6.7	8.7	60.3
Hotels & Restaurants	6.4	10.2	83.7	7.0	7.5	31.3	6.3	6.5	25.2	6.5	6.8	26.7
Bus. & Other Services	9.6	6.2	(25.4)	9.9	11.4	40.3	10.5	11.8	37.0	11.2	12.6	37.9
Public Administration	6.7	7.1	21.8	9.3	9.3	22.3	17.9	15.8	8.0	17.5	17.1	19.0
Not classified elsewhere	*	*	*	*	*	*	*	*	*	*	*	*

* not available

Source: Statistics Canada, Special data, Custom Products Service, Advisory Services, December 1993.

Table 2

Evolution of the Industrial Structure and Earned Income
Fredericton Metropolitan Area

	Distribution of Employment				Distribution of Employment %		Distribution of Earned Income %	
	1981	1991	Change	% Change	1981	1991	1981	1991
Total	35,250	43,070	7,810	22.1	100.0	100.0	100.0	100.0
Primary	1,615	1,370	(240)	(14.9)	4.6	3.2	3.1	2.8
Manufacturing	2,430	1,850	(580)	(23.9)	6.9	4.3	6.3	4.0
Construction	2,380	2,540	160	6.7	6.8	5.9	6.6	5.1
Transportation	2,605	3,295	690	26.5	7.4	7.7	9.5	9.8
Trade	6,495	7,375	880	13.5	18.4	17.1	14.5	12.7
Finance, Insur., Real Estate	1,350	1,905	555	41.1	3.8	4.4	4.2	5.2
Teaching	3,615	4,050	435	12.0	10.3	9.4	13.5	12.3
Health	2,345	3,760	1,415	60.3	6.7	8.7	7.0	8.7
Hotels & Restaurants	2,305	2,920	615	26.7	6.5	6.8	2.8	2.7
Business & Other Services	3,940	5,435	1,495	37.9	11.2	12.6	8.9	12.0
Public Administration	6,170	7,345	1,175	19.0	17.5	17.1	23.5	22.9
Not Classified elsewhere	*	1,220	*	*	*	*	*	1.8

* not available

Source: Statistics Canada, Special data, Custom Products Service, Advisory Services, December 1993.

was approximately the same as Saint John and Halifax, but much less than that of Moncton.

In the teaching sector, Fredericton's share of employment, 9.4 percent, was above average in terms of its rivals; 6.1 percent for Saint John, 6.9 percent for Moncton, and 7.5 percent for Halifax. It would seem that, despite the numerous institutions of higher learning in the Halifax area, the University of New Brunswick is much more dominant in terms of the population and work force in Fredericton. Despite the health sector being the fastest growing, the concentration of employment in this sector in Fredericton was much smaller than the other centres. Fredericton has only one regional hospital, while the others have more than one.

The proportion of those employed in the business and other services sector in Fredericton was slightly higher than that of Moncton and Halifax, but more than double that of Saint John's. The other sector where there was proportionately more persons employed in Fredericton was the public administration sector; 17.1 percent for Fredericton, 15.8 percent for Halifax, 9.3 percent for Moncton and 7.1 percent for Saint John.

It seems that Fredericton is transforming its economy from the goods producing sectors toward the service sectors at a faster rate than its rivals. We see that as this transformation is taking place, incomes are increasing. What stands out about Fredericton is its concentration of employment and growth in the service sectors, such as teaching, public administration, and the business and other services sectors. In the latter sector, much of the growth is linked to the increase in the number of software companies, engineering, and consulting firms, many of which have links with the Engineering and Computer Science faculties at the University of New Brunswick. There is growth in what might be called the knowledge-based industries.

Competing for Attention as a Centre for Knowledge Industries

In both its strategy papers and promotional plan, the city of Fredericton is positioning itself as an attractive community for well-educated white-collar workers of the baby-boom generation and younger. This is based on the strength of the city's physical attractiveness, and a variety of cultural activities, recreation and park areas not normally available in a city of Fredericton's size. And it is putting particular stress on the hope these amenities will attract - as well as keep people home to develop - companies in the knowledge industries sector. According to Paul Lavoie, Fredericton's director of economic development, this sector has "more opportunities than we can handle. Everyone will prosper. There is too much here to ignore."

A 1992 consultants' report for the city dealt with a number of the issues directly related to the three shocks that are the concern of this book.[6] The consultants reported they found a "broad consensus" that the city's economy needed diversification, "and that the future lies in the knowledge-based industries. The opportunities for this growth [are] seen as being primarily built around the academic institutions, the existing research/professional advisory service sector and proximity to the high technology centres of the New England States."[7] This report suggests both business and the universities could profit from stronger cooperation, whereby business can develop areas with economic promise that research has found feasible, and the universities' research role could profit from strong support from the business community. Much of that consultants' report has become city policy. One example is the current stress that the bilingual capacity of Fredericton should help it attract companies.

Part of the organizational work towards redefining Fredericton's economic role along knowledge industry lines included about half-a-dozen meetings of a Breakfast Club convened by mayor Brad Woodside. From those meetings a Knowledge Industries Steering Committee was formed to pursue those ideas that seemed most likely to succeed. A lot of people have gotten into the act - witness a conference organized by the UNB law school, in February of 1994, on the economic and other effects of information technology.

Lavoie says the major key to development is the telecommunication system: "That puts us ahead of everyone - that's the infrastructure we need." It has become a commonplace reference in almost all talk about the economic future of New Brunswick that it will be driven in large part by the quality of the telephone and telecommunication service available in the province. NBTel's fiber-optic ring around the province and the complete conversion of its system to digital switching has, among other effects, started to make call-forwarding and the rest of the modern message game a part of everyday life even in remote villages.

Information technology is certainly a key consideration for the provincial government, which a few years ago made the development of call-centre business one of its top priorities. And information technology is increasingly a key consideration for the economic future of the capital, given the government's stated goal of reforming its systems and operations through becoming a "model user" of information highway systems.[8] The province's information highway task force policy paper also talks about developing the province's potential as an "information highway pilot study centre."

Another significant development has been a recent acceleration of contact between the University of New Brunswick and various parts of the business community. "Fredericton has now begun to focus on what the university has as a resource," says Bill Paterson, UNB's director of contract research. "It is not uncommon for us to be asked to speak to someone who is visiting the city about the resources the university can put at their disposal to ramp up to competitiveness after establishment of a new firm."

As well, he says, "more and more things are being generated by the faculty, where the faculty is interested in seeing things commercialized." But that tends to happen with individuals, rather than the university as a whole. "We can't push the technology. We can respond to the pull reasonably well. The university is equipped with an attitude that is increasingly supportive of industry," Paterson says. "There is an increasing awareness in computer science, forestry and engineering about the kinds of problems industry has, and the ventures industry is interested in."

The university has a lot of irons in the economic fire, in various ways. A team of experts is providing valuable disease management support to the salmon aquaculture industry; another example is work being done by a university centre in pulp industry technology, to help perfect an environmentally-friendly alcohol-based system for pulping wood, for the Repap pulp and paper conglomerate.

But perhaps the most significant connection between the academic and the business worlds was made by Salem Masry, a professor of survey engineering who started a moonlighting business in the 1980s to develop applications and markets for the computer mapping and locational information systems being developed in the field. His business, Universal Systems Ltd. (USL), took over and developed a geographic information system, CARIS, that had been pioneered by the Canadian Hydrographic Service. Now USL has more than 40 employees, a long list of international clients, and lots of company in a "geomatics cluster" that includes several other smaller firms, as well as larger engineering and environmental consulting firms that have their own uses for geomatics technology. Geomatics is useful in a variety of fields, including mapping, construction location and design, geology, forest management, environmental monitoring, and navigation.

Nor is geomatics the only area in which software companies have established. More recently, there has been a rapid growth in companies developing training materials, ranging from remedial English and mathematics (Job Oriented Training) to instructional modules for people learning to use complex software packages (First Class Systems). Most recently, a number of companies have been working on developing Internet training programs for individuals in government and the private sector, and to develop distance education technologies and curriculum. Other areas of development have been custom hardware and software for the forestry industry, agriculture, and in publishing.

Certainly the software industry in New Brunswick has put down deep roots in Fredericton, in large part because of government demand for state-of-the-art service systems, and because of the steady flow of both graduates and the results of research and development from the University of New Brunswick. Of the 84 members listed in the 1993-94 directory of the non-profit industry group Software New Brunswick, 45 were in Fredericton. Among this group were almost all of the provincial branch offices of national and international firms - including IBM, Unisys, DEC and Brant - with software services and products in their quivers. Among the other cities, Saint John had fourteen members of SNB, Moncton eleven, the Miramichi area five, and nine firms scattered around the rest of the province. Membership in Software NB is not the only determinant of membership in the industry generally: a check of the yellow pages under computer consultants quickly reveals that several companies are not members, and at the same time that many, particularly smaller, software companies do not bother with yellow pages listings. Software and computer services generally is a difficult industry to pin down for statistical purposes, says George Nimegeers, an official of the provincial Economic Development and Tourism department whose brief includes knowledge industry development. "It's very dynamic, with people coming out of the woodwork, setting up in their basement, or coming out of companies. Statistical codes don't very adequately categorize what is going on."

Of a total of about $7.7 million in authorized ACOA assistance to New Brunswick computer services companies between 1988 and the end of March '94, only $2.6 million went to firms based in or near Fredericton.

It took some time to get people to think about Fredericton as having growth prospects in anything beyond secondary manufacturing: People did not think software appeared a viable area of expertise. But then, Nimegeers says, they saw that given the possibilities of interconnection through information technology, it looked like many doors could open. "We can create new products for consultants and engineers, publishers, film and video producers. Something of the nature of a knowledge industry might have a validity," especially where there is the potential to cross-fertilize.

Considerable attention and effort was being put into the city's being host in September of 1994 of a Canadian software show called Softworld '94. Hundreds of representatives of software companies from around the world - and chiefly North America - are expected to attend this event. The city's development department plans related efforts to get decision makers from target companies to come early to look around and meet key local decision makers. In any case, one of the conference's essential purposes is to act as a marketing opportunity for companies to demonstrate their software products, and to make contact with potential buyers and partners in marketing and development.

Moncton's success in the development of telecommunication business, by attracting call centres and back offices, too gained a lot of attention. Fredericton can point to some similar success, particularly in attracting a call centre for Canada Post. But there is, on the whole, a distinction that can be drawn between the communities' records in this field.

Call centres for telesales/teleservice and for handling invoices can be considered a close cousin to retailing: they apply new technology to dealing with customers in a variety of ways that is not, in function, different from the service the companies rendered in former times. The technology may deliver service to an individual customer or to a client department in the same corporation in a more immediate, complete and economical manner, but in most cases the customer is not supposed to notice any difference, other than that service is faster and better.

The nature of the knowledge industry business that Fredericton has developed to date is much less retailing than it is design and custom manufacture. The traditional leaders in this sector have been the engineering companies like ADI and Neill & Gunter, and the government-owned RPC, and there has been growth for environmental consultants like Jacques Whitford.

Most of the companies just referred to here, and above, are indigenous to Fredericton. Many of them - and certainly others not named - have prospered in large part through work done for NB Power and both the federal and provincial government, as well as work undertaken and paid for by the private sector to meet environmental and other standards. At the same time, the prospect of doing work for the government has also helped draw national and international computer and consulting companies to win contracts or to establish offices in Fredericton - among them Datacor/ISM, Systemhouse, Unisys, Brant, DEC, Andersen Consulting and the Irving-owned Maritime Information Technologies.

The analogy that contrasts Greater Moncton's success in "retail" telecommunication service with Fredericton's strength as a centre for the custom manufacture and refinement of knowledge solutions finds a further parallel, in the way Fredericton has decided to approach the question of how to market itself.

The city's strategic push to attract knowledge-based industry is likely to be less noticed within the region than outside it, and this as part of a deliberate strategic decision to focus recruitment efforts on people in the senior executive levels of target companies, and in particular companies in Ontario, Quebec and the northeast United States. And given a relative scarcity of human resources to nurture contacts, the city has chosen not to cast its promotional nets more widely, but rather has opted for intensive and in-depth attention to satisfying prospects, "[to put] Fredericton farther down the decision-making curve than it would be able to do if it tried to reach a wide audience."[9] Except insofar as it is looking for recognition of its specific expertise in areas such as geomatics and environmental technology, the city is not targeting people in other areas of Atlantic Canada.

A partial exception may be that one of its major goals in 1994 was for Fredericton to succeed in the increasingly-intense competition among cities for the honour of being considered the most business-like and business-friendly. The most sought-after prize in that competition is recognition in the *Globe and Mail Report on Business Magazine* as one of the top five centres in Canada. Moncton made that list twice in succession, in 1992 and 1993. In 1994, Fredericton is making a determined push for similar recognition, supplying the magazine's editors with a book that gives detailed answers to questions put by the magazine, together with various documents giving background information, and further the promise that various business and community leaders would call the editors prepared to talk about their own experience and impressions.

Lavoie says local leaders looked at the job done by Moncton to attract business - "They helped the whole province with its image, because they've impressed the hell out of people." And now, like Saint John, Fredericton has decided to gear up with a similar teamwork approach to attracting business opportunities. Fredericton considers its top rivals to be - in order - Moncton, Saint John and Halifax.

Prospects and Constraints

The factors that have made Fredericton a prosperous community - its role as a major headquarters for the provincial government, NB Power, its considerable federal military and civilian job base, as well as its strong base in advanced education - are, of course, all vulnerable to reductions in public spending. NB Power has already announced plans to scale back, as has the provincial government, which expects to reduce its province-wide work force by some 2,000 in a few years time.

But to a certain degree, those efforts to reduce the traditional bureaucracy are being undertaken with an ambition to make austerity pay dividends beyond simple savings in payroll and office expenditures. When the province announced the planned privatization of medicare claims administration to a consortium of private firms, it stressed that it expected there would be no net job losses. The development of new systems by the private companies was also expected to put them in a position to market the systems and expertise they would develop for other jurisdictions and clients. Given the high priority the United States now attaches to revamping its health financing system, the potential spin-offs could be enormous, even without (as now appears likely) an American adoption of the Canadian single-payer model of health insurance. Similar initiatives, such as the re-engineering of systems in the solicitor-general's department, might show like promise.

The Canadian Armed Forces presence in the Fredericton area is more likely to see growth than to decline, at least for the foreseeable future. This, paradoxically, is in part because two units are expected to be transferred from the to-be-closed CFB Chatham to CTC Gagetown. The base employment currently stands at 3,200 military personnel and 1,100 civilians. The base budget is about $235 million a year, including $168 million in salaries. There are plans for about $44 million in capital improvements at the base, towards the last third of the decade. But whether these plans come to fruition will depend on the fate of the Canadian military budget and CTC Gagetown's place within it: nearer-term capital spending plans totalling between $22 and $28 million were delayed or put on hold this spring.

A potential and general constraint may be a lack of self-confidence. According to the Vision 2000 report in 1992, the main hindrances to development along the lines contemplated had to do with "prevalent attitudes, value systems and practices." These included complacency because of the area's long-standing reliance on the government and education sectors, a general lack of a "customer-driven" mindset, resistance to change and a tendency to think small, uncoordinated and duplicated economic development efforts, distrust of government economic leadership, and "a lack of understanding of the need for and commitment to economic development."

The provincial government has made a splash in its initiative for developing an information highway policy, and its stated intention of making New Brunswick a leader in this field has a great deal of significance for the economy of Fredericton, not least because the information highway policy undertakes to help the development of knowledge industries through the province's own early adoption of the technologies, as a "model user/customer" of the highway and its services.

The degree to which the province does become a customer is likely to be a crucial concern to the software/knowledge industry sector. Just because a government is interested in a service or technology is no guarantee that it will pay for it in significant commercial quantities. In the past, the experience of some companies has been that governments will pay for a demonstration project, and urge companies to develop export markets, but decline, with regret, the opportunity to become a significant customer. The plea of poverty no doubt has its grounding in fact, but it denies precisely the support a company looking for customers elsewhere needs the most: Proof that a company's mastery of its niche has been recognized in its home market.

It may be natural to suppose there is a distinction to be drawn between a local sector mostly comprised of small, boot-strapping companies, and the local offices of large companies that might be presumed to be importing and retailing to the government off-the-shelf software systems and, sometimes, raw computer power and time. But people in the industry maintain the process of re-engineering government is so recent that there is relatively little on the shelf. The new systems of government administration and service delivery are being invented, tested and refined now. This same process, of course, has also been, and continues to be, applied to the development of private-sector call centres and tele-administration systems: The province's practical and policy direction is clearly to apply similar technology to its service delivery system. But the effects of this direction are only beginning to be felt.

At the moment, the most prominent portion of the locally-based computer services industry is geomatics, followed by companies in courseware development, says Wayne Gunter, manager of the southwest New Brunswick district office of the Atlantic Canada Opportunities Agency. He expects that both environmental technology and the telecommunication sector will be supported by government, and that telecommunication, in particular, will grow by "leaps and bounds." Video and film production companies in the Fredericton area have not made a big impact as yet, though that area has promise for multi-media initiatives. Most software companies are working on applications for markets outside Atlantic Canada, as well as inside.

And most of them are far from flush. "They don't have a lot of cash in their pockets, and financing is difficult for them," Gunter says. "They have to make believers of a lot of people." There is money available under the innovation portion of the Action Program, but ACOA wants to see some actual commercialization before it provides financial support. One recent form of such support has been a "mentoring" arrangement, under which nine companies got help with international marketing from a company in Boston, most of them to their profit.

To say that Fredericton has a busy sector of entrepreneurial computer service and software company start-ups is not to say that the sector as a whole has achieved a mature prosperity. Capital for software companies is notoriously scarce in Canada - in large part a function of the difficulty any liquidator would find in realizing salvage value from a product, most of whose value is expected to reside in the support and upgrades its creators would be able to provide for it, were they to continue in business. Financing software development firms is a problem in central Canada, and - as is true for firms of all kinds - the difficulties of finding equity financing are even greater in this region. When the New Brunswick government launched a community development bond program in 1993 to address part of this problem by offering to guarantee the initial capital investment that members of a community might place in ventures, part of the thinking was that the program could be of particular use to software companies. If there has, in fact, been subsequent local discussion of issuing even one such bond to support a knowledge industry company, it had not reached the ears of people contacted for this chapter.

One of the other impediments that a software development and knowledge industry in Fredericton, and in New Brunswick, generally faces is the lack of a local legal industry specialization in intellectual property practice. Local patent applicants are referred to central Canadian law firms that specialize in the field. Software - both in its programming structural design and in any content it delivers - falls into the category of copyright law, and there are no provincial lawyers specializing in that, either. A number of lawyers do handle matters of corporate identification and trademarks, but even that relatively elementary level of intellectual property law is only a minor part of local practices.

The argument generally heard in this region on the need for intellectual property protection is that a small start-up company should not bother with it, other than doing a relatively cheap search to establish that its efforts do not duplicate prior art. The argument goes that for small new enterprises the cost of obtaining wide patents, and of enforcing either a patent or a copyright, is almost always beyond the means of the aggrieved individuals involved. And therefore their scarce resources are held to be far better deployed in the actual development and marketing of the product. However, the ability to enforce legal protection of a product is essential when it is taken onto the world market, as it is expected that knowledge industry firms will do. Reaching for such larger markets requires marketing; marketing requires financial backing; and this cannot reasonably be expected for companies about to wander onto strange streets, the contents of their pockets unguarded and free for the plundering.

Lack of ready access to advice and local expertise on the fine points of standard and special terms and agreements on disclosure, joint ventures, and the assignment and compensation for the copyrightable contributions of others, can only be an impediment to an entrepreneurial software development community. Its prosperity might very well come more quickly, and be built on a sounder foundation, were the issue of intellectual property protection to be addressed pro-actively by both the legal and industrial policy sectors, and certainly by the knowledge industry itself. Proper intellectual property protection for commercial knowledge industries is no more a frill than is a functioning immune system.

Without some effort to balance awareness of, and access to, this legal expertise, knowledge industry companies here will work at a disadvantage to comparable companies closer to the centre of Canada's urban network - say, in Kanata or Cambridge in Ontario, or in the software cluster around Vancouver - who have readier access to more diverse sources of advice.

Re-engineering Government: Profit as Well as Savings?

The term "re-engineering" has in recent years come to be applied to informatics-based changes in both private industry and, increasingly, in government. The process of organizational reform for which re-engineering stands is not new: as one example, one can consider New Brunswick's well-established home care extramural hospital system, started some 15 years ago. While such changes may lead to more satisfied clients and greater financial efficiency, the best of them should pay for themselves even beyond that. The explanation and demonstration of how a workable reform functions could have major export potential, both in background and training materials and courses, as well as in what's known as "technical tourism."

NB Power, which has had a considerable effect promoting the growth of the engineering consulting industry in New Brunswick and particularly Fredericton, is nearing the end of its recent cycle of power plant construction. That will certainly eliminate the immediate local demand for the kind of plant systems engineering and environmental assessment work such projects call for. We may not need new power plants in Canada, but others do. Other utilities around the world may hire New Brunswick experts, such as in nuclear technology or in the design of scrubber systems: On that premise, 21 firms in

New Brunswick have established themselves recently as New Brunswick Engineering International, a "virtual" corporation designed to mix-and-match partners to compete for contracts that might otherwise flow just to large, vertically-integrated engineering companies based in large cities.

In addition, there may be new possibilities opening up in other directions. Providing training for Rumanian nuclear plant operations personnel is one area where opportunities are already being realized, as is the development of exportable technology for monitoring what is happening within the pipes of nuclear plants. In a different area, various New Brunswick companies have become expert in avoiding problems that can arise when inappropriate stone aggregate is used in major construction projects, and have been selling that expertise around the world. Power demand management systems and the development of "smart house" technology may be yet another area of opportunity.

As with those specific areas, the key to success for software companies in provinces like New Brunswick and Nova Scotia may also be to find their proper niche, says Ron Percy, director of the Information Technology Association of Canada for New Brunswick and chairman of Softworld '94. He considers it likely that local video game developers would have their lunch eaten by established competitors elsewhere. There is more promise, he argues, in providing the technical solutions and systems development that will support the re-engineering of government and business systems. And this road leads straight to - and straight from - the capital. Percy suggests that, given the quality of communications now possible, one can think of New Brunswick, as a whole, as a city. And he maintains that even the relatively small population of the province makes it easier to make big changes that can apply everywhere. A change in a system serving 750,000 people takes care of New Brunswick, but would be only a pilot or demonstration project in New York or Quebec. "The province is such a size that it is a good laboratory for re-engineering. We can work with the bureaucracy to recraft something. It's not hard to call the people you need to reach to get things going."

The software industry in New Brunswick is not big now, Percy says, "but it has all the ingredients to be another Kanata or Route 128 (the Boston-New Hampshire high-tech corridor)." Percy is a former president of Datacor/ISM, which started in business in the late 80s, taking on large out-sourcing contracts with the province of New Brunswick and the federal government, in addition to providing computer services to its initial co-owners, Blue Cross of Atlantic Canada and Bruncor (the holding company that controls NBTel). Now he is Atlantic vice-president and general manager of SHL Systemhouse, which is working with the New Brunswick Geographic Information Corporation to develop a complex system of land records applications. And while similar projects aimed at re-engineering the justice or health, finance, or income assistance systems for government may get the most attention, some of the busiest people working in re-engineering are doing their work for small and mid-range companies going through systems changes of their own.

The re-engineering of government systems to make use of information technology carries with it a range of transformative effects, and these go deeper than making it possible to go to an electronic kiosk to get information on a government program, or simply to pay a traffic fine. It can be expected to change the way people interact with government, and, therefore, how employees in government deal with the public. Some may not like these changes, and the resistance of such people can be expected to have at least short-term political impact, even if the eventual prospects of halting the informatic tide are as promising in this day as they were in King Canute's.

For a government, there are road hazards on the way to the information highway. Civil service resentment of perceived career ceilings for unilingual anglophones contributed much fuel to the local strength of the Confederation of Regions (CoR) party in the 1991 provincial election, and the Conservative party has made it clear it does not support Liberal government privatization initiatives. Significant job losses in the capital would never be accepted unopposed.

The McKenna government survived widespread public service labour resentment in 1991, and remained hugely popular into the summer of 1994. But in politics, tomorrow is always another day. The impact of health care cuts, and both school and municipal reorganization, has not been tested electorally. Austerity and turmoil, unbalanced by a perceived pay-off, is a hard sell. One question for the future of the new-economy drive for Fredericton may well be whether it is seen locally as a gain, or at least a palatable way of standing still. Another may also be whether any effort to strengthen the economy of the province's elite city, if seen to be at the expense of other regions, is politically acceptable.

Conclusion

If it does take root well, the re-engineering processes under way in the provincial government, and the growing interplay between the universities and the private sector, together may well transform the city from its former model, where all three sectors existed in discrete groupings with largely separate elite structures, whose members were more likely to mingle in the lobby of the Playhouse theatre or at Grand Lake than during their work. What may well emerge is a more functional capital, in which the boundaries between bureaucracy, academy and business are clearly porous, and becoming more so because of shared directions and endeavors.

It seems clear, at the same time, that it is impossible to confine the vision underlying such a new direction to Fredericton alone. The provincial government by definition has equal responsibilities and accountability to a citizen of Miscou Centre as to a citizen of Marysville; the University of New Brunswick is not the University of Fredericton, and as a university is not a garrison of scholars but a community's prime gateway to the world's knowledge; and the city's various knowledge industries know they will not thrive without reaching for at least continental, if not global markets.

The same economic logic by which New Brunswick has profited in its call-centre initiative, at the expense of Toronto and other Ontario cities can, of course, be applied within the province itself. If information from the centre can be fed easily anywhere in the province, this can both empower physically remote citizens, as well as enable the physical decentralization of government departments or departmental units. Such a centrifugal effect might, paradoxically, strengthen the centre, if it were a signal success for which other jurisdictions would crave both the tools and instruction in their use.

On the whole, Fredericton's declared goal of turning a government-and-academically-driven small city into an entrepreneurial complex ought to excite widespread practical attention, as well as intense interest from students of public administration. The development of modern systems of governance and public service, and the recruitment, particularly of the private sector, to apply its skills and imagination to the task, may provide part of the answer to the need to re-skill government, without increasing the civil service base. A practical and detailed solution, wherever it evolves, should be a valuable commodity in the new economy.

In terms of the three shocks - the reduction in public spending, globalization, and the development of the information economy - it can be said that the community of Fredericton is well on its way to learning how to swim in the backwash, even as the wave of public expenditure reduction continues to rise. It is at least plausible that the community has enough options at its disposal, and confidence to pursue them, to prosper in a changed economy.

In an age when all the talk about the future economy is about the development of knowledge industries and applying them to the more effective production of both goods and services, the future of cities like Fredericton ought to be bright indeed. But it is not assured. The key issue for the realization of that potential in knowledge industries may well be whether the community - and New Brunswick - are prepared to invest in those industries, even as the traditional flow of government funds declines in relative terms. This will require faith, confidence, and a willingness to invest from among local leaders, public and private. To withhold the essential support until the value and virtue of local efforts have been validated by national investors would be feckless, and quite possibly ruinous.

NOTES TO CHAPTER ELEVEN

1. City of Fredericton, Office of the City Administrator, "Economic Profile, 1993," pp. 1 and 3.

2. Bristol Communications Inc., "1994 Communications Plan for Fredericton Economic Development Inc.," February 28, 1994, p. 3.

3. See Statistical Appendix at the end of the book.

4. Statistics Canada, Census of Population, 1991.

5. Supplied by Ms Laurie Brown, Economic Development Officer, City of Fredericton, *via* a telephone interview on May 26, 1994. These figures have been confirmed by the Canada Employment Centre in Fredericton.

6. Coopers & Lybrand, Vision 2000 Economic Development Strategy, Key Findings and Recommendations.

7. Ibid., p. 26, 27.

8. *Driving the Information Highway*, the report of the New Brunswick Task Force on the Electronic Information Highway, NB ED&T, 1994.

9. Communications Plan for the Fredericton Economic Development Inc. (FEDI), prepared by Bristol Communications Inc., 21 February, 1994.

12

CHARLOTTETOWN:
A PERIPHERAL CENTRE AT THE CROSSROADS

J. Frank Strain

Introduction

Maritime urban centres are at a crossroads. Throughout much of the post-World War II era a complex interconnected set of economic, social, and political institutions shaped the pattern of regional and urban development in this part of the country. Although never static, these institutions provided a relatively stable environment within which business leaders and workers, farmers and fishermen, educators and students, as well as politicians, public servants and electorates could formulate plans and embark on concrete programs of action. These plans and programs ultimately generated the observed pattern of settlement and activity in the region.

But since the mid-1970s the social environment has become increasingly chaotic. The postwar institutions - the firms which dominated the postwar period, labour unions, the health and education systems, social welfare policies, and Canadian federalism - are experiencing significant problems. New social institutions are emerging. Whether we like it or not, Canada and the world are in the midst of a major transformation, and the Maritimes and its urban centres are along for the ride.

This paper examines this major transformation and its impact on one Maritime urban centre: Charlottetown, Prince Edward Island. The three major developments which lie at the heart of the current round of structural change - new global economic relations, technological change and the emerging knowledge economy, and changes in the role of government - have serious implications for Charlottetown. The objective of this paper is to combine some relatively simple theoretical ideas, empirical data, and an appreciation of past experience to "tease out" some of their implications.

The analytical approach adopted in the paper is heavily influenced by recent work on complex dynamical systems. Dynamic systems theory underlies much of the analysis in this paper. Significantly, this approach is beginning to have an impact on academic research (especially in biology, neuroscience, anthropology, physics, economics, history, etc.) and many believe this methodological framework has the potential to revolutionize the natural and social sciences. There are several very accessible introductions to ongoing work in this area. (in particular, see Waldorp, 1992 and Lewin, 1992) Interested readers are encouraged to consult these works.

Because the approach is new and requires new ways of thinking, it might be helpful to summarize the essential features of the approach, and its relationship to the analysis of this paper. Three features of the approach are critical.

First, the goal of the research with complex dynamic systems is not to produce precise predictions. Instead, it is to discover the generic structure of dynamic models, which, although are structurally simple, generate complex behaviour systems, and apparently have a "life of their own."

Second, discovering the underlying structure allows one to make predictions, but not about micro level outcomes; instead the predictions are made at the macro level. (This is the revolutionary aspect of complexity analysis. There is a strong reductionist tradition in scientific research where macro level outcomes are strictly viewed as a result of micro level developments.) The mathematics of complex systems which best describes "living systems," such as biological evolution, neuro-networks, spin glass, social history, turbulence in the flow of liquids and gases, and a variety of other natural and social processes, yields concrete predictions. For example: (a) "living systems" tend to persist in a state of homeostatis (stability) for periods, only to erupt into periods of rapid change (the mathematics here relates to the existence of attractors); (b) the periods of rapid change are relatively short (and the system tends to settle down again); (c) small changes spontaneously generate the rapid changes; and (d) "living systems" tend to become more complex over time but there is no tendency to degenerate into chaos; the systems are "self-organizing." The underlying structure of the mathematical models, which produce these outcomes, and which resemble the incredibly complex outcomes generated by "living systems," are remarkably simple.

Third, the dynamics of these complex systems are examined by searching for positive and negative feedback. Positive feedback results from interaction within the system, which moves the dynamic system toward an "attractor." Negative feedback results from interactions, which move the system away from an "attractor."

This paper incorporates a number of hypotheses from complex systems theory. For example, complex systems theory underlies the social structures of accumulation argument that capitalist societies tend to oscillate between periods of relative stability and periods of rapid change. Also, complexity theory is implicit in the arguments about the process of structural change in the paper. Rapid change occurs when negative feedback effects accumulate and push the system away from an attractor (institutions experience problems and the economy performs poorly), but the system eventually "hones in" on a new attractor (the institutional problems begin to be solved, new arrangements emerge, and economic performance improves), as positive feedback pushes the system toward a state of relative stability. This aspect of the theory is especially significant in the hypothesis that we will see new interconnected institutions develop out of the current period of structural change, and that the national welfare state, as we now know it in Canada, is unlikely to be part of the new institutional arrangement.

The theory also underlies the paper's main policy prescription. Complex dynamic systems are self-organizing. Policies which remove constraints on the ability of individuals to experiment with new ways of doing things are favoured in the paper because flexible, adaptive mathematical systems tend to be self-organizing, whereas tightly structured rule-constrained systems tend to chaos.

Although the theory does not yield precise predictions about concrete outcomes or a set of rules, which, if imposed on society, will assure a better life, it is far from vacuous. Instead, it offers predictions about the process (as opposed to outcomes), it suggests that one should be extremely sceptical about deterministic theories which ignore complexity, it generates policy prescriptions to improve processes, and it calls into question traditional policy prescriptions which proport to offer a path to a specific, desirable, outcome. Specifically, Charlottetown and other Maritime urban centres are viewed as part of a complex interconnected dynamic systems which continuously evolves over time. In this abstract framework change is endogenous. Changes spontaneously arising in one area can reverberate through the entire system affecting (perhaps even transforming) all economic, social, and political institutions through a complex of positive and negative feedback effects. Of course, because the system is extremely complex and because dramatic structural change is associated with relatively chaotic conditions, it is impossible to completely identify the structural characteristics of the underlying dynamic system. Thus complex dynamic systems theory is not used as the basis for a formal model-building exercise in this paper. Instead, complexity is used as an analogy to emphasize the fundamental importance of two features that complex nonlinear dynamic systems and socio-economic systems seem to share. First, the dynamic systems which seem to offer the best insight into our physical and biological world tend to operate "at the edge of chaos" where order and chaos achieve a special sort of balance. Social systems, too, exhibit this combination of order and chaos. Second, complex dynamic systems can experience dramatic transformations without completely degenerating into chaos. This property of adaptive or self-organizing complex systems is particularly important when the current round of structural change is put in historical context.

The opening section of the paper attempts to place Charlottetown and the current wave of structural change in historical context. Section two offers a brief discussion of the most important features of the current round of structural change. The third section looks at adjustments within the Charlottetown area over the past fifteen years. A final section is devoted to policy implications.

Charlottetown and Structural Change: An Historical Perspective

Charlottetown has been a permanent site of European settlement since the early seventeenth century when the French established Port La Joie within a sheltered harbour on the south coast of the Island. This makes Charlottetown one of the oldest settlements in the region: It antedates that in Halifax by at least three decades.

Much has changed over this three-hundred-year history, and it is possible to identify more than one major structural change which transformed the community. Although structural change is the central concern of this paper, an exploration of Charlottetown's adaptation to structural change in the past must be delayed until we explore some remarkable continuities in the settlement's history. There are two stable characteristics worthy of attention. First, the settlement of Charlottetown is and has always been the most important centre of commercial and government service provision in Prince Edward Island. The types and volumes of services provided have varied significantly over time but the basic role of the centre has not. Second, Charlottetown and Prince Edward Island have always been on the periphery of the wider civilization. Neither of these characteristics have changed during the 1980s, the beginning period of the current round of structural change, nor is it likely that these will change over the next twenty years.

Being on the periphery or at the margins of a civilization has implications for Charlottetown *per se*, and for the methods chosen in this paper to examine Charlottetown's adaptation to structural change. First, marginal regions are at the geographical fringe of the civilization. Thus interaction with other parts of the dynamic social systems is limited by the state of transportation and communication technology. Moreover, technical change in transportation and communication should be expected to have a significant impact. Second, marginal regions are on the cultural fringe of the civilization. Consequently, people in a marginal region must import culture from the rest of the world just to remain part of the civilization. (Note that culture is being defined very broadly here. Culture is embodied in the material goods we consume: for example, automobiles, televisions, and computers are essential features of the culture of today's North America; symphonies and dance troupes are not.) Finally, the cultural dependence creates economic dependence, since the marginal region must either export products in demand to the rest of the world; borrow (which assumes future exports), or be given, no strings attached, the cultural products they demand if they are to remain in the civilization.

Jane Jacobs (1984, pp. 34-5) in her book *Cities and the Wealth of Nations* clearly outlines the methodological significance of marginality for studies examining community history. Her reflections are worth quoting since they have strongly influenced the analysis of this paper (her original description was of the small settlement of Bardou in France. I have consistently substituted Charlotte-town for Bardou in the following quotation):

> Charlottetown is an example, in microcosm, of what I am going to call passive economies, meaning economies that do not create economic change themselves but instead respond to forces unloosed in distant cities. Time and again, like a toy on a string, Charlottetown has been jerked by some external economic energy or other. . . We could beat our brains out trying to explain Charlottetown's economic history in terms of its own attributes, right down to the [most detailed descriptions of politicians, business leaders, workers and work processes, etc. but] none of this would enlighten us at all as to why and how Charlotte-town's economy took the twists and turns it actually did. On that subject, the local clues stand mute, for the clues that in reality explain Charlottetown's twists and turns are to be found in distant city markets, jobs, city work transplanted, city technology, city capital. To under-stand both the changes that occurred in Charlottetown and why there were periods when nothing changed, we must look to clues that do not define Charlottetown in any way except as they have acted upon Charlottetown.

The pervasive influence of developments in the rest of the world on the human settlement in Charlottetown is easily illustrated. The original settlement at Port La Joie was European, established because Europeans, for the first time in history, possessed the capital, the technology and the motivation (potential profit from the exploitation of local fish stocks) required to initiate this type of venture. Unfortunately, the fish stocks did not actually yield profits for the early Island "developers" and the business failure left the small settlement stranded.

The community changed little until an outbreak of hostilities between England and France in the 1740s. When the English seized control of Nova Scotia and initiated a deportation of the Acadian population, large numbers escaped to the Island. The strengthening of the French fort at Louisbourg, too, was important, since it provided a source of export earnings as the Island began to produce agricultural products to supply the garrison. Nonetheless, the population in the area around what is now Charlottetown remained agricultural and scattered.

In the 1760s the English laid claim to the Island, and when the Island was granted independent colonial status, Charlottetown was designated as the centre for government and the site of a British garrison. The political and military institutions provided a focal point for a nuclear settlement, but growth was painfully slow. By the turn of the century there were fewer than 5,000 people on the Island, and perhaps 400 in Charlottetown. (Clark, 1959, p. 59) Moreover, the community was heavily dependent on funds from the British government, since the Island produced few exports.

But early in the nineteenth century, Charlottetown and Prince Edward Island were transformed by events in Europe. Hostilities between England and France during the Napoleonic Wars generated a bizarre sequence of government policies, which first effectively cut off England from its traditional Baltic timber suppliers, and secondly eliminated the American merchant marine from international shipping (see Easterbrook and Aitken, 1956, pp. 142-50 for a complete discussion). The change in the *general international environment* and *government policy* transformed the economies of the Maritime colonies. As Easterbrook and Aitken note:

> For the Maritime colonies as a whole the period from 1808 to 1815 was one of remarkable economic expansion. At the beginning of the period Nova Scotia and New Brunswick were hardly more than names on a map. Their settlements and towns were, for the most part, primitive pioneer communities, where men considered themselves fortunate if they could make enough from farming or the fisheries to support themselves and their families. By the end of the period the harbours and towns of the colonies were among the busiest and most prosperous of the Atlantic seaboard. Fortunes were being made and capital was being accumulated. Nova Scotia and New Brunswick had established themselves as active members of the North Atlantic trading system. Their merchants and ship captains had acquired the skill, the experience, and the confidence which, before many years had passed, would enable them to challenge the supremacy of New England. (p. 150)

Although Charlottetown and Prince Edward Island are unmentioned in the Easterbrook and Aitken account, they experienced the same transformation as Nova Scotia and New Brunswick. Indeed, by the 1830s the second largest shipping fleet in Atlantic Canada (the largest was in Saint John) was registered in Charlottetown, and the settlement had become a port of growing importance in the North Atlantic trading system. (Sager and Fischer, 1982) The development was clearly based on events outside Charlottetown itself; in particular, by the rapid growth of industrial England, which increased the demand for timber and ocean-going transport and the protection of the Baltic timber tariffs and the American Embargo Act.

Although this protection did not last long, the political events in Europe and the United States created a window of opportunity for the region. During this brief time capital was accumulated, information networks were generated, and skills were honed. When England moved to free trade in the 1840s (which might have transformed the region again), local business was able to compete successfully on the world market. By 1861 the population of Prince Edward Island had grown to 81,000, and that of Charlottetown to almost 7,000. (Clark, 1959, p. 87)

Two features of this period of growth are worthy of note. First, commercial economic activity in Charlottetown was largely based on initiatives by immigrants who had direct or indirect links with British firms. This provided a direct communication link with the prime markets for output and eliminated many potential marketing problems. Second, forest products were the most important export for much of the period. Because land was being cleared for agriculture, this was not a sustainable export base. Eventually, these exports would have to decline.

Nonetheless, the community's success in international trade not only sparked income and population growth, but also provided a financial base for the development of an elaborate network of commercial and community services in Charlottetown. Wholesaling, retailing and small-scale manufacturing establishments sprung up to service the growing Island population. Hospitals, education institutions, including two institutions of higher learning: Prince of Wales (1836) and Saint Dunstan's (1855) colleges, a court system, port facilities, a central market and entertainment centres were also established in Charlottetown. Like the wholesale, retail, and small-scale manufacturing establishments, the community facilities were designed to service the wider Island community.

The period of growth came to an end in the 1870s. The world economy experienced the chaotic conditions of "the first great depression" between 1873 and 1886, and many countries adopted protectionist measures to support their own floundering economies. Canada, too, turned inward, not only pursuing a strong tariff policy but also a policy of nation building based on a transcontinental rail system. The combination of protectionism, the new industrialism, western expansion, and technical change in shipping posed insurmountable challenges for the settlement at Charlottetown and the wider Island community.

The local economy stagnated as export earnings and living standards began to fall. Between 1881 and 1921 the Island's population declined from 109,000 to 88,000, as relative boom conditions in distant cities opened up opportunities for Islanders willing to leave their homes. Throughout the period of decline, Charlottetown remained the political and commercial centre for the Island, but it never became more. The small declining market in Prince Edward Island simply did not offer the opportunities for the new large-scale decreasing-cost industries developing in the heartland of North America. Nonetheless, Charlottetown did not experience the same population decline as the Island as a whole. (It continued to grow very slowly, reaching a peak in 1911 at 10,718, less than 300 more than in 1881.)

A number of relatively small-scale local successes (lobster canning in the 1880s and early 1890s and silver fox pelts early in the twentieth century) reduced the pain of stagnation and provided the export earnings required to import, and thus remain part of the wider civilization. Although living standards were lagging significantly behind those enjoyed elsewhere, the settlement at Charlottetown was not stagnant. Indeed, electricity, a central water and sewage system, and the telephone were introduced in the 1880s. The automobile made its appearance just after the turn of the century. By the 1920s roads were becoming a priority. Throughout the period local merchants stocked the latest in fashion. Nonetheless, the exodus of Islanders continued until the second depression hit, thereby eliminating the pull from the distant cities.

The depression and World War II sparked another major transformation in world economy. The most notable feature of the new social system was that many aspects of social life were being managed. Keynesian policies were introduced to manage demand. Social welfare policies of various types were introduced to manage social conflict and poverty. Collective bargaining legislation emerged to manage conflict between workers and management.

Management was not exclusively the domain of the state. Firms, too, reorganized to provide a more effective structure to manage the organization. As Galbraith (1967) noted, the large corporation relied heavily on an elaborate "techno-structure" dedicated to "planning." Even international economic relations were managed through arrangements like Breton-Woods and the General Agreement on Tariffs and Trade (GATT). The one area where direct management seemed to be unsuccessful - international political relations - generated the Cold War and provided the basis for significant state involvement in research and development, and in military spending.

In combination the postwar government and business policies helped stabilize the social environment, and thus provided a setting conducive to profit-making. Success fed success, as positive feedback and increasing returns dominated in the dynamic performance of the system. The resulting postwar social system provided the basis for a sustained period of expansion in the world economy which lasted through much of the 50s and 60s. However, by the early 70s cracks began to appear in the postwar social system, and the behaviour of the system became more chaotic. The system which had initially supported accumulation and profit-making was now causing problems. Although the breakdown of social institutions is complex (see Grant and Strain, 1991 for a discussion of some of the problems faced in Canada), a couple of important factors can be identified here to illustrate the types of things which contributed to the decline. The first factor was that management by the state opened an important arena to democratic control. State activity did not always support profit-making. Indeed, it often worked against it. Second, some policies had negative as well as positive feedback effects. On the one hand these policies aided profit seekers. (For example, government demand management policies assured markets for output, unemployment insurance did the same, while reducing the potential for social unrest accompanying unemployment, etc.) On the other hand, these same policies potentially threatened profits. (Demand management reduced unemployment and increased the relative power of labour, unemployment insurance reduced the relative power of management by reducing the threat of firing, etc.) As the system evolved business interests lost their ability to assure policies would support private profitability. Third, established capitalist nation-states gradually lost their ability to assure low-cost imports of raw materials from the rest of the world. The energy crises of the 1970s were the most dramatic manifestations of this. Finally, within the business firm, the planning apparatus, the legalistic system of industrial relations, and the vertically-integrated organizational structure, all of which had provided a basis for control of uncertainty eventually reduced the flexibility needed to adjust to rapid change.

In the Maritime provinces the postwar social structure of accumulation proved beneficial. Regional disparity in 1930 was severe. Personal incomes were approximately half those in Ontario. Roads and communication facilities were underdeveloped, the health and education systems were underfunded, and the typical person in the region did not have access to facilities common in other parts of the country (indoor plumbing, central heating, etc.). Indeed, the attractions of the centre and the lack of opportunities in the regions had generated relatively high rates of out-migration, especially among the younger cohorts. But, by 1993, typical residents of the Maritime provinces consumed the same goods as their counterparts in the centre, and had access to basically the same amenities (educational institutions, health care facilities, radio, telephone, automobiles, television, MacDonald's hamburgers, etc.), and they enjoyed comprehensive incomes (market plus in-kind - public goods and services - income) very similar to those of people in the rest of the country. Out-migration was also much less common, and in some years after 1970 the region actually experienced net in-migration.

The positive consequences are evident in Prince Edward Island's population statistics. After 1941 the Island population grew steadily. Although it took until 1971 for the population to climb back to the level achieved at the peak of Island prosperity in the previous century, the previous high-water mark was surpassed. The population now stands at 131,000.

Two factors underlay the relatively successful performance of Maritime provinces in the postwar period: the growth in exports generated by the growth in demand from distant cities, and the emergence of a national welfare state. The expansion of the North American economy increased demand for the Island's three major exports: agricultural products, fish products, and tourism. Higher incomes in these sectors increased demand for many non-traded goods and services. Many of these were provided from Charlottetown. The expansion of the welfare state was still more significant. Federal government departments began to open new offices in the provincial capital (symbolically, the largest building in Charlottetown in the 50s and 60s was the Federal Building, which housed the post office and many other federal government departments). National government transfers to persons (Old Age Security, Family Allowance, Unemployment Insurance, etc.) increased dramatically. Cost-shared programs helped finance expansion of the health care services and education sectors. Equalization allowed the provincial government to expand employment. The Prince Edward Island

Development Plan also contributed to the expansion of the provincial civil service. In sum, the various welfare state initiatives significantly increased incomes and civil service employment. Moreover, they increased demand for a wide range of non-traded goods and services which were supplied from Charlottetown. Thus Charlottetown benefitted directly and indirectly from the inflow of federal monies.

The citizens of Charlottetown created an extremely prosperous community with an elaborate division of labour in the postwar period. In some respects it resembles communities of similar size throughout North America. Its citizens have access to all the "amenities" of modern life, from Cat-Scan equipment to the MacDonald hamburger. Moreover, the citizens have access to amenities not available in most cities of similar size; the Confederation Centre (the home to live theatre and a major art gallery), a modern university, fine restaurants and a night life (supported in part by tourist dollars), and easy access to quality beaches and a picturesque countryside are notable attractions of Charlottetown life. The people of Charlottetown believe they have a quality of life which is as good as that enjoyed elsewhere, and perhaps better.

However, this quality of life has been built on a precarious foundation. Charlottetown is not, with the exception of tourism, an export centre. Instead, it remains, as it has since the 1870s, a centre for the provision of public and commercial services to its population and to the rest of the Island. The Charlottetown population supports its purchases of imports (few consumer goods are produced domestically) and thus its standard of living through the provision of services to the Island's producers of exportable products, and from the bounty flowing in from the rest of Canada through expenditures by the federal government. If most of the Island's imports were financed by exports sales, the situation would not be too disturbing. Unfortunately, they are not financed by export sales and the city and the province are incredibly dependent upon transfers from Ottawa.

The level of dependence is easily illustrated. Prince Edward Island is known as the garden province, and it is the most rural and agricultural province in the country. Yet an examination of agricultural statistics reveals that very few Islanders are engaged in agriculture, and further that the value of agricultural products is not very high. Table 1 shows that there were only 2,361 farms on the Island, supporting a farming population of less than 5,000. Moreover, the gross value of farm receipts was less than $300 million and net farm income was $50 million in an economy with Gross Domestic Product (GDP) just over $2 billion. Even if one assumes a fantastically large multiplier (say, of 10) on value added in the agricultural sector, agriculture would account for less than one quarter of economic activity on the Island as a whole. If one assumes a more realistic multiplier of 2, agriculture would only account for 5 percent of GDP. Clearly, the Charlottetown economy is not based on the provision of services to agricultural population, or to the population which indirectly owes its jobs to the province's agricultural base. Table 2 reinforces this conclusion, by illustrating the distribution of farms by gross receipts.

Table 1

Some Agricultural Statistics for Prince Edward Island, 1991

Number of farms	2,361
Total value of gross agricultural receipts	$280,567,000
Net income of farm operators from farm operations	$50,238,000
Gross domestic product, PEI	$2,078,000,000

Sources: Province of Prince Edward Island, 1993, *Agricultural Statistics,* Charlottetown: Department of Agriculture: Statistics Canada, *Provincial Economic Accounts,* Cat. no. 13-213.

Table 2

Farms Classified by Gross Receipts, 1991

Total Value of Gross Receipts	# of farms	%
Under $2,500	217	9.2
$2,500-4,999	184	7.8
$5,000-9,999	244	10.3
$10,000-24,999	383	16.2
$25,000-49,999	261	11.1
$50,000-99,999	355	15.0
$100,000-$249,000	434	18.4
Over $250,000	283	12.0

Source: Province of Prince Edward Island, 1993, *Agricultural Statistics,* Charlottetown: Department of Agriculture.

The fishery and tourism, although also important Island industries, do not generate as much activity as agriculture (the value of fish landings in 1989 was less than $73 million and estimated total gross tourist expenditure was less than $90 million). Thus they do not account for much of the economic activity on the Island. The Island manufacturing sector is slightly larger; it employs approximately 3,400 people with a value added of just over $100 million. But relative to total value added (just over $2 billion) the manufacturing sector is insignificant. In contrast, the federal government spent over a billion dollars on the Island in 1991. If taxes paid by Islanders are subtracted from this, the net federal spending amounts to $694 million (Statistics Canada, Provincial Economic Accounts, Cat. no. 13-213). This "gift" from the rest of Canada is clearly the basis of the Island economy and, even more so, the Charlottetown economy.

Any threat to the federal transfer system is a threat to the standard of living in Prince Edward Island and in Charlottetown. Unfortunately, the current round of structural change is threatening the federal transfer system. The following two sections of the paper focus on the critical elements of structural change and the adjustments which has occurred in Charlottetown over the past decade. But, before turning to these topics it is useful to quickly summarize the main points of this section.

1. The fate of Charlottetown is largely determined by events in distant cities. Changes in international economic relations, changes in technology, and changes in government policy formulated in far-off capitals have played an extremely important place in the Island capital's history.

2. Charlottetown has faced dramatic structural change in the past. It has always adapted. However, at least once, the adaptation was only partially successful and relative incomes fell and large numbers of the population left the province for more attractive regions. Figure 1, which illustrates population growth over the entire period of European settlement, provides a succinct summary of the Charlottetown's experience. The population is calculated using both the 1991 Census definition of the Charlottetown Census agglomeration area and the municipal boundaries. The former is designated as CA in figure 1.

3. Charlottetown is not now an export city. Nor does it depend heavily on activity in agriculture or the fishery. Instead, it is a community dependent upon the national welfare state which emerged in the postwar era.

Figure 1

Population: PEI and Charlottetown

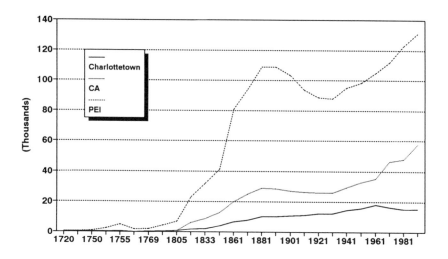

Source: A.H. Clark, 1959, *Three Centuries and the Island* (Toronto: Toronto University Press and Statistics Canada, Census, various years).

Structural Change in the Eighties and Nineties

Events in the 1980s have forced intellectuals (especially economists) to abandon their long-standing faith in continuity and gradual change. The very pillars of postwar Canadian society are being shaken. The industrial heartland of the country is in trouble as transnational companies reorganize their production on a global basis. The postwar "good jobs" in the highly-paid, highly-unionized manufacturing industries are disappearing as a result. New computer and telecommunication technologies (see Tapscott and Carson, 1992) are also whittling away the other "good" postwar corporate job category, as firms flatten their organization charts and lay off many middle-management workers. The professions (doctors, lawyers, accountants, university professors, etc.) will probably be affected over the next few years as well. Thus there is a fundamental change in the division of labour under way at the present time, and this is affecting every aspect of social life.

The transformation is also evident in industrial organization. The traditional engines of growth in the manufacturing sector are in trouble. Indeed, many "blue chip" companies of the postwar period (for example, IBM, General Motors, and Chrysler) are struggling just to survive. The adjustment in the manufacturing sector is occurring as production techniques become more flexible and products less standardized. Just-in-time inventory control methods and new billing and payment systems are reducing the demand for credit and capital. Moreover, service is becoming increasingly important in the manufacturing sector. More efficient purchasing strategies, increased emphasis on new product development, new innovative marketing strategies, and host of other developments have increased knowledge-intensive service work relative to traditional production work in this sector. Product service has become increasingly important as well. Today the purchase of an automobile is not just the purchase of a high-tech piece of machinery. It is the purchase of transportation, where the manufacturer practically guarantees that the car will take you from point A to point B (through elaborate warranties, guaranteed roadside service in the event of mechanical breakdown, and guaranteed replacement vehicles in the event the car needs to be serviced by the dealer). Similar product service arrangements are appearing in other industries as well.

The traditional service sector, too, is experiencing change. Thus far, change has been most dramatic in the financial services sector, where automated teller machines, debit cards, and expanding computer networks are beginning to threaten the branch banking model. But change is beginning to appear elsewhere as well. For example, lawyers now have access to large databases which are easily searched for information needed by clients (thereby increasing productivity dramatically). Computers are also poised to increase the productivity of doctors, especially in their "gate-keeping role," by providing a relatively cheap means to diagnose illness.[1] Computer communications, and the electronic highway, will allow accountants to work from centralized offices since they will not have to be close to their customers. The demand for clerical and secretarial services is down, thanks to easy-to-use word processing packages, electronic mail facilities, scanners, and database management programs. Even retailing is being affected, not only by tele-marketing, but also by dramatic reductions in the numbers of workers required to price products, take stock, and work cash.

The public sector has also experienced significant change. In the policy sphere, we see the Canada-U.S. Free Trade Agreement (FTA), the North American Free Trade Agreement (NAFTA), deregulation, and the death of Keynesian demand management policies in the face of chronic government deficits. Although some believe these policies are the underlying cause of structural change, it is probably more accurate to view them as a result of structural change. (In fact, in the nonequilibrium world of complex dynamic systems, everything is interconnected and these policies as well as the structural economic changes are fundamentally endogenous.) Economic and political change are occurring in concert, with changes in the public sector affecting the private sector, and changes in the private sector affecting the public sector.

As Courchene (1992) argues, one of the features of structural change is a diminution in the role and importance of the state generally, and of the nation-state in particular. Globalization and free trade constrain state action by forcing governments to play by the rules of the market. As well, state power is lost as nation-states surrender sovereignty to new supra-national institutions to assure the free flow of goods, services, and capital.

International and interprovincial trade data also indicate a rather dramatic shift from East-West to North-South trade. As a consequence, Canada is no longer a single economy, but rather a series of cross-border economies. (Courchene, 1992, p. 763) In this setting, centralized policy-making, whether with respect to macro-economic policy, transportation policy, or communications policy is less appropriate, and the case for a new regional approach is quite strong. This creates pressure to decentralize power from the centre.

Pressure to decentralize power is also a consequence of the growing importance of cities. As Jane Jacobs has argued, cities are the engine of economic development. Thus, in an integrated global economy, the linkages of importance are not linkages across countries but linkages between cities. As well, there are pressures to decentralize arising out of citizens frustration with "big politics" and their attempt to acquire more control over their lives.

The Canadian constitutional debate and the threat of Quebec separation must be seen in this context. Canada is not the only country currently experiencing "national problems." Witness the developments in Europe. There are many pressures moving us toward decentralization. The constitutional debate is a consequence of this.

The current round of structural change has not affected the public sector as much as the private sector, at least not yet. As Judith Maxwell (1993), former chairperson of the Economic Council of Canada, argues: "My sense is that we are in a kind of rolling depression. The depression started with the adjustment in resource industries in the 1980s, followed by restructuring in the manufacturing sector in the last five years. The adjustment in services and the public sector is still to come. The pain of a depression has been spread out, with the result that we have been able to avoid, so far at least, a crushing decline in living standards." (p. 105)

The debt crisis and the unwillingness of the public to accept further tax increases will force governments to restructure. Fortunately, computer technology has evolved sufficiently to allow governments to reap a number of productivity gains. We should expect government organizational charts, like those in the private sector, to flatten as many middle management positions are eliminated. The range of services offered will be reduced. And, most importantly, transfer programs will be redesigned. Just five years ago, significant cuts in the social policy envelope were unthinkable. Today, the "sacred trusts" of social policy are no longer sacred.

Given Charlottetown's dependence on the public sector, especially on the national government, the ongoing changes in the public sector pose a particularly important challenge. The high level of federal government spending provides the funds required to import the products the people of Charlottetown rely upon to support their standard of living. A decline in this inflow must reduce living standards unless the people of Charlottetown increase exports of goods and services sufficiently to offset the transfer decline. Indeed, expanding export industries is the big challenge facing the Maritimes, Prince Edward Island, and Charlottetown.

In the following section we examine the experience of Charlottetown over the past decade to see if the local economy is adapting to the new global economy, to new technology, and to the threat of a reduced federal role in the province. Is there evidence to support the hypothesis that the new technologies are centralizing? Or does the evidence suggest that the new technologies are decentralizing certain types of economic activities? Has there been a significant shift in industrial structure? In the occupational mix? Is there a high rate of investment in Charlottetown? Where are investments being made?

Charlottetown 1981-1991

If we are, as Judith Maxwell suggests, in a rolling depression in which the economy is experiencing a major structural shift in preparation for a renewed period of growth, any sector, region, or city which is to be successful in the new economy should show signs of internal adjustment. In Charlottetown's case, one would like to observe growth in export-oriented sectors, since the only way to preserve standards of living in the face of declines in transfers from the rest of Canada is to increase exports.[2] As well, one would like to observe other adjustments to the new economy: for example, the adoption of new technologies, people switching into new knowledge-intensive occupations, improving average levels of educational attainment, high rates of investment, and productivity growth.[3]

The starting point, therefore, is to look for new developments in the trade sector. The traditional export base lies in primary products. The two most important primary sectors - seed and table potatoes, and lobster - have been relatively stable export earners (ignoring the PVYn virus problem which plagued the potato industry for several years). Fortunately, the Island has earned a reputation as a high-quality producer of these food products, and it is well placed to enjoy some growth as markets for these products expand. However, the income elasticity of demand for potatoes is relatively low, and demand is unlikely to grow as fast as the economy generally. Lobster, on the other hand, is a luxury good and demand should grow faster than the economy as a whole. This primary sector export growth will help the Charlottetown economy but it is unlikely to be sufficient to counter problems caused by a reduction in transfer payments.

The Prince Edward Island manufacturing sector is small; it is largely tied to primary industry; and the majority of jobs are outside Charlottetown. A recent study by the Canadian Institute for Research on Regional Development (Desjardins and De Benedetti, 1993) provides some information on exports of this sector. One of the most remarkable findings of this study was that a significant proportion (43.5 percent) of the manufactured output of the province is consumed locally. Moreover, an additional 22.6 percent is shipped to New Brunswick and Nova Scotia. Thus the local market is extremely important and this sector is vulnerable to changes in transfer payments. Not surprisingly, the majority of manufactured exports are from the food and beverage industries.

Table 3 (which is calculated from data provided in Desjardins and De Benedetti, 1993) illustrates the destinations of manufactured goods exported from the Island. Over 40 percent of all exports go to Nova Scotia and New Brunswick, approximately 28 percent is shipped elsewhere in Canada, 18 percent is destined for U.S. markets (16 percent to New England), 10 percent goes to the European Community Countries, and the remaining 6.7 percent finds its way to the rest of the world.

Table 3

Manufacturing Shipments, 1991

Destination	Value of Shipment ($)	%
New Brunswick	53,391,210	22.7
Nova Scotia	40,804,754	17.3
New England	38,409,205	16.3
Ontario	33,000,855	14.0
European Community	23,981,151	10.2
Quebec	19,193,894	8.1
Newfoundland	10,786,589	4.6
The Rest of the World	15,699,276	6.7
TOTAL	235,266,934	100

Source: Based on Desjardins and De Benedetti, 1993. Table A2e, calculations by the author.

The Desjardins-De Benedetti study also provides some information on the recent changes in the export sector in Prince Edward Island. As part of their survey of Maritime manufacturing firms the authors asked whether the value of exports was increasing, decreasing, or remaining stable. The survey revealed that 22.3 percent of exporters experienced increases in exports, that 9.9 percent experienced a decrease in exports, and that 67.8 percent remained stable. The survey was conducted in the spring of 1992, a period which coincided with a serious recession in Canada and the United States. As a consequence, and with due allowance for the caveats of the authors, one can at least conclude that the existing export sector is in a relatively strong position. However, the size of the manufactured goods sector is still too small to provide much of a cushion should the Island experience a significant decline in transfer payments.

The export service sector in Charlottetown grew relatively rapidly after 1981. Although some of the growth can be attributed to tourism, most was a direct consequence of the relocation of the Department of Veterans Affairs (DVA) from Ottawa. DVA provides services to all Canadian veterans, thus the inflow of funds is tied to a service export. However, the number of veterans is decreasing and thus the demand for services should be expected to fall in the future. The opening of the Veterinary College at the University of Prince Edward Island is another export-oriented service sector development which had a substantial impact on Charlottetown. But, like the DVA, this service exporter is heavily dependent on government funding.

Private sector service exporters are more difficult to identify. Charlottetown, unlike Moncton, New Brunswick, has not developed a new integrated export service sector over the past ten years. However, the construction of the fixed link is likely to increase opportunities for engineering and construction trades. Charlottetown is emerging as the major centre for planning and design activities associated with the Link project and the skills acquired during the construction phase of the Fixed Link Project will provide a base for future service export activity in this area. The experience with the PVYn virus had the side benefit of creating expertise in composting techniques, and Islanders are now world leaders in composting technology. Thus there is some potential for service exports. However, the city will need to develop exportable services in a wide variety of areas if it is to make the transition to an export-oriented economy.

In sum, Charlottetown has barely begun to make the necessary transition toward an export-oriented economy. There are some hopeful signs, but much remains to be done.

Changes in the non-traded sector have been much more significant. New computer and communications technologies are being adopted by firms. The number of knowledge-intensive jobs has grown. The city is relatively well-integrated into North America-wide communication networks. Average levels of educational attainment are improving.

Tables 4 and 5 illustrate the most dramatic structural shifts in occupations over the 1986-1991 period for Prince Edward Island as a whole. The impact of technical change is evident in these tables. Bank tellers, telephone operators, mail and postal clerks, material handlers (labourers), library, file, and correspondence clerks were all among the declining occupations. Systems analysts, medical technicians, university professors, occupations in the life sciences, and production management occupations all appeared in the high-growth list. It is also interesting to note that visual arts were a high-growth area, whereas policing service occupations were declining. In general, the data seem to suggest adaptation to the new economy.

Table 4

Growing Occupations
Prince Edward Island, 1986-1991

Occupation	% Change 1986-91
University Teachers	111
Painters, Sculptors and Related Artists	110
Systems Analysts	109
Teachers' Aides	97
Medical Laboratory Assistants	88
Production Management Occupations	84
Farm Management Occupations	77
Occupations in Life Sciences	75
Fruit and Vegetable Canning, Preserving and Packing	75
General Office Clerks	71
Supervisors: Libraries, Museums and Archives	67
Surveyors	63
Inspectors and Regulatory Officers, Government	60
Supervisors: Food and Beverage Preparation	53
Excavating, Grading and Paving: Labouring Positions	51
Bartenders	50

Source: Statistics Canada, *Census 1991, The Nation, Occupations*, Cat. no. 93-327.

Table 5

Declining Occupations
Prince Edward Island, 1986-1991

Occupation	% Change 1986-91
Cashiers and Tellers	-66
Foremen: Wood Processing	-65
Private Police Agents and Investigators	-56
Inspecting, Grading, Testing, and Sampling Occupations	-55
Electrical Power Line Workers	-52
Lodging Cleaners	-46
Police Officers and Detectives, Government	-38
Material Handling, Labourers	-35
Personnel and Related Officers	-34
Telephone Operators	-34
Route Drivers	-32
Mail and Postal Clerks	-31
Painting and Decorating Occupations	-25
Occupations in Religion	-24
Deck Officers, Water Transport	-23
Library, File, and Correspondence Clerks	-21

Source: Statistics Canada, *Census 1991, The Nation, Occupation*, Cat. no. 93-327.

Table 6 shows changes in employment by industry for Charlottetown over the 1981-1991 period and comparative statistics on Halifax and Moncton. The information in table 6 needs to be interpreted carefully because Charlottetown is small and relatively small developments can have a significant impact on the rate of expansion. The index used for comparisons is the rate of change in Charlottetown divided by the rate of change in the comparison city. Thus, the number 1.6 for total (row) under Halifax (column) tells one that employment in Charlottetown expanded at 1.6 times the rate of expansion in Halifax. If interpreted carefully this index allows one to see differences across cities relatively easy.

Table 6

Employment Growth by Industry, 1981-1992
Charlottetown

Industry	% Change 1981-91	Halifax	Moncton
Total	36.5	1.6	1.6
Primary	25.4	22.7	0.8
Manufacturing	13.1	2.5	-2.9
Construction	22.5	0.9	2.1
Transportation	8.2	0.5	-0.5
Trade	19.5	1.3	1.2
Finance, Insurance, and Real Estate	11.3	0.7	0.7
Teaching	39.3	3.8	1.2
Health	29.3	0.9	0.5
Hotels and Restaurants	53.0	2.1	1.7
Business and Other Services	46.1	1.3	1.1
Public Administration	51.4	6.5	2.3
Not Classified elsewhere	n/a	n/a	n/a

Source: The author's calculations are based on census data provided to the Canadian Institute for Research on Regional Development, Université de Moncton by Statistics Canada.

Table 6 shows that employment in Charlottetown grew faster than employment in either Halifax or Moncton. Moreover, the table highlights the fact that employment in public administration, in hotels and restaurants, and in teaching, expanded at a much higher rate in Charlottetown. The high rate of growth in public administration is, in part, a consequence of the relocation of the Department of Veterans Affairs in the early 1980s. However, it should be noted that a comparison of census data in 1986 and 1991 for Prince Edward Island as a whole reveals that employment in the provincial government industrial classification increased by 42 percent. Thus the relative increase in government employment should not be attributed solely to DVA. Similarly, the growth in teaching is, in part, a consequence of growth in the University of Prince Edward

Island (especially with the introduction of the College of Veterinary Medicine). The growth in employment in hotels and restaurants is not surprising given the importance of tourism in the Island's capital.

Table 6 also provides some information on centralizing trends affecting Charlottetown. Halifax and Moncton are the two regional centres most likely to gain if technology allows increased centralization. Moreover, speculation about the relationship between technological change and industrial location suggest that trade, finance, insurance, and real estate, and business services are most vulnerable to centralization. The information in table 6 suggests that Charlotte-town actually increased its relative share of trade and business and other services employment. The introduction of the fixed link may well change things in the future, and it may be that much of Charlottetown's relative growth in these areas occurred early in the decade and that trends have reversed since. However, the data suggests that wholesale and retail services and personal business remain naturally protected sectors. On the other hand, the decline in Charlottetown's relative share in finance, insurance, and real estate employment suggests that this sector has been vulnerable to centralization.

Figure 2 provides an indirect measure of investment activity by reporting the value of building permits issued by the city. This table confirms the low level of manufacturing activity in Charlottetown and the complete dominance of commercial and government activity. The low level of investment is also striking and confirm Savoie's observation that "the Island has had a low level of business capital investment, which has consistently hovered at around 35-40 percent of the national average on a per capita basis." (1993, p. 192)

Tables 7 and 8 report information on educational attainment from the 1991 census. Table 7 shows that education levels among the over-15 population in Prince Edward Island are converging with those in the country as a whole. Given that the new economy will be based more on human capital and know-ledge-intensive work, this must be seen as a very positive development. Table 8 looks more closely at postsecondary graduates in commerce, in engineering and applied sciences, and in engineering technologies and trades. The proportion of the population with postsecondary training in these critically important areas are remarkably similar. Not surprisingly, the number of engineers per thousand over 15 years of age is smaller in Prince Edward Island (with limited industry, there are limited opportunities for engineers and applied scientists). The number of technologists and skilled trades people and the number of individuals with training in commercial fields are, however, quite similar to Canada as a whole. Indeed, the numbers of individuals with postsecondary training in commerce, management, and business administration (per thousand over-15 population) is greater in Prince Edward Island. Thus Charlottetown and Prince Edward Island have a skilled labour pool which is an extremely valuable asset when moving into a new knowledge-based economy.

Figure 2

Building Permits (thousands $)

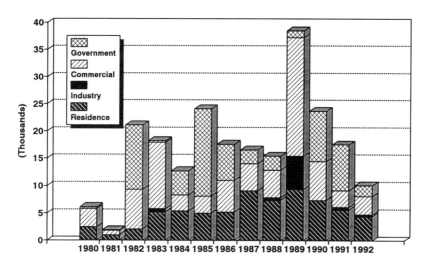

Source: Statistics Canada, Building Permits: Annual Summary, Catalogue no. 64-203.

Table 7

Educational Attainment
Prince Edward Island and Canada

Year	Less than grade 9		9-13		Some postsecondary		Degree	
	PEI	Canada	PEI	Canada	PEI	Canada	PEI	Canada
1971	36.9	32.3	43.2	45.9	16.7	17.1	3.2	4.8
1981	24.1	20.7	41.8	43.6	28.0	27.6	6.1	8.0
1991	15.7	14.3	42.7	42.6	33.1	31.7	8.5	11.4

Source: Statistics Canada, Census 1991, *Educational Attainment and School Atten-dance*, Cat. no. 93-238.

Table 8

Postsecondary Graduates
Prince Edward Island and Canada, 1991
(Graduate per 1000 Persons over 15 Years of Age)

Field of Study	PEI	Canada
Commerce, Management, and Business Administration	91	81
Engineering and Applied Sciences	5	13
Engineering and Applied Sciences, Technology and Trades	81	84

Source: Statistics Canada, Census 1991, *Major Fields of Study of Postsecondary Graduates*, Cat. no. 93-329.

The information in this section of the paper provides a base upon which we can draw to reach some general conclusions about Charlottetown's future. First, the export base of the city remains extremely weak. Thus, the city remains heavily dependent on transfers from the federal government. Without these transfers the size of the city would contract significantly. Second, the city's non-trade sectors have responded to changes in technology and in the economy. Moreover, the human capital base is relatively strong, a big plus in the new knowledge economy.

Clearly, the fate of the city will be determined by events in Ottawa. A substantial decline in transfers would result in significant unemployment, out-migration, and/or poverty. Since the tide has clearly turned against the Canadian transfer system, this is an extremely disturbing prospect. In the face of this, is there anything governments can do to ease the transition? This important question is considered in the concluding section.

Conclusions

The themes of this paper have been clear and disturbing. First, it was argued that Charlottetown is at a crossroads and the path it will take in the future depends heavily on developments beyond its control. In particular, dramatic changes in social institutions are occurring in distant cities, and there is a real possibility that the national welfare state (and its system of intergovernmental transfers) will be a casualty of those changes. This is by no means a certain outcome, but it is a very real possibility. Second, the paper argued that Charlottetown is a "passive economy" and its economic history has always been shaped by events in distant places. This exacerbates the control problem for policy makers in Charlottetown and Prince Edward Island, since their actions are unlikely to have a significant influence on the course of events. Finally, the paper drew on work on nonlinear dynamics to suggest that the changing fortunes of the Charlottetown economy must be seen as an outcome of an extremely complex evolving dynamic system which is in many ways unpredictable. Because everything depends on everything else the outcomes are very difficult to control through policy.

The themes of the paper may give rise to a defeatist attitude: That "one cannot have an effect, so why even try?" However, a closer examination of work on nonlinear dynamic models reveals very different lessons. The first of these was also drawn by Jane Jacobs when she argued:

> In its very nature, successful economic development has to be open-ended rather than goal-oriented, and has to make itself up expediently and empirically as it goes along. For one thing, unforeseeable problems arise. The people who developed agriculture could not foresee soil depletion. The people who developed the automobile could not foresee acid rain. Earlier I defined economic development as a process of continually improvising in a context that makes injecting improvisations into everyday life feasible. We might amplify this by calling development an improvisational drift into unprecedented kinds of work that carry unprecedented problems, then drifting into improvised solutions, which carry further unprecedented work carrying unprecedented problems. . .
>
> "Industrial strategies" to meet "targets" using "resolute purpose," "long range planning" and "determined will" express a military kind of thinking. Behind that thinking lies a conscious or unconscious assumption that economic life can be conquered, mobilized, bullied, as indeed it can be when it is directed toward warfare, but not when it directs itself to development and expansion. (Jacobs, 1984, 222)

The implications of this are clear. People experience problems, people improvise solutions, people drift into unprecedented work. Thus governments have an important role to play in creating an environment in which individuals have the power to improvise creatively. Assuring access to education and to information ensuring freedom from stifling regulations, and fostering entrepreneurship are policy initiatives which will support creativity and improvisation. Bureaucratic red tape, excessive regulation, and reliance on "expert planners" to tell people how to "do things right," will not.

The second important implication of nonlinear dynamic systems which challenges defeatist positions is that small initiatives can, in principle, generate large changes in outcomes. The "butterfly effect" in meteorological models (where a butterfly beating its wings over Peking can cause a storm in New York) is the classic illustration of this. The appropriate conclusion is not that policy initiatives are ineffective but instead that they are extremely important because they can (potentially) have a large effect. But, at the same time one should not be very surprised if most policy initiatives are ineffective. The goal of policy makers should be to "give it their best shot" and "hope for the best."

The challenge currently facing policy makers in Prince Edward Island and in Charlottetown is to create an environment in which citizens can react to the outside events by simultaneously taking advantage of any opportunities created, and trying to cushion the shock of decline. This is the only realistic strategy. Fortunately, Charlottetown is currently in a position to take advantage of any opportunities which might arise. It is an extremely attractive city (more so than ever, thanks to a major redevelopment of the waterfront and downtown core) with cultural amenities (restaurants, theatre, art galleries, etc.) which exceed those of cities many times its size. The population is well educated and deeply committed to trying to make a living on their Island. It has a vibrant university which is hooked into world-wide communication networks. Its basic infrastructure is in fairly good shape. And the Island itself offers scenic beauty and warm salt water beaches. The fixed link, free trade, the strong health and education system, Canadian gun control laws, low crime rates, and a relatively pollution-free environment are also assets which make the Island attractive.

These assets will not be much help if lower transfer payments were all the future appeared likely to offer. However, there will be other important developments in distant cities which can have a significant impact on Charlottetown. For example, the increase in crime, drive-by shootings, gang warfare, pollution, commuting times, etc. in the major North American cities are causing people to look elsewhere for a place to live. Charlottetown could be an attractive city for "life-style" immigrants. Southern California, the main centre of the new knowledge economy, is particularly vulnerable to life-style emigration, given the dual threats of geological and social earthquakes.

The arguments of Higgins (1993, p. 149) about Sydney, Nova Scotia, are of direct relevance to Charlottetown. He argues:

> A sophisticated small city, with a good university and a physically attractive setting, some cultural life, and special features can be attractive to top level managers, scientists, engineers, and technicians who have particular tastes. These are the key location factors for high-tech enterprises. Cape Breton doesn't need 100,000 such people: 10,000 would do nicely. For people of this kind, who like living on or near the sea, sailing, fishing, skin diving - and perhaps skiing - a city like Sydney could be very attractive.

There are many communities in North America which can offer "life-style immigrants" an attractive home. Thus Charlottetown cannot remain completely passive. It must make people aware of its existence, especially people in Southern California. Although the Maritimes' traditional links have been with New England, New England will not be the source of many life-style immigrants. The net must be cast a little more widely.

This type of promotional exercise will not necessarily pay dividends. (Boosterism in the late nineteenth century produced few gains for the Maritimes.) Unfortunately, success depends completely on the mood in those distant cities, and there is really nothing one can do about that. If developments in distant cities do not generate a movement of knowledge-based export activities to the periphery, and if transfers decline, Charlottetown, and the Maritimes generally, will face the very difficult problem of managing a shrinking economy.

BIBLIOGRAPHY

Anderson, P., K. J. Arrow, and D. Pines, "The Economy as an Evolving Complex System," *The Santa Fe Institute Studies in the Sciences of Complexity*, vol. 5 (Redwood City: Addison Wesley, 1988).

Arthur B., "Competing Technologies, Increasing Returns, and the Lock in by Historical Events," *Economic Journal*, 99, 1989, pp. 116-31.

Clark, A.H., *Three Centuries and the Island* (Toronto: University of Toronto Press, 1959).

Courchene, T.J., "Mon pays, c'est l'hiver," *Canadian Journal of Economics*, XXV, 1992, pp. 759-89.

Courchene, T.J., "Path - Dependency, Positive Feedback, and Paradigm Warp: A Schumpeterian Approach to Social Order," in Elisabeth Reynolds (ed.) *Income Security in Canada: Changing Needs, Changing Means* (Montreal: The Institute for Research on Public Policy, 1993), pp. 43-82.

Desjardins, P.-M. and G.J. De Benedetti, *A Study of Atlantic Canada's Interprovincial Trade and Foreign Exports for 1991*, Research Report no. 11 (Moncton: Canadian Institute for Research on Regional Development, 1993).

Easterbrook, W.T. and H.G.J. Aitken, *Canadian Economic History* (Toronto: Macmillan, 1956).

Galbraith, J.K., *The New Industrial State* (New York: Mentor and Plume Books, 1967).

Grant, H. and F. Strain, "Social Structures of Accumulation in Canada, 1945 - 1988," *Journal of Canadian Studies*, 26(4), 1991, pp. 75-93.

Higgins, B., "Entrepreneurship and Economic Development: The Case of Cape Breton," in D.J. Savoie and R. Winter (eds.) *The Maritime Provinces: Looking to the Future* (Moncton: Canadian Institute for Research on Regional Development, 1993), pp. 125-56.

Jacobs, J., *Cities and the Wealth of Nations* (New York: Random House, 1984).

Lewin, Roger, *Complexity Life at the Edge of Chaos* (Toronto: Maxwell MacMillan, 1992).

Maxwell, J., "Comments on Courchene and Osberg," in Elisabeth Reynolds (ed.) *Income Security in Canada: Changing Needs, Changing Means* (Montreal: The Institute for Research on Public Policy, 1993), pp. 101-8.

Sager, C.W. and L.R. Fischer, "Atlantic Canada and the Age of Sail Revisited," *The Canadian Historical Review*, LXIII(2), 1982, pp. 125-50.

Savoie, D.J., "Regional Development: The Case of Prince Edward Island," in D.J. Savoie and R. Winter (eds.) *The Maritime Provinces: Looking to the Future* (Moncton: Canadian Institute for Research on Regional Development, 1993), pp. 189-214.

Tapscott, D. and A. Carson, *Paradigm Shift: The New Promise of Information Technology* (New York: McGraw Hill, 1993).

Waldorp, Mitchell M., *Complexity: The Emerging Science at the Edge of Order and Chaos* (Toronto: Touchtone Books, 1992).

NOTES TO CHAPTER TWELVE

1. Lawyers and doctors remain extremely powerful in our society and they have resisted any encroachment on their position. But as the technological revolution continues, many of their traditional functions will be better handled by para-professionals (see Courchene, 1992 for a related discussion of para-professionals).

2. There are only three ways to secure imports: (1) trade (exchange goods and services you produce for the goods and services produced by others); (2) borrowing (borrow today to buy the imports, export in the future to pay off the loan); and (3) gifts (receive the imports free of charge). A significant proportion of imports are currently secured free of charge *via* the transfer system. But this situation is unlikely to persist in the future. One can only borrow, if there is someone willing to lend. Potential lenders are unlikely to be forthcoming, given the current economic structure (they would need to be confident that exports will increase sufficiently to cover repayment). Thus, increasing exports today is fundamental. It is possible, in theory, to imagine an import substitution strategy based on protectionist measures. But given the general move to freer trade, it is impossible to believe this type of policy is feasible in practice.

3. However, these changes are still of secondary importance, since, if the changes are only occurring in the non-traded sectors, they will be of little help in adjusting to a decline in the role of federal transfers. Whether or not a good or service is traded, depends on the cost of delivering the product. Technological change will, over time, result in changes in transport and communication costs. Unless local provision remains the cheapest form of provision, local producers will face competition from outside. Thus, productivity increases in the non-traded sector are extremely important. However, these productivity increases will not result in new exports, unless local producers are leaders who, through technological change, begin to penetrate the non-traded sectors of economies elsewhere. (This is precisely what happened with the introduction of the improved roads and shopping mall. Producers of retail services located in Charlottetown were suddenly able to compete with the local store in small Island communities. The disappearance of the small local store was a consequence of this technological change.)

CONCLUSION

George J. De Benedetti
Rodolphe H. Lamarche

When we assembled the team for this project, our intent was to determine which of the urban centres in the Maritimes were on the trajectory of modern development, and which were not. We were also interested in discovering whether the Maritime urban system had become more integrated, i.e., whether the connections among the Maritime cities had become stronger. We discovered during the course of the book's progression that leadership and organization would be important factors in the healthy growth of the individual cities and the Maritime urban system itself. Some authors addressed this directly, and others have alluded to the importance of leadership and organization.

What did we discover about the specific cities in our study? Halifax, the largest of the centres, is blessed by many attributes. One would expect that its beautiful harbour, its architecture, its other urban amenities, its advanced medical and numerous educational institutions, and its great Maritime traditions would propel this city well beyond the others in the new economy. Professor Higgins doubts the likelihood that Halifax will develop into the dominant Maritime regional metropolis that it should be. It all depends on how quickly and effectively it can find within itself the leadership capable of guiding it into the twenty-first century. The city is indeed "in a fragile equilibrium" in this regard.

Leadership is a major issue. One has only to consider the difficulties the city faced in devising a plan to clean up its harbour. The leadership for a time found itself incapable of summoning its people around this one timely and well-defined goal. There are other issues that call for leadership and resolution, including the long-term survival of its great port and the restructuring of its medical and educational institutions. At this onset of the information age, the role of Dalhousie as the flagship of Maritime universities should be reinforced with vigour.

Halifax stands on a "knife-edge." Professor Higgins argues that it is no longer true that "the growth of Halifax is the *sine qua non* of a prosperous Maritime urban system" because the information highways will make it possible for other centres in the Maritimes to hook up with other urban areas, without the need for an urban system centred on Halifax.

How will Sydney fare in the new economy? Like all other industrialized areas of the country whose economies were based on heavy industry and natural resources, Cape Breton and its main urban centre, Sydney, will experience great difficulty in moving towards an economy based on human resources and knowledge. Yet it must. The University College of Cape Breton has made a start in leading the transition from the old to the new economy. Education traditionally has been funded separately from regional development efforts, and now the province of Nova Scotia is cutting back on educational expenditures. A greater effort should be made at both the federal and provincial levels to invest regional development monies in information activities and institutions.

Metro Sydney faces the additional difficulty that, unlike most other industrial centres, it has only a small and dispersed population base and consequently a smaller pool of entrepreneurs, leaders and visionaries. Amalgamating most of the urban centres of Cape Breton into a single metropolitan region would not necessarily solve this problem. The outcome would depend on the dynamics operating within the new regional council. There is documented evidence that there are two processes commonly found at work in newly amalgamated regional authorities. One process almost invariably succeeds by promoting unified and coherent regional growth and development; the other generally leads to a squandering of funds and hopes on fractional efforts typical of ward-type politics. When such regional councils are headed by strong leaders who are capable of generating agreement on common goals and pushing aside parochial agendas, development occurs. However, when municipal leaders insist on advancing their own local agendas, development efforts at the regional level fail. (Sabourin, 1994)

The University College of Cape Breton is one of the main assets of the Island. It will be up to its Board of Governors and its academic leaders to ensure the college is able to prepare the region for the new economy.

The three New Brunswick urban centres, each located within a two-hour drive of each other, could be viewed as one economic region because their economies are interdependent and complementary. Saint John is the largest of the three, and an important industrial centre of the Maritimes. During the period when the city was busily engaged in constructing a number of modern frigates for the Canadian navy, Saint John built up a large, highly skilled industrial labour force, and a very large network of high-tech connections, all of which were skilfully directed by the Irving corporations. The city is also the financial and technical innovation centre for NBTel, one of Canada's most advanced telecommunications companies. These two factors alone should be sufficient to propel the city well into the twenty-first century. However, it does have a number of difficulties to overcome. First the pollution levels in the city are still too high to make it an attractive centre, and it also does not have the urban and physical amenities that Halifax has. Secondly, Saint John must shed its reputation, merited or not, as a centre that has been infertile ground for small entrepreneurial firms. It could well develop into the province's largest manufacturing centre for high-tech goods, as New Brunswick gears up for the new economy.

Moncton is New Brunswick's second largest city. It has already begun to develop within the new economy, and for a number of reasons. It is ideally situated geographically. One has only to examine the map of the region, on page 6, to see how central it is to the transportation infrastructure of the Maritimes.

Once the fixed link to Prince Edward Island is complete, Moncton will be at the junction of two highway networks, one going East-West from Charlottetown to Saint John and another going North-South from Halifax to Fredericton and beyond. Moncton has strong leadership at the provincial and municipal levels, so that it is not likely to become immobilized by conflicts over local agendas. So dynamic is the economic planning system of Greater Moncton that it must be given credit for getting the city past the effects of the recent loss of the huge CN repair shops. The community has a large pool of entrepreneurs. Some of the younger ones come from the business, engineering, and other faculties of the universities and colleges in the area, others from the smaller centres in the immediate surrounding region of Moncton, as described in Dorothy Downing's chapter on "High-Tech in Small Towns," and some others from among the former employees at the CN Shops. Furthermore, Moncton has a skilled bilingual labour force and is the centre for a number of NBTel's information services based in the impressive Blue Cross Centre. As NBTel develops large scale information networks, Moncton would be an excellent base for the development of bilingual aspects of the service, and government should encourage such endeavours. Finally, Moncton is only beginning to awaken to the importance of urban amenities and to changing the image it projected in the past. After some prodding from federal agencies, the city is in the process of improving its physical appearance and community services.

Donald J. Savoie and Yves Bourgeois concluded that Moncton is less vulnerable than Halifax, Fredericton, or Charlottetown, to reductions in public spending, and that Moncton entrepreneurs are aggressive in identifying new markets globally. They also warned that Monctonians might become smug and complacent about their recent successes; that Moncton's future success is not independent of other Maritime centres; and that success is contingent on "planning its future development efforts in full collaboration with other centres in the region." So Moncton could fare very well in the new economy.

Fredericton is the province's third largest centre and the home of one of Canada's best engineering schools. Because it is a centre where we find a fairly large number of software, consulting engineering, and environmental firms and because both civic and provincial leaders are focusing Fredericton's development on knowledge-based industries, we think Fredericton will flourish in the new economy.

And what about Charlottetown? Frank Strain says it best when he concludes that the prospects for the future of Charlottetown are disturbing. But Charlottetown and Prince Edward Island have so many amenities that are not readily found elsewhere that it is inconceivable that this city will not make it in the new economy. It may well become the home for a number of small high-tech firms. To achieve this, the city leaders cannot remain passive, but must make people aware of Charlottetown's existence and draw to it the kind of entrepreneurs the city needs to guide it into the new century, build the new industries it needs and still maintain the quality of life for which the region is famous.

If we now turn to the first six chapters of the book which deal with the Maritime urban system as a whole, what have we learned? From Larry McCann's historical review we find that stress and change are not new to the Maritime urban centres. Some have been able to cope with change, and others not. From Chapter Two, we find the Maritime urban system is being gradually drawn into a single national pole dominated by Toronto. There is the possibility that the existing small Maritime urban system is in danger of being supplanted by a new system where each Maritime centre is directly tied to Toronto with only marginal ties to other centres in the area. We also learned that the loss of a single head office in the region does more damage to the integrity of the Maritime sub-systems than a similar loss in a larger centre. But then the four lane highways under construction and the coming telecommunication networks should increase the links among the urban centres in the Maritime urban system. Chapter Three gave us some indication of the strengths of the links between the Maritime centres and centres in the U.S.A. and how these links are evolving.

Chapter Four indicated how difficult it would be to restructure the Maritime economy to make it viable and strong for the twenty-first century. The process must be managed, otherwise the stress will be so great as to lead to social and political instability. Chapter Five showed the extent of the involvement of federal agencies in the urban centres of the Maritimes, and the areas most likely to bear the brunt of reductions in public spending. Finally, Chapter Six outlined a number of success stories in the smaller Maritime urban centres, and how some of these centres might fare in the new economy. Downing described well how a number of entrepreneurs have already pulled their enterprises into the twenty-first century. But how do you find, attract, and support such dynamic people? It should certainly be one of the major objectives of our regional planners.

We trust the success stories in Chapter Six will awaken the creative instincts of a younger generation of Maritime industrialists and entrepreneurs. We also hope that experienced and successful entrepreneurs in the region will feel the need to share their capacity for leadership and responsibility.

One should not overlook the difficult work that ACOA has achieved so far in fostering entrepreneurship. One of its main tasks, it seems, was to study the workings of the entrepreneurial process and further its development in the Atlantic provinces. The agency seems to be having some success in spite of the difficulties of such a task.

Events of the next few years will determine whether the following decades will be ones of cumulative expansion or cumulative decline. Static and dynamic forces of about equal strength hold the Maritime economy as a whole in a more or less steady state, which might be interpreted as "equilibrium," or alternatively as stagnation. The static forces are those of conservatism, reluctance to change, clinging to "natural forces and traditional know-how" in the vain hope of thereby returning to past glories. The dynamic forces are those favouring the necessary shift to "human resources and knowledge," the surge of innovative entrepreneurship, much of it in small enterprises, some of it in small towns, applying a high level of science, technology, and knowledge to producing sophisticated services and manufactured goods. So which will win?

The authors of this volume are on the side of optimism, and faith in the long-run victory of the dynamic forces. The number and nature of the new breed of entrepreneurs, together with the number and nature of the academic institutions in the region, constitute an irresistible force, before which the sticky mass of static forces will not prove immovable.

In the end, what does the new economy hold for the Maritime urban centres? What are the reasonable expectations we might hold? We must remember that the information economy is already present to a degree in the Maritimes and that many firms have already adopted high-tech innovations to penetrate today's markets. We should also expect the leaders of the provinces and the urban areas to set out common goals, provide the organizational, financial, and regulatory supports required by the entrepreneurs of the region. These leaders should also be aware that without their aggressive input, the process of change will go awry and their regions will be crippled for a long time to come. Inevitably, some regions will lose and some will gain, as past experience has shown. The pursuit of strategies of development has to be sure-footed and diligent, and this requires leadership and organization if we are to have success in the new economy. Policies must encourage innovative entrepreneurship, and the expansion and improvement of the region's academic institutions. If all of these processes operate together and in concert, as they should in a functional urban networks, then the future of the Maritimes will be bright.

REFERENCE

Sabourin, Vincent, "La planification stratégique du développement régional selon l'approche en modèles des grappes industrielles: leçons de la démarche associée à la réforme Picotte," Paper presented at *l'Association Canadienne Française pour l'Avancement des Sciences* (ACFAS) (Montréal, 1994).

STATISTICAL APPENDIX

Growth of the Labour Force by Industry
In Canada, the Atlantic Provinces and Selected Urban Centres, 1981, 1991

INDICES 1981-1991	Lab. Force* 1981	Lab. Force* 1991	Growth 81-91	% Growth 81-91	Dist. of Emp.	Dist. of Emp.	Income** 1981	Income** 1991	Income 91 1981 dollars	Income 91 % of Canada
CANADA										
Total	13,129,270	15,509,250	2,379,980	18.1	100.0	100.0	not avl.	23,167	13,860	100.0
Primary	940,465	907,715	(32,750)	-3.5	7.2	5.9	not avl.	20,330	12,162	100.0
Manufacturing	2,458,260	2,155,575	(302,685)	-12.3	18.7	13.9	not avl.	27,071	16,195	100.0
Construction	835,685	941,815	106,130	12.7	6.4	6.1	not avl.	24,525	14,672	100.0
Transportation	1,027,915	1,083,355	55,440	5.4	7.8	7.0	not avl.	30,243	18,093	100.0
Trade	2,230,045	2,501,150	271,105	12.2	17.0	16.1	not avl.	18,731	11,206	100.0
Finance, Insur., & Real Estate	688,525	827,430	138,905	20.2	5.2	5.3	not avl.	28,705	17,173	100.0
Teaching	864,690	1,015,750	151,060	17.5	6.6	6.5	not avl.	28,618	17,121	100.0
Health	968,170	1,356,535	388,365	40.1	7.4	8.7	not avl.	24,458	14,632	100.0
Hotels & Restaurants	819,620	998,960	179,340	21.9	6.2	6.4	not avl.	10,047	6,011	100.0
Business & Other Services	1,300,705	1,777,020	476,315	36.6	9.9	11.5	not avl.	21,969	13,143	100.0
Public Administration	995,190	1,155,875	160,685	16.1	7.6	7.5	not avl.	29,189	17,462	100.0
Not classified elsewhere	not avl.	788,090	not avl.	not avl.	not avl.	5.1	not avl.	13,930	8,334	100.0
Atlantic										
Total	1,061,475	1,232,150	170,675	16.1	100.0	100.0	not avl.	18,834	11,268	81.3
Primary	95,490	95,955	465	0.5	9.0	7.8	not avl.	16,832	10,070	82.8
Manufacturing	167,200	153,845	(13,355)	-8.0	15.8	12.5	not avl.	19,198	11,485	70.9
Construction	75,035	79,185	4,150	5.5	7.1	6.4	not avl.	17,824	10,663	72.7
Transportation	87,195	87,855	660	0.8	8.2	7.1	not avl.	25,566	15,295	84.5
Trade	181,905	201,005	19,100	10.5	17.1	16.3	not avl.	14,835	8,875	79.2
Finance, Insur., & Real Estate	37,925	42,530	4,605	12.1	3.6	3.5	not avl.	23,812	14,246	83.0
Teaching	76,540	86,920	10,380	13.6	7.2	7.1	not avl.	26,779	16,021	93.6
Health	86,560	114,305	27,745	32.1	8.2	9.3	not avl.	21,387	12,795	87.4
Hotels & Restaurants	61,345	75,795	14,450	23.6	5.8	6.2	not avl.	8,250	4,936	82.1
Business & Other Services	83,750	108,230	24,480	29.2	7.9	8.8	not avl.	14,892	8,909	67.8
Public Administration	108,530	136,595	28,065	25.9	10.2	11.1	not avl.	25,062	14,994	85.9
Not classified elsewhere	not avl.	49,930	not avl.	not avl.	not avl.	4.1	not avl.	11,079	6,628	79.5

* Labour Force: Population of 15 years and over having worked since January 1st 1980 and January 1st 1990 respectively.
** Income: Average Employm

INDICES 1981-1991	Lab. Force* 1981	Lab. Force* 1991	Growth 81-91	% Growth 81-91	Dist. of Emp.	Dist. of Emp.	Income** 1981	Income** 1991	Income 91 1981 dollars	Income 91 % of Canada
Halifax, N.S.										
Total	156,295	191,185	34,900	22.3	100.0	100.0	12,198	23,314	13,948	100.6
Primary	2,235	2,260	25	1.1	1.4	1.2	11,153	21,075	12,608	103.7
Manufacturing	12,015	12,660	645	5.4	7.7	6.6	13,769	26,498	15,852	97.9
Construction	8,130	10,250	2,120	26.1	5.2	5.4	12,306	23,385	13,990	95.4
Transportation	13,365	15,680	2,315	17.3	8.6	8.2	15,233	28,407	16,995	93.9
Trade	28,205	32,410	4,205	14.9	18.0	17.0	9,359	17,781	10,638	94.9
Finance, Insur., & Real Estate	10,285	12,060	1,775	17.3	6.6	6.3	13,688	26,311	15,741	91.7
Teaching	12,920	14,245	1,325	10.3	8.3	7.5	15,093	28,669	17,151	100.2
Health	14,910	19,895	4,985	33.4	9.5	10.4	11,278	24,143	14,444	98.7
Hotels & Restaurants	9,860	12,340	2,480	25.2	6.3	6.5	5,125	10,070	6,024	100.2
Business & Other Services	16,460	22,545	6,085	37.0	10.5	11.8	9,442	19,761	11,822	89.9
Public Administration	27,910	30,135	2,225	8.0	17.9	15.8	15,712	31,313	18,733	107.3
Not classified elsewhere	not avl.	6,705	not avl.	not avl.	not avl.	not avl.	not avl.	13,918	8,326	99.9
Sydney, N.S.										
Total	53,210	51,045	(2,170)	-4.1	100.0	100.0	10,339	18,434	11,028	79.6
Primary	5,260	4,115	(1,145)	-21.8	9.9	8.1	14,208	24,486	14,649	120.4
Manufacturing	7,870	4,510	(3,360)	-42.7	14.8	8.8	12,179	17,849	10,678	65.9
Construction	3,545	3,085	(460)	-13.0	6.7	6.0	9,645	16,115	9,641	65.7
Transportation	4,820	3,745	(1,075)	-22.3	9.1	7.3	13,547	24,417	14,608	80.7
Trade	9,500	9,455	(45)	-0.5	17.9	18.5	7,251	14,254	8,527	76.1
Finance, Insur., & Real Estate	1,485	1,380	(105)	-7.1	2.8	2.7	11,712	23,142	13,845	80.6
Teaching	3,995	3,925	(70)	-1.8	7.5	7.7	14,892	29,708	17,773	103.8
Health	5,930	5,860	(70)	-1.2	11.1	11.5	9,245	21,308	12,748	87.1
Hotels & Restaurants	2,995	3,610	615	20.5	5.6	7.1	4,171	8,375	5,010	83.4
Business & Other Services	4,065	4,070	5	0.1	7.6	8.0	6,692	13,741	8,221	62.5
Public Administration	3,745	4,380	635	17.0	7.0	8.6	10,594	21,712	12,989	74.4
Not classified elsewhere	not avl.	2,910	not avl.	not avl.	not avl.	not avl.	not avl.	10,051	6,013	72.2

* Labour Force: Population of 15 years and over having worked since January 1st 1980 and January 1st 1990 respectively.
** Income: Average Employment Income.

INDICES 1981-1991	Lab. Force* 1981	Lab. Force* 1991	Growth 81-91	% Growth 81-91	Dist. of Emp.	Dist. of Emp.	Income** 1981	Income** 1991	Income 91 1981 dollars	Income 91 % of Canada
Saint John, N.B.										
Total	57,340	65,940	8,595	15.0	100.0	100.0	12,191	21,998	13,160	95.0
Primary	675	1,110	435	64.4	1.2	1.7	10,101	23,949	14,327	117.8
Manufacturing	8,775	9,810	1,035	11.8	15.3	14.9	15,882	31,440	18,809	116.1
Construction	4,610	4,105	(505)	-11.0	8.0	6.2	15,446	21,185	12,674	86.4
Transportation	7,245	6,350	(895)	-12.4	12.6	9.6	15,746	29,973	17,932	99.1
Trade	10,850	11,790	940	8.7	18.9	17.9	8,446	15,819	9,464	84.5
Finance, Insur., & Real Estate	3,125	3,070	(55)	-1.8	5.4	4.7	13,307	25,586	15,307	89.1
Teaching	3,265	4,030	765	23.4	5.7	6.1	14,072	25,180	15,064	88.0
Health	5,800	7,530	1,730	29.8	10.1	11.4	11,231	22,357	13,375	91.4
Hotels & Restaurants	3,650	6,705	3,055	83.7	6.4	10.2	4,108	8,737	5,227	87.0
Business & Other Services	5,490	4,095	(1,395)	-25.4	9.6	6.2	9,649	16,347	9,779	74.4
Public Administration	3,855	4,695	840	21.8	6.7	7.1	14,365	26,869	16,074	92.1
Not classified elsewhere	not avl.	2,650	not avl.	not avl.	not avl.	not avl.	not avl.	11,800	7,060	84.7
Moncton, N.B.										
Total	48,845	59,765	10,925	22.4	100.0	100.0	11,298	20,792	12,439	89.7
Primary	680	890	210	30.9	1.4	1.5	7,094	15,920	9,524	78.3
Manufacturing	4,725	4,510	(215)	-4.6	9.7	7.5	12,083	23,352	13,971	86.3
Construction	2,910	3,220	310	10.7	6.0	5.4	10,846	20,512	12,271	83.6
Transportation	7,405	6,135	(1,270)	-17.2	15.2	10.3	16,511	29,769	17,810	98.4
Trade	10,875	12,710	1,835	16.9	22.3	21.3	9,496	17,482	10,459	93.3
Finance, Insur., & Real Estate	2,575	3,020	445	17.3	5.3	5.1	12,708	25,027	14,973	87.2
Teaching	3,105	4,125	1,020	32.9	6.4	6.9	14,203	27,243	16,298	95.2
Health	3,720	6,115	2,395	64.4	7.6	10.2	9,607	22,031	13,180	90.1
Hotels & Restaurants	3,430	4,505	1,075	31.3	7.0	7.5	4,496	8,659	5,180	86.2
Business & Other Services	4,855	6,810	1,955	40.3	9.9	11.4	7,767	15,883	9,502	72.3
Public Administration	4,565	5,585	1,020	22.3	9.3	9.3	14,714	28,110	16,817	96.3
Not classified elsewhere	not avl.	2,140	not avl.	not avl.	not avl.	not avl.	not avl.	12,102	7,240	86.9

* Labour Force: Population of 15 years and over having worked since January 1st 1980 and January 1st 1990 respectively.

** Income: Average Employment Income.

INDICES 1981-1991	Lab. Force* 1981	Lab. Force* 1991	Growth 81-91	% Growth 81-91	Dist. of Emp.	Dist. of Emp.	Income** 1981	Income** 1991	Income 91 1981 dollars	Income 91 % of Canada
Fredericton, N.B.										
Total	35,250	43,070	7,810	22.1	100.0	100.0	11,480	22,092	13,217	95.4
Primary	1,615	1,375	(240)	-14.9	4.6	3.2	7,651	19,274	11,531	94.8
Manufacturing	2,430	1,850	(580)	-23.9	6.9	4.3	10,562	20,792	12,439	76.8
Construction	2,380	2,540	160	6.7	6.8	5.9	11,265	19,268	11,527	78.6
Transportation	2,605	3,295	690	26.5	7.4	7.7	14,823	28,318	16,941	93.6
Trade	6,495	7,375	880	13.5	18.4	17.1	9,022	16,333	9,771	87.2
Finance, Insur., Real Estate	1,350	1,905	555	41.1	3.8	4.4	12,566	25,913	15,502	90.3
Teaching	3,615	4,050	435	12.0	10.3	9.4	15,167	28,886	17,281	100.9
Health	2,345	3,760	1,415	60.3	6.7	8.7	12,127	22,001	13,162	90.0
Hotels & Restaurants	2,305	2,920	615	26.7	6.5	6.8	4,889	8,915	5,334	88.7
Business & Other Services	3,940	5,435	1,495	37.9	11.2	12.6	9,182	21,002	12,564	95.6
Public Administration	6,170	7,345	1,175	19.0	17.5	17.1	15,401	29,685	17,759	101.7
Not classified elsewhere	not avl.	1,220	not avl.	not avl.	not avl.	not avl.	not avl.	13,675	8,181	98.2
Charlottetown, P.E.I.										
Total	24,085	32,850	8,795	36.6	100.0	100.0	10,200	19,277	11,533	83.2
Primary	1,570	1,970	400	25.5	6.5	6.0	7,522	17,759	10,624	87.4
Manufacturing	1,595	1,805	210	13.2	6.6	5.5	10,541	19,198	11,485	70.9
Construction	1,755	2,150	395	22.5	7.3	6.5	10,945	18,860	11,283	76.9
Transportation	1,810	1,960	150	8.3	7.5	6.0	13,439	25,519	15,267	84.4
Trade	4,345	5,190	845	19.4	18.0	15.8	8,313	14,134	8,455	75.5
Finance, Insur., & Real Estate	975	1,085	110	11.3	4.0	3.3	13,674	24,853	14,868	86.6
Teaching	1,870	2,605	735	39.3	7.8	7.9	13,108	26,534	15,874	92.7
Health	2,680	3,465	785	29.3	11.1	10.5	10,164	21,622	12,936	88.4
Hotels & Restaurants	2,025	3,100	1,075	53.1	8.4	9.4	4,619	8,499	5,085	84.6
Business & Other Services	2,320	3,390	1,070	46.1	9.6	10.3	7,835	15,785	9,444	71.9
Public Administration	3,140	4,755	1,615	51.4	13.0	14.5	14,251	28,290	16,925	96.9
Not classified elsewhere	not avl.	1,375	not avl.	not avl.	not avl.	not avl.	not avl.	10,448	6,251	75.0

* Labour Force: Population of 15 years and over having worked since January 1st 1980 and January 1st 1990 respectively.
** Income: Average Employment Income.

CONTRIBUTORS

Maurice Beaudin is senior researcher and assistant director for the Canadian Institute for Research on Regional Development. He is the author of two books: *La lutte pour le développement: le cas du Nord-Est*, published by Les Presses de l'Université du Québec and *Les défis de l'industrialisation des pêches au Nouveau-Brunswick* published by Les Éditions d'Acadie, Moncton, 1992. He is also the author of numerous articles on the Atlantic economy. He is currently working on his Ph.D. dissertation at l'Université de Nantes, France. The dissertation deals with the difficulties of restructuring the economy of the small communities in the Gulf of St. Lawrence.

Yves Bourgeois received, with high honours, a degree in political science at l'Université de Moncton. In 1993 he became the recipient of a Rhodes scholarship and is presently studying at Oxford University.

George J. De Benedetti is an associate professor of economics and a former head of the Department of Economics at Mount Allison University. He is a past-president of the Atlantic Canada Economics Association, has served on the Research Advisory Committee of the Atlantic Provinces Economic Council, is a member of the Board of Directors and a visiting fellow at the Canadian Institute for Research on Regional Development, and a frequent commentator in the press, CBC Radio, and television. He has written a number of articles on the Atlantic economy.

Dorothy Downing is an Australian. She began her career in Melbourne during World War II as a film editor of war action footage in the film unit of the Netherlands East Indies Bureau of Information. In Canada she wrote film scenarios, and shooting scripts at Carillon Films, Montreal, and wrote radio scripts about Canada for the CBC International Service. In New York she produced and directed film documentaries about New York for Atlas Television. In Boston she edited cultural and educational films at WGBH. She has co-authored three books with Benjamin Higgins, *Indonesia: Crisis of the Millstones*, *Japan and South East Asia*, and *Economic Development of a Small Planet*.

Benjamin Higgins is fellow in residence at the Canadian Institute for Research on Regional Development and visiting fellow in the Department of Economics, Research School of Asian and Pacific Studies, Australian National University. He holds degrees from the University of Western Ontario, the London School of Economics, Harvard University and the University of Minnesota. He has been professor of economics at McGill, M.I.T., Texas, California/Berkeley, and Montreal. He has been an economic advisor to the governments of Australia, Canada, and the United States and a number of developing countries. He has devoted the last four decades mainly to the problems of economic development of less developed countries and to the regional development in both developing and industrialized countries.

Rodolphe H. Lamarche is professor of geography at l'Université de Moncton and an associate researcher at the Canadian Institute for Research on Regional Development. He is the author of *Capitalizing on the Information Economy*, co-editor of *Telecommunications: A Strategic Perspective on Regional, Economic and Business Development* and published articles and chapters on the impact of the information economy on the Canadian urban system and regional development. He is currently associate editor of the *Canadian Journal of Regional Science*. His current research focuses on the impact of information activities on the Atlantic regions.

Larry McCann teaches urban and historical geography at the University of Victoria. Prior to moving to Victoria in 1992, he was Davidson professor and director of Canadian Studies at Mount Allison University. He has served on the Planning Committee of the National Capital Commission in Ottawa and on the board of various Canadian learned societies. He is the editor of *Heartland and Hinterland: A Geography of Canada*, a standard text used in courses on the geography of Canada, and of other books on the historical, urban, and cultural development of the Maritimes and Atlantic Canada. His current research focuses on the links between urbanization and economic development, as well as planning, architecture, and suburbanization, in major Canadian cities at the turn of the twentieth century.

Donald J. Savoie holds degrees in politics and economics from l'Université de Moncton, University of New Brunswick, and Oxford. He was appointed to the Clément-Cormier Chair in Economic Development at l'Université de Moncton in 1990 where he also teaches public administration. He founded and directs the Canadian Institute for Research on Regional Development. He is the author of numerous books. Some of his best known books include *Thatcher, Reagan and Mulroney: In Search of a New Bureaucracy*, *The Politics of Public Spending in Canada* and *Regional Economic Development: Canada's Search for Solutions*. He is the editor of numerous books and the author of many articles dealing with public policy and economic development. He has served as an advisor to a number of international agencies, foreign governments and to federal, provincial and territorial government departments and agencies. He was made an officer of the Order of Canada (1993) and Fellow of the National Academy (1992).

Frank Strain is associate professor and head of the economics department at Mount Allison University. His research, which focuses on Atlantic Canadian economic history, fiscal federalism, and Canadian public policy, has been published in a variety of academic journals and edited volumes. Dr. Strain holds degrees from the University of Prince Edward Island, the University of New Brunswick and the University of Manitoba.

Paul Villeneuve received his Ph.D. in Geography from the University of Washington in Seattle in 1971. He has been associated with the department of geography at l'Université Laval in Quebec City, where he now heads the Centre de recherche en aménagement et développement. His research has been published in a number of journals including, *Les Cahiers de Géographie du Québec*, *The Canadian Geographer*, *Urban Geography* and *The Canadian Journal of Regional Science*.

Guy Vincent was appointed an assistant professor of geography at l'Université de Moncton in 1992. His research fields are in urban and social geography, with a special emphasis on inner city issues and the North American urban system. He earned his Ph.D. degree from l'Université Laval in 1993 with a dissertation entitled, "Une nouvelle centralité urbaine au Canada."

Eugen Weiss is a Moncton-based journalist who has been covering aspects of Maritime regional and urban development for twenty years. He first wrote about urban renewal issues, and Interlake regional development, for the Winnipeg *Tribune* in the period from 1970 to 1972. In recent years, he has written a number of stories about high-tech businesses and related developments in the Fredericton area and in the rest of New Brunswick. He received his BA in political science from the University of Manitoba in 1971.

Printed by
The Tribune Press Ltd.
Sackville, N.B.